Innovating to Compete

Richard E. Walton

with the assistance of
Christopher Allen and Michael Gaffney

INNOVATING TO COMPETE

Lessons for Diffusing and Managing Change in the Workplace

Jossey-Bass Publishers

San Francisco   •   London   •   1987

INNOVATING TO COMPETE
Lessons for Diffusing and Managing Change in the Workplace
   by Richard E. Walton

Copyright © 1987 by: Jossey-Bass Inc., Publishers
                       433 California Street
                       San Francisco, California 94104

                       &

                       Jossey-Bass Limited
                       28 Banner Street
                       London EC1Y 8QE

Library of Congress Cataloging-in-Publication Data

Walton, Richard E.
   Innovating to compete.

   (The Jossey-Bass management series)
   Bibliography: p.
   Includes index.
   1. Shipping—Personnel management.   2. Shipping—
Management.   3. Industrial management.   4. Comparative
management.   I. Title.   II. Series.
HE736.W35   1987   658.4′06   87-45426
ISBN 1-55542-056-7 (alk. paper)

Manufactured in the United States of America

The paper in this book meets the guidelines for
permanence and durability of the Committee on
Production Guidelines for Book Longevity of the
Council on Library Resources.

JACKET DESIGN BY WILLI BAUM

FIRST EDITION

Code 8738

The Jossey-Bass
Management Series

Consulting Editors
Organizations and Management

Warren Bennis
University of Southern California

Richard O. Mason
Southern Methodist University

Ian I. Mitroff
University of Southern California

To Andy, Marg, Beth, John,
and in memory of Richard

Contents

Preface

This book is about the capacity for innovative change, setting forth what comprises this capacity and how it can be strengthened. What is reflected here is an interest in adaptive social and organizational innovations—innovations that help a company or a national industry compete. For example, the U.S. auto industry has recognized the importance of such innovative changes as flexibility in work assignments and worker participation in management in its effort to become competitive in terms of quality and costs. Also, the semiconductor industry may recognize that changes such as cooperative research and development may be essential if America is to maintain a leading position in this world industry.

The capacity for innovative change may exist in social systems of any scope—a plant, company, industry, or country. This book breaks new ground in its primary focus on the innovative capacity of a national industry. This unit of analysis has recently received increased attention, primarily as a way of calibrating an industry's competitive strengths and weaknesses in world competition. This book explores one underlying source of that strength or weakness: an industry's ability to innovate in social and organizational terms.

I first realized the need for a theory of innovative change in large systems in June 1983. I was working on a committee sponsored by the National Research Council to make recommendations for more "effective manning" (staffing practices that are economically and socially effective as well as safe) in the United States shipping industry.* This specific problem triggered my interest in developing a general approach that would apply to other settings and other types of innovation. The problem that prompted the formation of the committee arose because America's merchant vessels employed larger crews than their competitors and were burdened with higher operating costs. High costs combined with the U.S. government's policy to reduce subsidies to the shipping industry made it increasingly urgent to develop shipboard innovations that would permit U.S. ships to be operated effectively with smaller crews.

The committee, which consisted of employers, labor and government representatives, and academics, was charged with studying work innovations in other traditional, high-wage maritime countries and assessing the relevance of these innovations to the U.S. shipping industry. I was part of a delegation of the committee that visited Norway, Sweden, Denmark, Holland, the United Kingdom, and the Federal Republic of Germany. We met with shipowners and their industry associations, seafaring unions, relevant government agencies, and academics. The committee also received reports on Japan.

The innovative changes practiced in many of these countries included role flexibility, delegation of decision making to officers, participation in work planning by other crew members, increased continuity of employment, and social integration. However, implementation of these practices, even if they were judged to be highly appropriate to the U.S. setting, would depend on many factors, such as economic incentives and disincentives for change; social values and beliefs; institutional constraints; and the

*At the request of the Maritime Administration, the National Research Council established the Committee on Effective Manning. Members of the committee included persons with backgrounds in maritime trade unions, ship operations management, vessel design, social change, and U.S. government supervision of vessel operations and safety. See the committee's report: National Research Council. *Effective Manning of the U.S. Merchant Fleet* (Washington, D.C.: National Academy Press, 1984).

knowledge, skill, and choices of shipowners and other actors in the
industry.

To develop a systematic understanding of the capacity for
innovative change, I framed my preliminary observations on the
shipping industry as a puzzle to be solved as follows:

> The maritime sectors of the eight countries—Japan,
> the United States, and six northwestern European
> countries—had been under mounting economic
> pressure since the early 1970s. Role flexibility and
> other work innovations first developed about 1970
> could help these high-wage shipping industries
> compete in an increasingly competitive market. These
> innovations, which represented radical departures
> from traditional shipboard organization, had much in
> common with work innovations in other industries.
> Twelve years after well-publicized project ships had
> first experimented with these innovations, they had
> been adopted to a large extent by Norway, Holland,
> and Japan, to a moderate extent by the United
> Kingdom, Sweden, and West Germany, and almost
> not at all by Denmark and the United States.

What accounts for the differences in the development and
diffusion of these particular new work forms? What determines and
affects an industry's general capacity for innovative change?

If the enabling conditions in the more innovative of the eight
countries can be identified, U.S. shipowners, officials of seafaring
unions, and government policymakers can be helped to originate
and implement more effective staffing concepts and policies. Even
more important, if the varying experiences of these eight shipping
sectors in their struggle to survive and prosper can be understood,
decision makers in other American industries will be better able to
assess and strengthen their own industries' capacity for innovative
change. Thus, while this book is about a general problem, theory,
and method, the vehicle used to develop the theory and exemplify
the method is a comparative study of innovative change in the
shipping sectors of the eight countries.

Audience of the Book

This book is written for two broad audiences: practitioners and scholars.

The practitioner audience includes business and labor leaders, government officials, and organizational consultants who are concerned with adapting industry practices to meet competitive conditions. Many managers may believe they know the work reforms required for competitive purposes, but most will acknowledge that they do not know how to introduce and diffuse these innovations throughout their companies. Many labor leaders and government officials, often more concerned about the survival of whole industries than individual companies, experience frustration when trying to decide what changes are needed to improve competitiveness and how to promote these changes throughout an industry. This book provides concepts and methods that practitioners can use in promoting innovative change.

The scholarly audience is also composed of several groups, the first being researchers interested in innovation and the diffusion of innovation. This book proposes a theoretical framework for explaining why social systems are capable or incapable of innovative change. The book also provides evidence of the relative importance of different aspects of the structure and dynamics of this capability.

A second group includes researchers concerned with work reform. Shipboard organizational innovations are similar to work innovations recently developed in such American manufacturing and service industries as the auto, steel, paper, refining, food-processing, aircraft-manufacturing, airline, and insurance industries, to mention only a few. The study presented in this book provides new insights about the crucial importance of the nature of the models that guide work reform. To be effective, models should embrace changes in many policy areas—for example, participation, employment continuity, and flexibility—each of which reinforces the others. Also, models must be responsive to multiple stake-holders—to employee groups as well as employers. Without discounting the importance of tactical choices made by individuals in managing the innovation process (an element usually empha-

sized in previous research, including my own), this study provides
persuasive evidence about the influence of economic, social, and
institutional factors on organizational change.

A third academic group addressed includes students of
industrial planning and adjustment. The workplace changes in the
shipping industry are an instance of industrial adjustment. The
theoretical framework presented in this book applies to other forms
of industrial adaptation, including new long-term relationships
between auto manufacturers and their select vendors, cooperative
research and development arrangements among competitors in the
domestic semiconductor industry, and managed adjustments of
production capacity (as, for example, in the remarkably viable
Canadian steel industry). The findings reported in this book
confirm that to promote industrial adjustment, we must go beyond
the revision of economic policies (the customary targets of diagnosis
and action in the industrial-planning field) and direct attention to
institutional reform. Crucial institutional reforms include encouraging cooperative rather than adversarial relations among stakeholder groups (business, labor, and government); fostering internal
cohesion within these groups; and establishing forums and other
mechanisms for dealing with issues of common concern.

Students of comparative organization and management are a
fourth category of scholars. The theory presented in this book is
"tested" empirically by comparing the innovative performance of
the eight countries. Interestingly, national differences in social
values and beliefs about participation, delegated authority, and
social integration (which are directly relevant to the work
innovations) were less important in explaining the diffusion of
innovations than were national differences in institutional
arrangements that facilitate or hinder the innovation process.
Although values and beliefs and institutions are each aspects of
national culture, cross-cultural studies have focused more on the
ideational (values and beliefs) than the institutional aspects of
culture. This study suggests that comparative management and
organizational studies give these two aspects of culture more
balanced attention.

Overview of the Contents

In Part One I set forth my approach to innovative change. In Chapter One I discuss why innovative change is particularly important in American industry today and why the shipping industry is a good vehicle for studying innovation. In Chapter Two I discuss the elements of innovative capacity, the interactions among them, how they are influenced by environmental trends, and how they can be managed by policymakers.

After proposing the general theory, I explore what changes were made (Part Two) and why the changes were made or not made (Part Three). Finally, I address the question: What does it all mean? (Part Four).

In Part Two I describe the four adaptive changes in shipboard organization that each of the eight countries made or failed to make during the seventeen years between 1966 and 1983. In Chapter Three I examine first the trends that created problems for the maritime shipping industry during this period, and second, the four innovations that were generic ways of coping with the trends. In Chapter Four I round out the account of the four changes by focusing on the amount of innovative change that took place within each of the eight maritime sectors and by ranking each country on its innovative performance.

In Part Three I apply the theory developed in Part One to the events described in Part Two, focusing on the particular development within the eight maritime sectors. I examine the role of each of the constituent elements of a capacity for innovative change (Chapters Five through Nine). My primary purpose is to assess the influence of each of these elements on a maritime country's rate of change. My secondary purpose is to demonstrate an analytic method that can be used to aid the policymaking process.

Having set forth the theory and method, recounted how the four innovations fared in the eight maritime industries, and applied the theory to the particular events, I conclude by considering what it all means. In Chapter Ten I summarize the comparisons of the countries; in Chapter Eleven I explore what the findings mean for the theory and the diagnostic methods; and in Chapter Twelve I derive the implications for action by American industry.

Acknowledgments

I was helped immeasurably by others during the project that led to this book. One was Michael Gaffney, staff officer for the National Research Council study, who led the U.S. delegation to the European countries and later visited Japan. His trip notes supplemented my own interview notes for most of the European countries, and they also provided an important source of data on innovative change in Japan. As a scholar of shipboard innovations and as a former seafarer himself, he contributed to my general understanding of shipboard organization issues. The second person to whom I feel especially indebted is Christopher Allen, who collaborated with me during the middle part of the project. Trained as a political scientist with a strong background in European politics, Allen was a postdoctoral fellow at the Harvard Business School during the academic years 1984 to 1986. He performed field research on the U.S. shipping industry, checked and improved my understanding of the broader political and economic contexts of the European countries included in my sample, and generally engaged me in dialogue about the puzzle I was trying to solve.

I was assisted in other ways. David Moreby, dean of the Maritime College at Plymouth Polytechnic in England, read the manuscript at several stages and helped me identify errors and omissions in my description and analysis of this industry. Moreby, who holds a master's license and who engages in extensive activities in the shipping industry throughout the world, was identified repeatedly by others familiar with the industry as the person most knowledgeable about the northwestern European shipping sectors included in my sample. I received a similar critique from Jacques Roggema, before his untimely death, about the soundness of my interpretations as well as the accuracy of my facts. Roggema, a Dutchman, was instrumental in the pioneering efforts to introduce change in the shipping industries of Norway, Holland, and the United Kingdom.

I also wish to acknowledge the generous and helpful comments from colleagues who critiqued the manuscript, including Barbara Ankeny, Chris Argyris, Sam Camens, Robert Drazin, Arthur Friedberg, Robert Guest, Richard Hackman, Charles Heckscher, Rosabeth Moss Kanter, Robert McKersie, Andrew Pettigrew, George Lodge, Jerome Rosow, Stephen Schlossberg, and Shoshana Zuboff. I owe a special thanks to Thomas McCraw, whose critical comments and insightful suggestions on an early draft of the manuscript helped remind me how much work remained to be done. Ray Corey, in his role as the school's director of research, was helpful during the early stages of the project in providing personal encouragement and institutional support. Finally, I appreciate the editorial help I received from Jane Lewin and Bill Ellet, and the expert assistance given this project by Jill Wierbicki in my office at Harvard.

Boston, Massachusetts   Richard E. Walton
August 1987

The Author

Richard E. Walton is the Jesse Isidor Straus Professor of Harvard Graduate School of Business Administration. He received his B.A. degree (1953) and M.S. degree (1954) from Purdue University in economics and his Doctorate of Business Administration from Harvard University (1959). He also pursued postdoctoral studies in social psychology at the University of Michigan (1962-63) and the University of California, Los Angeles (1966-67), and he taught at Purdue from 1959 to 1969.

Walton has served on the editorial boards of several journals and is director of Berol Corporation. He has consulted with many companies, government agencies, and labor unions on matters ranging from the management of conflict to the management of innovative change, and he has published extensively on both subjects. His most recent books include *Managing Human Assets* (1984, with others), *Human Resource Management: A General Manager's Perspective* (1985, with others), *Human Resource Management Trends and Challenges* (1985, with others), and *Managing Conflict: Interpersonal Dialogue and Third Party Roles* (1987).

Innovating to Compete

PART ONE

New Perspectives
on Innovation, Change,
and Competitiveness

In Part One the competitive need for innovative change and a framework for understanding and managing innovative change are reviewed. Chapter One assesses the urgent need for innovative change in American industry, using the auto and steel industries as examples. Diverse organizational innovations, including the new work practices emphasized in this book, are essential to regain competitive strength in these and other industries. To promote the desired change, we need more powerful theories to explain innovation and more effective methods to manage innovation. And because the shipping industry analyzed in this book is a microcosm of the competitive forces requiring adaptation, it is a particularly suitable vehicle for exemplifying the theory and method proposed.

Chapter Two sets forth a general theory for explaining a social system's capacity for innovative change. This theory includes the sources of motivation for change, the type of direction essential to change activities, and critical aspects of the innovative change process itself. It also clarifies how motivation, direction, and process can influence each other and how they may be shaped by both environmental trends and policymakers.

1

Chapter 1

The Competitive Need for Organizational Innovation in American Industry

American Industry's Stake in Innovative Change

The report of the President's Commission on Industrial Competitiveness in 1985 and recent studies by the U.S. Commerce Department confirm that America has lost its competitiveness in a broad range of manufacturing industries, including steel, autos, textiles, machine tools, robotics, semiconductors, consumer electronics, telecommunications, rubber, and commercial aircraft.[1] Perhaps autos and steel dramatize best the loss of America's competitive edge.

The U.S. auto industry has in recent decades yielded to foreign competition in the domestic market in particular and in the world market in general. During the period from 1972 to 1981, imports in the U.S. market rose from 15 percent to 27 percent.[2] The most severe setback came between 1979 and 1981, when the U.S. share of the total auto production of Japan, the United States, and Europe (West Germany, France, the United Kingdom, Italy, and Sweden) declined from 35.4 to 27.4 percent.[3] Among the weaknesses of the U.S. auto industry were high labor costs. For example, by the early 1980s the Japanese auto companies needed only 65 percent of the labor required by American automakers to produce a comparable product.[4] This yielded a U.S.-Japan employment cost difference per vehicle of about $2,000.[5] To make matters worse for American automakers, they had fallen behind the Japanese in quality as well as cost.

The American steel industry has also been losing ground competitively. Foreign imports jumped from less than 5 percent in 1959 to more than 16 percent of total domestic requirements by 1980. During the same period, the U.S. share of world steel production declined, going from 28 to 17 percent. Productivity growth rates declined, and employment fell by 25 percent, from 450,000 to 340,000.[6] The industry was marked by many plant closings, which inflicted severe pain on both individual steel-workers and local communities.

The international competitiveness of autos and steel, like that of other American manufacturing industries, has declined for many reasons, one of which is that the industries have lagged in adopting new organizational strategies that are responsive to changing competitive demands.[7] Autos and steel therefore illustrate well the urgent need for the type of change treated here. Both autos and steel have made workplace adjustments (such as wage and work-rule concessions and introduction of simple forms of laborsaving technology) that do not involve organizational innovation. They have also made changes of the kind we are interested in: innovative changes, that is, changes requiring the development of new and different forms of organization.

By exploring the agendas for innovative changes in the auto and steel industries, the progress they have made, and the work they still have left to do, we can underscore the need for better concepts and methods of innovative change.

Recent Innovative Change in the Auto Industry. In response to heightened competition, a number of radical changes have occurred and are occurring in the automobile industries of the United States, Europe, and Japan.[8] They include innovations in the organization and methods of the production process. The notions that it costs more to produce high quality and that large inventory buffers are needed to achieve high process yields are being reversed. A closely related reversal in policy with respect to suppliers is also coming about: Instead of using many suppliers, each of whom is dealt with at arm's length, companies now are beginning to deal with a few select suppliers, whom they nurture, support, and provide with market intelligence and technical know-how. Another revolutionary concept deals with coordination and control. Instead of bringing information from the bottom up and sending instructions down, auto manufacturers are learning that by moving knowledge, skills, and decision making to the plant floor, they make many of the old supervision and information/control systems redundant. Other innovations include multiple skilling and flexibility in work assignments, the use of work teams in the production process, policies that promote employment continuity, and structures for sharing management's power and responsibility with employees and their unions.

Adaptations of these innovation developments, several of them pioneered by the Japanese, are deemed relevant to their situations by automakers in the United States, West Germany, Sweden, France, the United Kingdom, and Italy.[9] Thus, the competitive strengths of the auto industries in these countries will depend partly on the pace and effectiveness with which those changes and others like them are developed and diffused. At the present time, the United States is somewhere in the middle of the pack in implementing a number of the changes, for example, those involving the reorganization of work at the plant floor.[10]

Innovations in the organization and management of work in U.S. auto plants and the accompanying development of new forms of union and management collaboration have occurred under the banners of "quality of work life" (QWL) in General Motors (GM) and "employee involvement" (EI) in Ford. Both QWL and EI are sponsored jointly by the companies and the United Automobile Workers (UAW). These initiatives, especially the ones in GM, were launched before management and labor became familiar with similarly inspired practices in Japan.

General Motors pioneered the changes in the auto industry in the mid 1970s. In 1974 managers in GM and leaders in the UAW began to sponsor activities that involved workers in efforts to improve their immediate work situation. Over the next twelve years GM and the UAW developed participative mechanisms and other changes in work organization that have increased production flexibility, improved product quality, and enhanced the quality of work life.

For example, when Buick's foundry operation in Flint, Michigan, was replaced with a new torque converter business in October 1980, local management and union officials developed new ways of running the renovated plant. They formed work units of eight to fourteen employees, with each unit responsible for performing all the work in its respective areas—production, housekeeping, material control, and quality control. All hourly employees other than skilled tradesmen were classified as "quality operators." Supervisors became "advisers" and were expected to facilitate the development and functioning of the work units. Pay was based on the individual's skill and knowledge rather than on a fixed and closely defined job description. Status distinctions—for example, in dress, cafeteria, and parking—were diminished or eliminated.

Organizations founded subsequently for GM production became increasingly comprehensive in their transformation of the traditional automobile plant. Not only are the roles of workers and managers changing, but so are the concerns and activities of union officials. "Issues once considered the sole prerogative of management, such as scheduling, work standards, and discipline, today are increasingly the focus of joint management-union teamwork," according to Alfred Warren, GM's vice-president of industrial relations.[11]

By 1987, GM and the UAW had created an ambitious model of an automobile-manufacturing organization designed to enlist the full commitment of employees. The organizational model was already functioning in the GM-Toyota plant in Fremont, California, and it was planned for the new GM car division, Saturn, which would begin producing cars in 1990. Both organizations feature the following innovative changes:

- few hierarchical layers, facilitating vertical communication
- self-managing work teams as the building blocks of the organization, reducing the support and supervisory overhead required
- few job classifications, making possible high flexibility in assignments
- major investments in training in technical and social skills, supporting both self-management and flexibility
- few status distinctions and the placement of all employees on salary, signaling increased respect for the contributions of all GM employees
- high levels of employment security for senior employees, giving them a more certain stake in the prosperity of the enterprise
- union representatives on strategic planning and operational management committees, creating a type of partnership between capital and labor that until recently was unprecedented in the United States
- a policy that decisions will be made by consensus, reducing the reliance on unilateral authority systems and contractual forms

After each generation of work reforms has proven effective in a few pilot plants, GM management and UAW leaders have sought to spread it to other plants. The rate of diffusion to other GM facilities has been steady, but it has been slow relative to the competitive need for improvements. Almost a decade after the effort began, only one-third of all GM plants had been significantly affected by work innovations, one-third had begun to change, and one-third had changed very little. By 1987 virtually every facility has at least begun to change, but the leaders of both union and management place great importance on accelerating the rate at which innovations are effectively diffused. They believe that both UAW jobs and GM's position in the world car market are at stake.

Recent Innovative Change in the Steel Industry. The steel industry developed high labor costs and inefficient operating practices during the 1950s and 1960s, when profitable American steel-making industries and the strong steelworkers' union, the United Steelworkers of America (USWA), were not worried about foreign competitors. However, by the early 1970s the leadership of the USWA fully understood that "in the final analysis, our union's success in improving the steelworkers' standard of living will be tied to the viability of the steel industry and its long-term productivity growth."[12] Similarly, some steel executives recognized that significant increases in productivity would require the willing cooperation of labor and changes in work practices. Thus the basic industry agreement between steel companies and the USWA in 1971 included a provision for a Joint Advisory Committee on Productivity. Despite the positive intent of the parties, the Joint Committee failed in its promise to change workplace practices and improve productivity.

Almost a decade later, in April 1980, the parties entered into another agreement to produce work-place reforms, the Labor-Management Participation Teams (LMPT) Agreement. This time the agreement was followed by meaningful change. Implementation began at a pilot plant in 1981, and within a year twelve other plants in Bethlehem, Jones and Laughlin, National, Republic, and U.S. Steel had launched LMPT change activities, involving one hundred plant-floor teams. By 1985 twenty-three steel plants covered by the basic steel-industry agreement had implemented five hundred participation teams, each organized around a work unit and containing from seven to thirteen workers and one to three supervisors.

Teams have addressed both performance and quality-of-work-life subjects, including use of production facilities, safety and environmental health, scheduling and reporting arrangements, absenteeism, overtime, incentive coverage and yield, job alignments, contracting out, energy conservation, and transportation pools.[13] The following are cited as examples of the improvements generated by LMPT teams:

- Delays on a roll change at a welded tube mill, which were found to have been caused by worn dust covers, were eliminated, producing potential savings of $42,000 per year.
- A standard operating procedure was developed to reduce excess rolling for each order on a cold mill, which was costing $713,043 per year.

- A material was devised for protecting the rolls at one rolling mill when they were placed in racks for storage, saving $21,000 each year.[14]

Sam Camens of the USWA terms the LMPT teams' accomplishments "breathtaking," noting that their "enthusiasm, drive, and success have become the talk of all industry periodicals."[15] Benjamin Boylston of Bethlehem Steel's industrial relations staff agrees, stating that at Bethlehem "the antagonisms of the past [are giving] way to new relationships based on mutual trust, cooperation, and commitment to common goals."[16]

Nevertheless, as important and promising as these developments are, they involve only a small percentage of the basic steel work force, and the changes represent only a beginning in the transformation that steel management and labor had already envisioned for the industry. Thus, the early positive results have served to intensify both parties' interest in enlarging the industry's capacity for innovative change.

The Problem Broadened. The stories about the beginnings of innovative change in the auto and steel industries are not unique. Indeed, while the leading companies in other U.S. industries may be more or less advanced than GM and Bethlehem Steel, most of them have similar histories. They have implemented innovations in pilot facilities, judged them successful, and then experienced a frustratingly slow spread of these approaches to other facilities. This pattern can be found in AT&T, Goodyear, Procter and Gamble, EXXON, Alcoa, Kellogg, Polaroid, Weyerhauser, Cummins Engine, McDonnell Douglas, General Electric, Rockwell International, Honeywell, and Digital Equipment Company, to cite only a sample of the U.S. companies that have been pioneers in their industries in work reforms similar to the ones pioneered by General Motors in the auto industry and Bethlehem in the steel industry. Viewed from a broader perspective, the rates of development or diffusion of work innovations, within given industries, such as autos and steel, and throughout U.S. industry as a whole, have been accelerating but more slowly than needed, given the urgency of improving the American competitiveness.

The more extensive discussions of steel and autos help dramatize the need for innovative change but should not be taken as an indication that the capacity for change is important primarily for distressed industries. As the sample of companies cited in the preceding paragraph indicates, the work-innovation trend affects a diverse set of industries, ranging from basic industries, such as steel and aluminum, to high-technology industries, such as telecommunications and computers.

Innovative capacity is becoming a more urgent issue throughout all parts of American industry, not only because of intensifying competitive pressure but also because of the increasingly important role that advanced information technology can play in competing strategies. A recent study sponsored by the National Research Council investigated the human resource policies implemented in sixteen leading U.S. plants that had introduced advanced manufacturing technology within recent years.[17] The study committee, which I chaired and which was composed of business executives, labor leaders, and academics, concluded that the potential of this new generation of technology can only be fully realized when implementation of the technology is accompanied by parallel social innovations, including many of the work innovations already initiated in the auto and steel industries.

Toward More Powerful Explanatory Concepts and Diagnostic Methods

The discussion of America's stake in innovative change raises a number of questions that underscore the need for more powerful concepts about the capacity to innovate and for more effective methods of assessing the capacity in practice.

At the national level, I cited the lead role Japan has played in pioneering several new concepts in the world auto industry. Japan's advantage in other export industries also has been based in large part on organizational innovations, including involvement mechanisms at the shop floor; symbiotic relations between manufacturers and their suppliers; cooperative research and development ventures among companies in the same industry; and collaborative planning at the sector level by business, labor, and government. These organizational forms have generated greater motivation, lower investment in inventory, more rapid development of manufacturing process technology, and the ability to shift resources from declining sectors to growing industries. The question is, why do some countries, in this instance Japan, appear to have better overall records than many others, such as Britain and perhaps the United States, in developing new organizational solutions in industry?

At the company level, the role General Motors played in pioneering work reforms in the U.S. auto industry raises the question, why in the same national industry do some companies adapt more rapidly than others?

Similarly, at the plant level, why does management choose to close down some facilities because it cannot see a way to implement organizational change, while it readily succeeds with change programs in other plants that are no better equipped technically?

Moreover, I referred earlier to the American steel industry's false start in its effort to address the productivity problem. Why do some initiatives for change (such as the steel effort in 1971) fail and others (such as the steel effort in 1981) succeed?

Many specific reasons can be given to explain why more innovative change has occurred in one country, company, plant, or time period than in another. Perhaps in one case the innovation was more soundly conceived and therefore offered a better solution to the system's problem or problems. Or if the same innovation was in question, then perhaps the competitive need for change was simply greater in one situation than in another. Or in one case social values and beliefs may have been more sympathetic to the innovative effort that succeeded than to the one that did not. Still another factor may have been operative: Perhaps the process of implementing the innovation was more effective in one situation than in another, either because it encountered fewer institutional constraints or because it was more skillfully managed.

Together these explanations cover a wide range of factors that can potentially influence the capacity to innovate. Often the actual record of change can be explained only by considering all of these possibilities. Therefore, we need an analytical framework that embraces such a broad range of factors and clarifies how they may relate to each other. The approach I propose attempts to meet these requirements and also to clarify how the capacity for innovative strength can be enhanced.

Thus, the proposed theoretical framework allows us both to explain and to diagnose. It allows us to explain why some social systems are more innovative than others, and it allows us to diagnose a given system's strengths and weaknesses in innovating. The diagnosis can then be used by policymakers in business, labor, and government as they decide what policies to institute and where.

The capacity for innovative change is the same conceptually whether it refers to a plant, a company, a national industry, or an entire country. But while the ideas can be applied to social systems of any scope, the primary focus of this book is on the innovative capacity of a national industry. The emphasis on the industry level breaks new ground, especially in the United States. In many of the European and Asian countries with which American companies compete, business, labor, and governmental bodies have long considered the competitive strength of specific industries—such as the Japanese shipbuilding industry, the West German steel industry, and the Swedish car industry—and have taken concerted action to strengthen competitiveness on an industry-by-industry basis. In the United States, only recently have we begun to give serious attention to the national industry as a unit of analysis for assessing competitive strengths and weaknesses. Thus, it is not surprising that, to date, little attention has been paid to one underlying source of strength or weakness—an industry's ability to innovate in social and organizational forms.[18]

Shipping Industry: A Vehicle for Understanding Innovative Change

Although the approach presented in this book is broadly applicable, I concentrate on a specific set of work innovations that were pursued in the maritime shipping industry in eight countries during the period from 1966 to 1983. The shipboard innovations are role flexibility, continuity of employment and assignment, delegation and participation, and social integration. The countries whose records in developing and diffusing the reforms I compare and analyze are the United States, Japan, and the six European countries of Denmark, West Germany, Holland, Norway, Sweden, and the United Kingdom.

Shipping is a suitable industry for developing and applying the approach to innovative change for several reasons.

First, as a fairly typical worldwide industry, shipping illustrates the competitive dynamics common to many worldwide industries, including autos, steel, machine tools, and textiles. New competitors, including newly industrialized countries, have provided major increments of industry capacity at the same time that growth in demand has slowed.

Second, within the shipping industry itself, the United States is competitively weak, as is true within numerous other industries. In fact, many U.S. industries, including shipping, may not survive without government assistance or protection.

Third, the sources of weakness within the U.S. shipping industry are similar to the sources of weakness within other U.S. industries. They include higher labor costs, relatively inefficient and ineffective use of human resources, older plants and equipment, and outmoded technology. Moreover, inefficient labor practices and aging capital stock are interrelated. Companies are discouraged from investing in new equipment when they cannot expect to operate it more effectively. And the failure to develop new plants and equipment deprives industry of the catalyst for change that accompanies the design and start-up of a new facility.

Fourth, the basic options available to U.S. shipping companies for improving their competitive positions are analogous to the options available to other U.S. companies. U.S. shipowners can transfer vessels to a flag of convenience, such as Liberia, and hire Third World crews, just as U.S. manufacturers can build a plant overseas and hire cheaper labor. Alternatively, like their counterparts in other U.S. industries, U.S. shipowners can stay in the United States and adapt their practices, including the way they organize and manage work. A cornerstone change for the shipping industry—and for other U.S. industries—is role flexibility. In shipping, this involves crossing traditional boundaries, such as that between deck and engine room. In other industries, it may mean combining crafts or assigning workers to do both maintenance and production work. In any case, it means broader jobs and more contingent responsibilities.

Not only is shipping as an industry a good microcosm of the challenges of world competition, but the countries selected for study also lend themselves to a comparative analysis.

During the period in question, the eight countries competed with each other as well as with other maritime nations. Firms in almost all countries could buy from the same shipyards and purchase fuel at the same price. The countries shared a common maritime tradition, especially in terms of shipboard organization, mostly inherited from the British. Yet, by the start of the period of interest here, there were already some differences among the eight countries, the effects of which turn out to be instructive. The main difference was shipping labor costs, which were high internationally in all of these countries but varied considerably from one country to another. (Staffing costs were the most controllable operating cost.)

The six European countries were all subjected to the same broad manpower trends, business cycles, and cost pressures, although these factors were felt with different degrees of severity and were handled somewhat differently by the governments involved. The United States and Japan had moderately different economic patterns. The eight countries illustrated different levels and forms of government support for shipping.

The shipboard changes throughout the eight-country sample were directionally similar, yet the amount of innovative change that was ultimately made varied widely from country to country. By 1983 the innovations had been widely adopted in three countries (Norway, Holland, and Japan), moderately adopted in three countries (the United Kingdom, Sweden, and West Germany), and hardly adopted at all in two countries (Denmark and the United States).

We turn now to the consideration of a theoretical framework that will be used to explain these differences.

Chapter 2

A New Framework for Understanding and Managing Innovative Change

What are the major components of a social system's capacity for innovative change? How do these elements relate to one another? What external forces modify them? Together, the answers to these questions constitute a theory of innovative change[1] and define a framework both scholars and policymakers can use: scholars, to explain differences among social systems; policymakers, to diagnose the strengths and weaknesses of a particular system and then act to strengthen it. The term *social system* applies to competitive entities of any scope—plants, companies, industries, and countries.

The Components: The What, Why, and How of Innovative Change

All the components of the theory, working in combination, must provide answers to three fundamental questions about any innovation: (1) What change is to be made? (2) Why is the change to be made? (3) How can the change be put into effect?[2] In other words, *what* model or vision guides the movement toward change? *Why* is the proposed innovation considered desirable? Specifically, what prompts an awareness of the need for the innovation, and what affects the climate of acceptance? *How* will the innovation be developed, implemented, and diffused? Specifically, what institutional conditions and managerial skills affect the process by which the innovation develops and spreads throughout a social system?

Without an adequate vision of the form the innovation will take, whatever energy is generated will be dissipated. Without a critical amount of motivation, neither the energy to initiate change nor the readiness to implement it will be present. Moreover, even given a clear sense of direction and a high degree of drive, the process will not advance without an ability to manage it. Direction, motivation, and skills in dealing with the innovation process must all be present. Their strength or quality will have a direct bearing on the success with which an innovation is developed and diffused.

The "What": Visions and Guiding Models. Innovation cannot be effective unless it is guided by a vision made manifest in a model. A model is a general concept of the future organization and evolves from an understanding of the limitations of traditional organization and experimentation with alternatives. It can include such features as more flexibility, greater participation, and the employees' increased financial stake in the commercial success of the business.

The model must be strong. That means it takes into account the fact that policies often affect other policies—that organizations are systems, and therefore the effectiveness of each policy depends on its being consistent with other policies.[3] An organization cannot work well unless all its policies, technical systems, and structural features are adequately aligned. Innovations based on models that deal with only one policy often fail because they are too simple. Many U.S. companies have learned the hard way that when techniques such as quality circles, management-by-objective programs, or work teams are introduced without supportive changes in training, rewards, and selection procedures, the changes are doomed.

Strength in a model also means that it responds to the interests of all the different groups with a stake in the proposed changes. When an innovation is based on a model that affects both the employer and the employees but does not protect the interests of both groups, the innovation will fail.

For example, a change may be too focused on the interests of the initiating party. This happened recently in American industry, when production managers negotiated agreements with unions for fewer job classifications within a plant. Some managers addressed only their own need for more efficient production and ignored the workers' concerns, such as finding challenges on the job and influencing their immediate work situations. These managers ultimately gained less in efficiency from their revisions in job classifications than did the managers who addressed both their own interest in efficiency and the workers' interest in personal development.

The abortive effort at innovative change in the steel industry in 1971 (see Chapter One) was also weakened by the model that guided it. Sam Camens of the United Steelworkers of America attributed what he called "the total failure" of this effort to the fact that the committee focused exclusively on productivity and did not attempt to improve the relationships between employee and employer and between union and company. Thus the program engendered mistrust in the average steelworker, who looked on it as "another speed-up, crew-cutting process which would inevitably mean more short-term layoffs."[4]

The vision reflected in the second steel effort, the one based on the Labor-Management Participation Teams (LMPT) Agreement, differed sharply. According to a union official who helped develop and implement the LMPT Agreement:

> We read, consulted, planned, and even took joint
> labor-management trips to Japan. Out of all this came
> a clear picture. Planning had to begin with the
> understanding that long-term success could only come
> from cultural change fostering voluntary plant floor

teams. The teams, with proper training in joint problem solving, would be able to improve the quality of products, increase production, and make improvements in equipment, environment, and working conditions; and thus they would produce a stronger steel industry, a more involved and dignified workforce, better union-management understanding, and more employment security.[5]

Compared with the first model, the second was more comprehensive and better integrated the interests of stakeholder groups. Thus, not only did it have the power to inspire management and unions and to enlist the participation of a growing proportion of the labor force, but also it would work.

Hence, a general theory of the capacity for innovative change begins with a proposition about the models that guide innovation.

Proposition One: Guiding Model

The capacity for innovative change is enhanced by the soundness of the model that guides the development of the innovations. A model is sound if it (1) affects and aligns a group of interrelated policies and (2) integrates the interests of multiple stakeholders.

The "Why": Economic Necessity as Motivator. The importance of economic necessity in triggering innovative change in the workplace has long been recognized.[6] Competition directly motivates the search for more efficient work methods. But competition, or economic forces, influences the organization of work indirectly as well. Competitive disadvantage motivates managers to develop changes in products, in technical processes, and in laborsaving technology.[7] All three, in turn, produce innovations in the social organization of the workplace.[8]

The postulate that economic pressure triggers innovation has much anecdotal support. For example, after the auto industry promoted work reforms at the plant level for a half-dozen years, company and union officials observed that more progress had been made at components plants than at assembly plants. The difference between the two? Components could be supplied by vendors, so workers as well as managers at the components plants were under greater economic pressure than their counterparts at the assembly plants.[9]

In accounting for Bethlehem Steel's initiatives beginning in 1981, a member of the company's industrial relations staff wrote that changes in human resource policies, which had been "unthinkable" when profits were satisfactory, became the "focus of our corporate planning process" when imports seriously cut into Bethlehem's market share.

> Our strategic studies led us to conclude that additional capital expenditures alone would not solve the corporate profitability crisis—we simply could not spend our way into profitability. Trend lines of productivity improvements, cost increases, and potential price increases indicated that non-capital-intensive ways of improving our productivity and profitability had to be found. We identified four major productivity factors that profoundly affected our steel operations: technology, energy, capital, and human resources. The prospect of productivity improvement in the first three areas appeared limited by associated costs; the human resource area, however, held out real possibilities.[10]

Economic pressures for change can come from product markets and labor markets.[11] A systematic study of change in the U.K. firm Imperial Chemical Industries (ICI) between 1960 and 1984 found three periods characterized by high levels of organizational change and innovation. Each of these periods was associated with increased economic pressure on ICI businesses.[12] Market pressures, however, may be neutralized by government policies that protect companies and labor from the full effects of world competition or may be reinforced by policies that sharpen the incentives for change.

Organizational innovations are economic investments, requiring up-front infusions of money and effort to realize a stream of benefits over time. Therefore, they are facilitated by longer planning horizons. If competitive pressures are so acute that they threaten survival in the short run, the effect may be to discourage the investment in innovation. The opening of new facilities, however, presents uniquely favorable opportunities for investing in work innovations: Less incremental time and money are required to implement the innovations, and the economic incentives for labor to accept them are usually stronger and more apparent.

Thus, another component of the theory can be formulated.

Proposition Two: Economic Necessity

The capacity for innovative change is influenced by the economic pressures on those who have the power to initiate change. The pressures are exerted by the market and by policies. The capacity is also strengthened by (1) the extent to which the economic incentives of other groups are aligned with the economic incentives of the initiating group and (2) the length of the planning horizons.

The "Why": Social Context as Motivator. Economic necessity, however credible as a motivator of innovation behavior, cannot always explain differences in that behavior. For example, during the 1970s many American companies pioneered reforms even though they were under less economic pressure than their domestic competitors. Sometimes it is the social context within the leading companies that proves more conducive to innovation. In addition to economic necessity, then, we need to consider the motivation provided by social values and other aspects of the social context.

"Social context" refers to social values, attitudes, and beliefs *in relation to the innovation in question.* The term also refers to the political concerns managers and labor representatives have about the innovation and its potential effect on their own status or power.

Social attitudes and beliefs can vary among plants in the same company, among companies in the same industry, and among industries in the same country, and such beliefs will certainly vary from one country to another. Even within a single plant, groups may differ sharply in their social attitudes toward a proposed change in work structure. For example, the expansion of workers' influence is often supported by upper management and welcomed by workers but disapproved of by first-line supervisors. The crucial question is whether those differences significantly affect the development and diffusion of an innovation that is otherwise adaptive to the environment.

The answer given by most managers and social scientists is yes. They probably believe that social values shape how change is accepted as firmly as they believe that economic necessity triggers change. It is widely accepted, for example, that some successful practices of Japanese companies would not work well in the United States, and vice versa. Comparative studies that include analyses of many of the countries treated in this book arrive at the same general conclusion.[13]

Proposition Three: Social Values

The capacity for innovative change is strengthened by the extent to which the social context supports the innovation in question. The alignment between the social values of the groups affected by the innovation and the social effects these groups anticipate after the innovation is in place are particularly important.

The "How": Institutions and the Process of Innovating. The implementation of innovations is a process that usually passes through several phases. First, a concept is formed. Next, it is embodied in a new structure or procedure, is tested and evaluated, and is possibly redesigned. Finally, a new structure or procedure judged to have merit is diffused throughout the facility, company, industry, or country. The effectiveness of the process depends on the institutional context within which the process takes place and the abilities of those who manage the process.

The institutional context for a national industry consists of the following:

- Organized labor—how is it structured (for example, by craft, by industry, or by enterprise), and how unified is it?
- Employer associations—are there any, and if so, how internally cohesive are they?

- Regulatory agencies that affect the industry—how well coordinated are they?
- Relationships among labor, management, and government— what structures and mechanisms link them, and what is the quality of those links?
- Laws and government policies—do they cover practices in the workplace?[14]

Overarching and shaping all these institutional elements are society's beliefs or ideologies—both past and present—about the appropriate roles of business, labor, and government.[15]

Institutional factors can facilitate or obstruct three functional requirements of the innovation process: the emergence of sponsors for innovative change, the development of consensus about the change, and the transfer of information and social technology relevant to the innovation.

These functional requirements are best fulfilled when key groups—business, labor, and government—are unified internally, linked by mechanisms for dealing with common concerns and differences, and oriented toward cooperating with one another.

Internal unity, a linking mechanism, and a predisposition to cooperate are especially important for developing a consensus about change. However, the amount of consensus required will itself depend on the institutional situation. For example, in some settings a company is required to secure the approval of government or labor before implementing a change in roles, pay, perks, employment contracts, or training programs. The requirement may be set by law, administrative policy, or previous contracts. Where the approval of one of the other parties may not be formally required, the party initiating the change may nevertheless find it prudent to secure prior approval and thereby ensure effective implementation. The more stringently institutions impose a requirement for approval, the more the institutions must have a capacity for facilitiating consensus if effective innovation is to occur.

Proposition Four: Institutions

The capacity for innovative change is strengthened to the extent that institutions (for example, labor, management, and govern-

*ment) are unified internally, linked by problem-solving mecha-
nisms, and oriented cooperatively. Institutions' capacity to facilitate
consensus must be commensurate with the amount of consensus
they require.*

The "How": Competence and the Process of Innovating.
The innovation process is influenced not only by institutions but
also by the competence of those individuals who manage the process
and develop, implement, and diffuse innovations. These people
must demonstrate the ability to learn, exercise good judgment, and
implement skillfully.[16] Individuals must manage the same three
process requirements as those affected by institutional factors,
namely, ensuring adequate sponsorship, a workable consensus, and
timely and accurate transfer of information about the innovation.

Sound organizational prototypes do not emerge automatically when the institutional context is favorable to change, and
successful trials do not automatically lead to adoption of a change.[17]
Choices made at every stage of the process can influence the quality
of the outcome. Decisions must be made about where to search for
alternative solutions, whom to involve in formulating a new
approach and sponsoring a trial of it, how many simultaneous
trials to pursue, how to assess trials in order to generate findings
credible to potential adopters, and so forth.

Fortunately, during the past decade we have been learning
(mostly by trial and error) about making wise choices and
implementing them skillfully to diffuse new work forms.[18] At GM
plants, for example, management and the union have found that
change is promoted by the following conditions:

- the emergence of champions within both the union and
  management
- the use of symbols (for example, joint appearances by managers
  and union officials)
- the reeducation of managers and union officials
- the careful placement of managers skilled at producing change

More generally, the experiences of GM and the UAW have
demonstrated how leaders can initiate processes that will help build

an understanding of and consensus about the need and direction for change. Their experiences have shown that it is important to promote several projects simultaneously, ensure that people learn from trial, reinforce success, and oversee the revision of critical policies and practices. These form only a small sample of the activities that must be managed competently.

Proposition Five: Competence

The capacity for innovative change is strengthened by the skills and knowledge of the individuals who manage the innovation process.

Relative Importance of the Components. The five components of the capacity for innovative change are not always equally significant. Sometimes the explanations for differences in the ability to innovate lie more with one element than with another.

In addition, although economic, social and institutional attributes are potentially relevant to organizational innovations, all of these attributes may not apply in every given situation. In any particular case, the researcher or policymaker must ask a series of questions about the work innovation.

- Is it potentially relevant to economic performance? If the answer is yes, then Proposition Two (economic necessity) comes into play.
- Is it potentially relevant to the social attitudes and beliefs of the people affected by the change? If the answer is yes, then Proposition Three (social values) comes into play.
- Does it depend on the approval or assistance of two or more institutions? If the answer is yes, then Proposition Four (institutions) comes into play.[19]

Unlike the economic, social, and institutional components, the quality of the guiding vision (Proposition One) and the competence of the people managing the process (Proposition Five) influence all forms of innovation. But under certain circumstances, vision and competence are more influential than usual. An example of such a circumstance is when a work reform has complex implications for those affected by it.

After gaining a preliminary understanding of the work innovations implemented in shipping, I could confirm that all five of the proposed elements of a capacity for innovative change had been relevant. Taken as a whole, the shipboard innovations

- Could be combined in a variety of ways to form alternative organizational models
- Affected economic performance
- Were relevant to social values and beliefs
- Required institutional approvals
- Relied on competent tactical choices by individuals

However, because shipboard reforms involved a number of discrete innovations (including, for example, role flexibility and employment continuity), each may have been affected differently by the five components.

Chapters Five through Nine will assess what components were generally more influential in shipping and why. It will also assess whether the five elements were differentially relevant to the several discrete innovations.

Levels of Operation of the Components. As we have already noted, the theory of innovative change applies to entities at the national, industry, company, and plant levels, each of which can be thought of as a distinct social system.[20] At the national level, the theory applies to the national economy; the social values of the country as a whole; the national institutions for management, labor, and government; and the relevant skills and knowledge generally characteristic of the country. At the industry level, one examines the economics of the specific industry within the national economy, the industry's unique culture, the institutions particular to the industry, and the competencies that characterize the industry. At the company level, one examines the economic position of the company within its industry, the philosophy and culture of the company, its institutional relations with unions, and the competencies of the individuals within the company. Similarly, a plant will have its own unique economic incentives, social climate, institutional context (including corporate structures), and competencies.

Regardless of the level of one's primary interest, however, one must also take into account conditions at the other levels. An innovation may simultaneously be influenced by conditions and policies at the national level, at the industry level, and so forth. Thus, in diagnosing the strengths and weaknesses of the innovative capacity of a social system at one level, and in deciding on actions that policymakers should take, one has to be able to move between levels. Policymakers need to determine at what level key bottlenecks have developed and at what level interventions or initiatives are likely to have the most leverage. They will then know where to focus their attention. Will changes in national economic policy lead to innovations in the workplace? Will it be more fruitful to focus on an industry's institutions (for example, the craft structure of the unions or consortium arrangements among the firms)? Is the phenomenon one that only individuals at the level of the firm will be able to influence?

The three levels of nation, industry, and company all shaped the patterns of innovative changes in shipboard organization. A study of shipping permits one to explore not only the conditions that in one instance determined the relative importance of each level but also how coordinated action on different levels may be required to produce innovative change.

The Internal Dynamics of Innovative Capability

As we have seen, each of the five basic components of the capacity to innovate directly influences the amount of change a system can make. But equally important in determining innovative capacity are the relations among the five factors, which are not static but continually evolving. Thus, innovative capacity may increase or decrease over time.

In particular, the combination of motivational forces and the nature of the process determine the form of the model,[21] as shown by the solid lines in Figure 2-1. For example, when the economic and social interests of different groups are brought directly into the

Figure 2-1. Factors Influencing the Development and Diffusion
of Innovations.

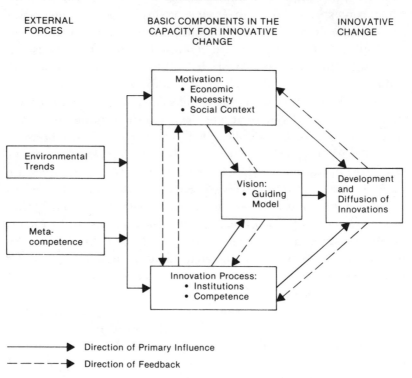

EXTERNAL   BASIC COMPONENTS IN THE   INNOVATIVE
FORCES   CAPACITY FOR INNOVATIVE   CHANGE
                                 CHANGE

————————▶ Direction of Primary Influence

– – – – –▶ Direction of Feedback

process, they are more likely to be reflected in the guiding concepts. Similarly, when the process is limited by few institutional constraints and is managed competently, the resulting model is more likely to include an adequate set of interrelated policies and to integrate the interests of different groups.

Other relationships among model, motivational forces, and process factors may or may not be found in any particular setting, but all possible patterns of influence must be allowed for. Two such patterns involve (1) the model and the motivational forces and (2) economic incentives and institutional arrangements. The design of the model may not only reflect the motivational forces but may also lead to their being further redefined. Furthermore, the policy aspects of the economic incentives may have a reciprocal relationship to the institutional arrangements producing the policies. These possible interactions are shown by the dotted lines in Figure 2-1.

In addition, the strength of the several factors may change with experience and exposure to the innovation. This is particularly true for competence and social approval. Whatever the initial competence of the individuals who manage the innovation process, the ongoing experience itself will add to their skills and knowledge about how to engineer the required consensus, manage participative processes, conduct and evaluate trials, and disseminate findings. Similarly, after participants have direct experience operating within the new organizational forms, they may revise the social assessments they made when those same organizational structures were only proposals. The participants' attitudes and beliefs (about participation, for example) may change in either direction, becoming more or less favorable to the innovation. These feedback dynamics are also shown by the dotted lines in Figure 2-1.

External Forces: Environmental Trends and Metacompetence

The capacity to innovate is dynamic not only in the sense that it is modified as the components themselves interact, but also in the sense that external factors may alter the components and cause an increase or decrease in the capacity. External forces take two forms: (1) broad market, technological, and political trends that alter the economic, social, and institutional contexts and (2) deliberate initiatives that modify the economic policy framework, social context, and institutional arrangements to make them more favorable to innovative change.

Developments in the environment, such as the oil crises of the 1970s, can radically alter the magnitude as well as the nature of economic pressures on particular industries. Similarly, rising levels of education and new social legislation can affect the social attitudes and expectations of employees in the workplace. Changes in political regimes and economic conditions can affect the power equation and the relations between labor and management.

Metacompetence describes the ability to manage the context for innovative change.[22] Like the competence required to manage the process of innovation, which may be called "tactical," metacompetence is highly purposeful; however, because it operates outside the arena where process competence and the other four basic elements operate, it may be called "strategic." Tactical competence operates within the scope defined by existing economic forces, social values, and institutions, so it influences the activities of the immediate work innovation. Metacompetence—the most strategic element of a capacity to innovate—reflects the ability to assess the effects of the five basic elements and to strengthen one or more of them.

Proposition Six: Metacompetence

Metacompetence acts to modify the five basic components and hence to influence future activity. It can influence economic policies so that they sharpen the incentives for employers and labor to change, promote broad movements that shape values and beliefs, and reform institutions so that they allow or even promote innovative change.

Ultimately, a theory of innovative change must include metacompetence, which is crucial not only for changing the economic policies, social beliefs, and institutions that limit a system's capacity for innovation but also for capitalizing on the economic forces, social discontent, and institutional idiosyncrasies conducive to innovation.

Summary

The capability of a social system (facility, company, industry, or country) to develop and diffuse organizational innovations depends on a combination of five interacting components. The capability is strengthened to the extent that innovative change is (1) guided by models that are sound; (2) motivated by economic incentives that are strong and that align the interests of all groups with a stake in the change; (3) supported by values and other social factors sympathetic to the innovation; (4) facilitated by institutions with a structure and climate that make it easier to sponsor, reach consensus, and process information about innovations; and (5) managed by individuals with the relevant competencies.

The five components influence each other in a variety of ways. For example, the first component, the vision or model that emerges to guide innovation, is itself a product of economic incentives and social beliefs as well as institutional constraints and the abilities of those who manage the innovation process. In addition, the components, especially social attitudes and competencies, may change as a direct result of innovation activity, just as they may affect it. These types of internal dynamics cause the capacity to continually change.

The capacity is also modified by two types of external forces. First, broad trends in the environment may change the economic, social, and institutional elements, either increasing or decreasing the innovative capacity of the social system in question. Second, policymakers concerned with promoting innovation in a particular industry or company may act strategically—may exercise metacompetence—to sharpen or supplement the inherent market forces for change, arouse social motives supportive of a class of innovation, and reform the institutional framework to enable innovation processes.

This innovative change theory is meant to be used as a general research framework and policy tool for guiding a discovery process. Therefore, the theory identifies the major components of the capacity for innovative change but does not specify their relative importance to the overall capacity. It also identifies the many possible interactions among the five components but does not specify all of them. A few relationships, particularly between the model and other elements, can be generalized. Other possible interactions will depend on particular features of the situation that can be discovered only with analysis. In short, the framework provides guidance about the questions to ask and the places to look for answers, more than it specifies what those answers will be.

PART TWO

Adaptation to Change
A Shipping Industry Case Study

In Part Two we begin to analyze details of the shipping industry. Chapter Three addresses two questions: What broad forces affect the industry and require adaptation? What is the form of the industry's innovative responses to these forces? These questions outline the general empirical problem the theory of innovative change will address. The same questions should also guide preliminary steps in diagnosing and strengthening innovative change in a particular national industry or company.

The answers to these two questions in the shipping case are far from unique. Many of the forces operating in other world industries are exemplified by the shipping industry. Economic pressures have mounted because low-wage countries have entered the competitive arena, and because the industry has excess capacity. Shifts in social beliefs have raised expectations about egalitarian treatment and participation in the workplace. Automation and other laborsaving technologies have reduced the size of work forces, modified the skills required, and altered the way work is organized. A major theme to the adaptive responses to these several forces in many industries, including shipping, is increased flexibility in the use of human resources.

Chapter Four asks: How much innovative change has actually occurred to date in the eight shipping sectors? The ranking of the innovation records of the eight countries presents the essential facts that the theory attempts to explain. A similar assessment of past innovative achievements should also be the point of departure for a diagnosis of the strengths and weaknesses of the innovative capacity of particular social systems. Diagnosis does not necessarily require comparison of as many systems as the eight compared in this study and need not be as systematic. Diagnosis may compare achievement in only two or three social systems, or it may merely assess achievement against expectations. The comparison may involve similar industries or different ones. The important point is that comparisons such as those in Chapter Four can motivate a diagnostic process in other settings, just as they can provide an analytic task for an explanatory theory.

Chapter 3

An Industry's Responses to the Need for Change

Until recently, seafarers knew exactly what to expect when they signed on a ship.

> The officers and crews were always cordoned off into separate classes. Officers socialized with officers; crewmen mingled with crewmen. When the crew, known in sailing parlance as "ratings," received a reasonable order from the captain or a mate, they rarely questioned it. The schedule of work activities—who would do what and when—was drawn up by the officers and adhered to by the crew; a work assignment was not a collaborative exercise or a matter for discussion. There were no suggestion boxes. . . .
>
> There was little or no flexibility in work assignments. . . . If you came on as a navigator, you navigated. If your status was that of an engineer, you worked on the engine. No one was expected to work in the engine room one day and on the bridge the next.

Work roles were frozen by contract between management and the maritime unions.

That's what the sailors were accustomed to on
American vessels.[1]

The specific reference here is to American ships, but the
pattern was similar in most traditional maritime countries. Around
1970 things began to change, first in one country, then another, and
another, until by 1983 all but two of the eight countries studied had
at least some vessels operating with radically different shipboard
organizations: The role structures were more flexible, the employment and assignments of seafarers provided more continuity, the
authority structures were characterized by mutual influence, and
shipboard organizations were more egalitarian and integrated
socially.

Work innovations in the shipping industry from 1966 to
1983, the period covered by this study, were shaped by many factors.
They were an adaptive response to certain trends, especially
economic, technological, and social. And they were constrained by
tradition and institutions. This chapter outlines these general
features of the industry and how they impinged on the eight
industrialized maritime countries included in the study as a group.
In subsequent chapters these features help explain differences in the
innovation records of the countries. This chapter also describes the
major shipboard innovations, setting the stage for analysis in the
next chapter of the spread of these innovations in each of the eight
countries.

Economic Context

The shipping industry comprises companies that operate the world
oceangoing fleet. The fleet grew from eighteen thousand to twenty-
six thousand ships and tripled its tonnage capacity between 1966
and 1983.[2] It included several types of vessels, each handling a
different type of trade. Tankers hauled mostly crude oil. They
represented nearly half of the tonnage in 1981 but only a fifth of the
ships. Bulkers carried homogeneous loads of dry commodities, such
as coal, iron ore, and grain. General-cargo vessels typically carried

heterogeneous loads of manufactured goods, processed foods, or other packaged products. General-cargo vessels represented about one-fourth of the tonnage but two-thirds of the ships.[3] Shipowners operated in two distinctly different types of services: liner trades and tramp shipping.[4] The liner service operated like a railroad, carrying general cargo for many shippers from point to point on a regular schedule at announced rates. In tramp shipping each trip was scheduled individually and usually involved a contract to carry a full shipload of a single bulk commodity. Freight rates for tramp shipping were highly sensitive to fluctuations in the supply of tonnage capacity and the volume of seaborne trade.

The liner services were typically managed by conferences, especially in the areas covered in this study—Europe, the United States, and Japan. A conference was a group of shipowners of one or more nationalities that served a group of ports on a given route. Members of the conference would agree to a sailing pattern and charge identical rates. Freight rates in the liner services tended to be more stable than those in tramp shipping.

General trends in shipping industry supply and demand shifted midway in the period covered by this study, creating two distinct periods. From mid 1960 through 1973 the tonnage of seaborne trade grew every year, averaging 7 percent growth per annum. Demand often stretched the available capacity of existing ships. The picture changed dramatically during the period from 1973 to 1983. Growth first slowed, and then the total volume of seaborne trade actually declined. The ten-year period saw no net growth in trade (see Table 3-1). By 1983 the industry was in a major slump and had been for several years.

Several other developments, combined with the recession in seaborne trade, threatened the prosperity and survival of the maritime countries in the study.

The fleets of a number of newly industrialized countries and of members of the Soviet bloc grew more rapidly than world seaborne trade.[5] Countries in both groups aggressively promoted their national fleets, escalating the competitive conditions in many of the markets in which the established maritime fleets participated. Another type of fleet, called flags of convenience (FOC), also grew. FOC ships were registered in Liberia, Panama, and a few other

Table 3-1. Growth and Decline in Tonnage
of World Seaborne Trade, 1965–83.

Year	Percent variation per annum
1965–66	+8
1966–67	+5
1967–68	+10
1968–69	+11
1969–70	+7
1970–71	+7
1971–72	+4
1972–73	+12
1973–74	+4
1974–75	−6
1975–76	+9
1976–77	+3
1977–78	+2
1978–79	+8
1979–80	−3
1980–81	−4
1981–82	−7
1982–83	−2

Source: OECD, 1983, p. 22.

small countries that accepted vessels with any national ownership. (For a definition of this term and others unique to the shipping industry, see Exhibit 3-1). Owners in the traditional maritime countries who reregistered their ships under an FOC could often gain economic advantages, such as tax benefits, relaxed regulations, less expensive crew, and more flexible staffing practices. By 1983 FOC fleets accounted for over 25 percent of the world fleet. The loss of ships to FOC fleets was greater in the more cost-competitive segments, tanker and bulker. For example, the Liberian fleet became the predominant world tanker fleet, largely owned or chartered by the multinational petroleum companies.[6] The eight countries as a group experienced considerable losses from their national fleets to FOC's. By 1983 more than twenty-eight hundred vessels owned by shipowners in these countries were operating under foreign flags.[7]

Exhibit 3-1. Glossary of Terms.

Billets	Positions on the shipboard staffing roster
Bosun	Unlicensed supervisor of deck ratings
Deck officers	Licensed (officer) personnel responsible for navigation and cargo
Deck ratings	Ratings in the deck department
d.w.t.	Dead-weight tonnage: the total lifting capacity of a ship
Engineering ratings	Ratings in the engine room
Engineers	Licensed (officer) personnel responsible for the engine room
FOC	Flag of convenience: denotes registration of vessels in foreign nations that offer favorable tax structures and regulations. Countries with significant registries are Liberia, Panama, Bahamas, Cyprus, and Bermuda.
General-purpose (GP) ratings	Also sometimes referred to as multiple-purpose crew, ships' mechanics, dual-purpose crew. The GP is certified to work in both the engine room and on deck. More advanced forms of general-purpose positions were called ships' mechanics and ships' operators.
grt	Gross registered tons: a common measurement of the internal volume of a ship. One ton equals 100 cubic feet.
Integrated officer	The form of officer role flexibility developed in Japan
Master	The top officer position on the vessel, sometimes referred to as captain
Ratings	A British term for the nonofficer complement of the crew. Ratings are referred to as "unlicensed" crew members in the United States.
Ro-Ro	Roll-on/roll-off: ships designed to allow trucks to drive on and off with cargo
Seafarers and crew	Both terms are used in this book to refer to all shipboard members, including officers. Occasionally the term *crew* has been used to refer to nonofficers only.
Seamen	Ratings, usually deck ratings
Semi-integrated officer	The form of officer role flexibility between deck and engine work developed in Holland

Trends in shipping economics affected operators. From 1966 to 1973 wages increased sharply in the eight countries in our study. For the countries as a group, this was a period of general prosperity, low unemployment, and strong unions. Almost all of them experienced particularly severe manpower shortages in shipping, causing them to raise maritime pay even more rapidly than wages in shore industries. Because the rapid growth in shipping during this period outstripped capacity, freight rates rose to cover the steadily increasing costs. Then the industry changed dramatically. The years from 1973 to 1983 were marked by overcapacity and increasingly depressed freight rates. Coincidentally, interest rates and fuel costs increased dramatically, before subsiding somewhat at the very end of this period. Despite general reductions in crew sizes during the ten-year period and major increases in fuel prices and capital costs during the 1970s, the crew continued to represent one of the larger costs for the countries in our sample. Consider the cost breakdown in 1980 for a sixty-thousand-dead-weight-tonnage (d.w.t) modern bulker in the United Kingdom fleet,[8] the fleet with the lowest pay scales in our sample:

Fuel expenses	30%
Crew costs	24
Capital costs (interest and depreciation)	28
Other	18
	100%

Crew costs on the U.K. vessel were almost one-fourth of total costs and over 40 percent of operating costs. In a comparable vessel in the Third World crew costs would be one-third the United Kingdom's; in the United States they would be more than double the United Kingdom's.[9]

Shipowners in the eight countries responded in various ways to these trends. One response was to increase the average size of the vessels in the fleet, increasing labor productivity and achieving other operating economies. Shipowners also shifted the mix of their fleets, often out of tankers or bulkers and into general-cargo vessels, which usually competed less heavily on the basis of freight rates.

They also attempted to carve out new niches within these three segments based on technical and marketing innovations, examples being containerization of general-cargo vessels, intermodal (road-rail-sea) transportation systems, roll-on/roll-off ships (called Ro-Ro's, the vessels are constructed to allow heavy vehicles to drive on and drive off with cargo), and highly specialized liquid-gas carriers. They also stepped up the introduction of automation. In modernizing their fleets, the countries studied often sold their ships to the newly industrialized countries, which added to the surplus capacity in the industry.

The growth and decline of particular national fleets was influenced not only by industry economics and the adaptive responses of shipowners but also by the amount and nature of assistance that governments provided their flag fleets.

Some countries reserved coastal and other domestic shipping for national fleets. Many unilaterally reserved some portion of their import and export cargoes for their own fleets.[10] The developing countries were pushing for a multilateral cargo-sharing agreement that called for an even division of liner conference cargoes between trading partners, with a smaller percentage reserved for third nations (called *cross-traders* because they hauled cargo between two other countries).[11]

Virtually every country with a national fleet subsidized it directly or indirectly.[12] Subsidies included income-tax breaks for operators and seafarers, preferred credit for new construction, and operating subsidies. They also included support for industry research and development and maritime education. In many cases where the country had both a significant shipping industry and a shipbuilding industry, it linked support for the two industries by subsidizing shipyards and inducing operators to purchase home-built ships. The eight countries studied provided varying levels of financial support from their shipping industries, but taken as a group they did not provide levels of support that differed materially from the rest of the world industry.

As a group the shipping sectors of the countries in our sample emerged from the period 1966 to 1973 in reasonable shape. They expanded their total capacity but at a slower rate than the world industry as a whole. The eight countries included most of the

Table 3-2. Prestudy History of Flag Distribution of Merchant Oceangoing Fleet (Thousands Gross Registered Tons and Percentage of World Fleet).

	1919		1939 Sept. 3		1948 Dec. 31		1958 Dec. 31		1965 Dec. 31	
	Thousands grt	Percentage	Thousands grt	Percentage	Thousands grt	Percentage	Thousands grt	Percentage	Thousands grt	Percentage
United Kingdom	16.3	34.0	16.9	27.5	16.0	22.0	19.2	16.8	20.4	13.2
United States	9.8	20.5	8.7	14.2	26.2	36.0	24.2	21.2	19.3	12.5
West Germany	3.2	6.7	4.2	6.8	0.1	0.2	3.9	3.4	5.3	3.4
Japan	2.3	4.8	5.4	8.8	1.4	1.9	5.5	4.8	11.3	7.3
British Commonwealth	1.9	4.0	1.9	2.8	3.4	4.5	2.9	2.5	4.6	3.0
France	1.9	4.0	2.7	4.5	2.5	3.4	4.3	3.8	4.9	3.1
Norway	1.6	3.3	4.7	7.6	4.2	5.8	9.6	8.4	15.6	10.1
Holland	1.6	3.3	2.8	4.6	2.6	3.6	4.3	3.8	4.5	3.0
Italy	1.2	2.5	3.3	5.4	2.1	2.9	4.9	4.3	5.5	3.7
Sweden	0.9	1.9	1.4	2.3	1.8	2.5	3.3	2.9	3.9	2.5
Denmark	0.6	1.3	1.1	1.8	1.0	1.4	2.0	1.7	2.5	1.6
Greece	0.3	0.6	1.8	2.8	1.3	1.8	1.9	1.7	6.9	4.5
Russia	0.5	1.0	1.2	1.9	1.3	1.7	2.6	2.3	7.5	4.9
Spain	0.7	1.5	0.9	1.5	1.0	1.4	1.3	1.4	1.8	1.2
Panama	—	—	0.7	1.2	2.8	3.9	4.4	3.8	4.7	3.1
Liberia	—	—	—	—	—	—	11.1	9.7	19.3	12.5
All other	5.1	10.6	3.7	6.3	5.2	7.1	9.0	7.5	16.0	10.4
World	47.9	100.0	61.4	100.0	72.9	100.0	114.4	100.0	154.0	100.0
U.S. reserve fleet (inc.)	—	—	—	—	13.1	—	14.4	—	10.4	—

Source: Adapted from O'Loughlin, 197, p. 60.

world's major traditional merchant navies, having claimed 74 percent of world fleet tonnage before the Second World War (see Table 3-2). They started the period in 1966 with a total capacity of 111,600 d.w.t. and 48 percent of the capacity of the world fleet.[13] In 1973 the tonnage had grown to 189,900 d.w.t., but their share of world trade had declined to 43 percent.[14]

During the more difficult period from 1973 to 1983, the ability of individual shipowners in our sample to sustain their competitiveness depended on innovations, good judgment, and good fortune in many areas—marketing (for example, identifying market niches where they could sustain a competitive advantage), sourcing and selling assets (for example, negotiating favorable terms for new construction and timely sales of existing vessels), technology (for example, developing appropriate laborsaving automation and fuel-efficient engine plants and superstructures), and the human resource policies I will discuss in the final section of this chapter.

Despite the resourcefulness of many shipping companies during the period from 1973 to 1983, the capacity of the eight countries shrank as a percentage of world capacity from 43 to 26 percent and absolutely from 189,000 to 171,300 d.w.t.[15] The northwestern European region especially slipped at the expense of a few larger fleets, for example, Greece and the USSR, and some smaller fleets, for example, Singapore, the Philippines, and Korea. All six European countries lost a share of the total world fleet in terms of both number of ships and tonnage capacity. Japan's position also declined in both respects. Of the countries in our sample, only the heavily protected U.S.-flag fleet increased its share of world tonnage capacity, but only slightly, while losing share of ships slightly.

The eight countries lost (-) or added (+) the following total d.w.t. capacity and ships in their fleets during the decade ending in 1983 (see Table 3-3). Capacity increases or decrease of the flag fleet were of particular importance to shipowners and governments. Governments were also interested in the interrelationship of this sector to other national industries, such as shipbuilding, oil, and automobile transport.

Table 3-3. Change in Shipping Capacity, 1973 to 1983.

D.W.T. Capacity		Number of Vessels
United States	+57%	–10%
Denmark	+14	–13
Japan	+7	–20
Holland	+5	+3
Sweden	–19	–33
Norway	–20	–52
West Germany	–22	–38
United Kingdom	–43	–58

The unions were more interested in changes in the number of ships. The loss of ships under the national flag translated directly into the loss of jobs, because reregistered ships hired foreign ratings and mostly foreign officers.

The size of a national fleet is influenced by its competitive performance, but other factors are also important. This can be illustrated by reviewing the experiences of the countries in this study. The eight countries encountered differing degrees of difficulty, depending on conditions in the industry segments in which their ships were initially employed. Clearly Holland, Denmark, Japan, and the United States did better at maintaining their share of the world fleet capacity and preserving jobs, but they provided their fleets more generous government assistance. Norway and the United Kingdom suffered the greatest declines in tonnage, but both were heavily engaged in the more competitive cross-trading. They also received less financial support from their governments. It is safe to conclude that, of the two large cross-traders, Norway was more successful than the United Kingdom. While such a conclusion is plausible, it must be regarded as highly tentative in the absence of more direct indicators of competitive performance.

The absence of a simple relationship between a country's competitive performance and the maintenance of its share of the world fleet has further implications for the analysis of innovation. While I will attempt to make a persuasive case that work innovations that reduced crew sizes were one of several factors enhancing the competitive performance of national fleets, this is not reflected in a correlation between innovativeness and maintenance of shares of world capacity.

Technology Developments

As noted above, economic pressures encouraged the developed countries to modernize their fleets with larger, more specialized, and more automated vessels. Larger and faster ships increased labor productivity and achieved other economies. Both tankers and bulker vessels were designed for particular cargoes and trade routes. Examples were specialized liquid-gas carriers and Ro-Ros, designed to transport long lengths of steel.

The major technical innovation in the liner trades was the development of an intermodal container system, based on standardized twenty-foot or forty-foot containers, each eight feet wide and eight and a half feet high. The containers could fit on rail cars, trucks, and ships. The containers decreased port time, minimized wastage from handling, and decreased labor required to handle cargo on the docks and on board. Containerization required large investments. For example, in 1977 a containership cost $25 to $30 per cubic foot to build, compared with $7 to $8 per cubic foot for a conventional break-bulk cargo ship. The thirty-ton-capacity crane required to lift containers cost $1.7 million.[16]

Many forms of automation and other changes in vessel design, technology, and equipment decreased labor costs.[17] Engine-room automation consisted of remote sensing of operating conditions, which eliminated round-the-clock watch keeping in engine spaces. Maintenance requirements were reduced by equipment designed to be maintenance free, by systems that automatically monitored the condition of equipment, and by use of epoxy paints and special coatings that required less maintenance. Mechanical innovations were applied to moving and anchoring, including self-stowing line baskets, constant-tension winches, and smaller and lighter lines. Microprocessors aided cargo operations, performing such tasks as calculating load and monitoring hull stress, while satellite telecommunications made possible dependable, high-

Table 3-4. Crew Reductions in Recent Decades.

Name of Ship	Year Investigated	Number of Crew	Type of Ship
Hakonesan Maru	1961	50	Conventional liner
Arizona Maru	1962	45	Conventional liner
Shizuoka Maru	1963	45	Conventional liner
Kasugasan Maru	1952	35	Automated liner
Mishishipi Maru	1964	34	Automated liner
Munetama Maru	1977	27	MO[a]-oil tanker
Hikawa Maru	1977	25	MO-oil tanker
Kojusan Maru	1977	24	MO-iron ore
Tarumaesan Maru	1978	17	Containership
Kushiro Maru	1978	17	MO-paper carrier

[a]MO designates unmanned engine room.

Note: This table is adapted from an article reporting on successive studies over two decades of work on board Japanese vessels. The pattern is generally illustrative of the decline in crew sizes in the most progressive shipowners in the countries studied.

Source: Adapted from Koishi, 1981, p. 261.

quality voice, telex, and computer communications between the ship and shore offices and between seafarers and their families.

The combined effect of laborsaving technology, different operating strategies, and work innovations was a dramatic decrease in crew sizes over the period studied: from the high forties to the high teens in the most progressive companies in our sample. The reductions achieved by leading parts of the industry during this period are illustrated in Table 3-4.

Traditional Shipboard Organization and Shipping Institutions

All of the maritime countries in the sample borrowed their shipboard traditions as well as some of the supporting institutions from the British, which is not surprising in view of the fact that Britain claimed over one-third of the world fleet as late as 1919 (see Table 3-2).

I begin by describing the traditional shipboard organization and some of the duties associated with various positions in the organization.[18] The master, or captain, is in charge of the ship. Beneath him duties are divided among three departments: deck, engine, and catering (or stewards). Masters are promoted from the deck department.

The deck department is headed by the chief officer or first mate, who plans and supervises the handling of cargo and the maintenance of the ship and much of its equipment. Second and third mates are junior officers responsible for navigation charts and equipment, lifesaving equipment, and other duties that assist the first mate. The deck department includes a foreman drawn from the ranks of deck ratings. The nonofficer crew members are referred to as ratings in many countries and as unlicensed seamen in the United States. The foreman of deck personnel may be called a bosun, or, in the United Kingdom, a deck petty officer. There usually are two levels of deck ratings, called ordinary and able-bodied seaman in the United States and seaman grade I and grade II in the United Kingdom. Both may be employed in the same way, but able-bodied seamen possess higher skills.

The engine department is the responsibility of the chief engineer, who oversees the main propulsion machinery, electrical plant, refrigeration plant, and ventilation system. The engineering-officer complement may comprise, in addition to the chief engineer, first, second, third, and fourth engineers. These officers perform such duties as controlling the speed of the main engines; maintaining proper steam pressure and water temperature; and overseeing inspection of engines, pumps, and generator. Engine-room ratings include positions representing at least two levels of skill. Sometimes a foreman, called a petty officer motorman in the United Kingdom, relays instructions from engineers to ratings.

The stewards', or catering, department is headed by the chief steward, who is responsible for menus, the galley, galley stores, and ship's linen. He is assisted by cooks and other attendants. Finally, radio officers operate the radio communication equipment.

Seafarers usually are educated and trained by a combination of specialized maritime academies, apprenticeship experiences, and company programs.

Traditionally, many conditions of seafarer employment were set out in a country's laws or regulations, and others were covered by union agreement. Both ratings and officers in all eight countries were represented by trade unions. The extent of unionization varied within the rest of the world fleet, which included the Soviet bloc countries and newly industrialized countries, such as Taiwan and Korea, with weak union movements.

The number of separate unions representing seafarers varied throughout our sample. In Holland one union represented all ratings and a second all officers; in the United Kingdom deck officers, engineering officers, masters, radio officers, and ratings were represented by five different unions. In both countries each union was a national union, representing all seafarers within the designated craft classification. Among the countries studied, only in the United States (and West Germany to a minor degree) did multiple unions compete to represent the same group of seafarers.

Typically in my sample, an industry shipowners' association negotiated with the national unions on matters affecting pay, hours of duty, staffing levels, shipboard living conditions, sea and shore leave time, and travel expenses. Agreements often prescribed minimum terms for the industry, and individual shipowners might agree to more generous terms.

Seafarers were employed by two contrasting mechanisms. The traditional mechanism was casual employment through hiring halls, usually operated by the unions themselves, where the seafarer contracted for a specific sailing. The other employment mechanism was the conventional one for industry generally in the countries we studied, hiring seafarers to become regular company employees. Regular employment for seafarers involved alternate periods of sea duty and shore leave. Some countries in the sample had converted completely to regular employment relationships, others continued to rely very heavily on union hiring halls, and others fell between these extremes.

In addition to the terms negotiated between the shipowners and unions, employment conditions were set by law or government regulation. Government rules usually prescribed the minimum staffing scales for ships operating under the national flag. Minimums were prescribed for certain classes of crew, such as deck officers and marine engineers, and for the overall crew. The scale typically varied according to the size of the ship, type of equipment, and trade route. Regulations also prescribed the qualifications and certification procedures for each category and class of seafarer.

I can illustrate some additional types of laws and regulations and the rigidities they created in shipboard organizational practices. The following examples are taken from the U.S. regulations.[19] One staffing rule required a radio officer, a position no longer necessary in some cases owing to technological advances in telecommunications. A U.S. statute expressly required three watches, which in many cases was obviated by automation, especially in the engine room. A "crossover law" stipulated that the seafarer could not serve in both deck and engine departments in a single voyage. Deck and engine licenses were divided by statute, which precluded a dual-purpose license. Moreover, many statutory classifications of ratings preserved customary practices. They refered to "able seaman," "coal passer," "wiper," "qualified member of the engine department," "oiler," "fireman," and "watch tender."

National regulation of workplace conditions was pervasive in this industry for many reasons. Shipping posed high inherent risk of accident and loss of life as well as loss of property and damage to the environment. The young age at which boys traditionally went to sea made protective legislation especially appropriate. The casual nature of maritime labor historically meant that, for all intents and purposes, seafarers were employed by the industry. Regulations ensured that the seafarer knew what to expect when he signed on any particular vessel; similarly, shipowners knew what to expect from the seafarers they signed up for a voyage. The mobility of production capacity (vessels) in this industry and the commodity nature of much of the service provided fostered intense competition. The competition sometimes encouraged shipowners, many of whom owned one or a few vessels, to cut corners on safety.

National regulations in the countries studied were typically formulated by government departments through discussions involving unions and shipowners' associations. The discussions occurred within a structure of representative committees, and each focused on some aspect of the industry, such as staffing.

An agency of the United Nations, the International Maritime Organization, also proposed standards and issued regulations relating to standards for training, certification, leave time, and watch keeping.[20] International oversight of shipboard staffing reflected the fact that the accident involving a ship from one country could cause loss of life, property damage, and environmental pollution in other countries.

Innovations in Shipboard Organization

Economics and technological developments not only affected the way shipowners competed but also altered the daily lives of seafarers. Indeed, the developments were changing the very meaning of seafaring, as two journalists on the maritime beat report.

> Much of the age-old glamour associated with "going-to-sea" has disappeared: the seafarer may still get some time off in port to see the local sights, working on old, simple tween-deckers. But aboard sophisticated capitally intensive vessels, port time must be reduced to a bare minimum, measured in hours rather than

days, and during this period the ship is at its busiest. Some seafarers rarely even see a port—they just work between offshore terminals.

The seafarer has always worked in a unique environment—a few people labouring round the clock in a rigid hierarchy and yet, people do choose the occupation. But the changing nature of shipping has meant that some of the attractive, even romantic, parts of the job have all but gone and at the same time, new and deeper pressures have been introduced into the work. Increased technology, smaller complements and the never-ending search for greater operating efficiency combine to induce more stress; and opportunities for relieving tension are less available. The important process of "role changing," which happens ashore all the time, provides a valve to release stresses built up at work: just decorating the house or a trip to the pub with friends.[21]

The economic and technological trends and the decreasing appeal of seafaring underlay the work innovations in the shipping industry between 1966 and 1983. The innovations involved four types of change:

1. From a strict hierarchical, departmental structure with narrow, fixed roles to one in which roles are more broadly defined and assignment patterns more flexible
2. From rotary hiring halls through which seafarers hire on for specific voyages to ongoing employment relationships between seafarers and shipowners; and from a high turnover of onboard personnel to a pattern in which more individuals return to the same ship after shore leave
3. From a pattern of central authority to more delegated authority and participative decision making
4. From a rigid, castelike social structure to one that is more flexible, with a deemphasis of status symbols and encouragement of greater social integration.[22]

These four dimensions of change were common across many manufacturing and transportation industries in many countries, confirming that the shipping innovations were part of a broader pattern of industrial change. But the changes were particularly dramatic in the maritime industry, because it had developed an extreme version of the traditional hierarchical, departmentalized, socially segregated, limited employment relationship organization.

Toward Role Flexibility. Until recently, crew members of deep-sea vessels would not consider crossing departmental lines to perform work in another department. The deck, engine, and catering departmental boundaries were usually reinforced by tradition, union agreement, and law and functioned satisfactorily on conventional cargo ships. The deck and engine departments could operate relatively independently. Each had adequate manpower within its own ranks and could provide personnel with a balanced mixture of watch-keeping, operational, and maintenance tasks.

The disadvantages of maintaining a strict departmental structure resulted from two types of technical changes. First, although containerization and other innovations reduced the cargo-handling responsibilities of deck personnel, they also reduced the time in port and thus substantially increased the proportion of time spent on basic navigational watch keeping. At the same time, the automation of the engine room decreased the round-the-clock watch-keeping duties of engine-room personnel. Thus, the earlier balance of tasks in each department changed, and in complementary ways, but the departmental structure and specialized training precluded the use of engineering officers for deck watch duties. Second, automation decreased the size of the crew complement in both departments, making it more difficult to meet fluctuations in work loads from within a department.

The primary rationale for role flexibility was the ability to handle peak loads anywhere in the ship with fewer personnel. The shortage of manpower that developed from 1966 to 1973 increased the interest of some shipowners in using scarce personnel more flexibly. Then the cost pressures that developed from 1973 to 1983 generated a stronger financial incentive for shipowners to employ costly personnel more flexibly in order to permit a decrease in crew sizes.

The trend toward shipboard role flexibility affected six of the eight countries. In the late 1960s companies in several countries gained permission from unions and the government to use engine-room ratings on deck and vice versa. The practice was referred to as interdepartmental flexibility. Later, ratings who were cross-trained were approved as a new standard in many countries. They were often called general-purpose (GP) ratings. Under the earlier forms of interdepartmental flexibility, ratings could do only menial tasks when assigned outside their home department, but the GP was fully qualified in both departments, at least in principle.

Still later—in the late 1970s—role flexibility was extended to officer ranks. In one of the two countries that had implemented change of this type, they labeled the new position "semi-integrated officer," signifying that an officer had a primary role in one department (deck or engineering), for which he or she had received extensive training, and a secondary role, drawing on basic training in the disciplines of the other department. Additionally, one country trained and certified ratings to perform watch-standing duties previously requiring an officer. Shipowners in many other countries were interested in developing both of these forms of flexibility affecting the work performed by officers.

We saw above that some technical changes were influencing the move toward role flexibility. The effect of other technical changes was to ease its implementation. Location on the bridge of remote controls for the engine room as well as for navigation control permitted multiskilled officers to handle both deck and engineering duties. Similarly, mechanical innovations, for example, self-stowing line baskets and constant-tension winches, decreased the brute strength required for duties on deck and therefore permitted duties to be more readily included in a single general-purpose rating classification.

Toward Continuity of Employment and Vessel Assignment. As pointed out above, seafarers traditionally were hired from an industry pool or a union hiring hall. A seafarer did not have an ongoing employment relationship with a shipowner and may never have sailed with the same shipowner in any two consecutive voyages. This casual employment relationship met shipowners' needs for flexibility in response to their fluctuating requirements for seafarers. At the same time the autonomy of the seafarers became a part of their tradition, which some of them valued highly. Even where seafarers sailed with the same shipowner on consecutive voyages, they did not sail with the same crew on the same vessel.

The disadvantages of casualism and instability in vessel assignments grew over time. The voyages themselves became shorter as vessel speed increased and port time decreased. Routes that took months in the early 1960s were subsequently completed in weeks. In addition, unions were negotiating shorter stints of sea duty and more time ashore. Prior to the mid 1960s, it was common for seafarers to serve continuously on the same ship for periods exceeding twelve months. Subsequently, the typical service period was decreased to four months. These two developments meant that the policies of casualism produced progressively higher rates of turnover.

Casualism was erased by legislation before the mid 1970s in several European countries. The requirement of shipowners to offer regular and continuous employment to seafarers was part of broader legislation enlarging the social obligation of employers. Increasingly, shipowners in many of the other countries studied also achieved service continuity by policies or by informal means.

Some shipping companies, especially those committed to implementing other innovations, went further and worked to achieve assignment continuity. One pattern was to assign three full crew complements to two ships; under this arrangement each crew took two months of leave for every three months at sea. Other companies, usually in Sweden, assigned two crews to one ship, based on a pattern of equal leave and sea time. Whatever the pattern, the objective of crew continuity complicated personnel planning and incurred manpower costs, a fact that caused shipowners to continue to assess the costs and benefits of the practices in their particular circumstances.

Toward Participation and Delegated Authority. The idea of ratings planning their own work and involved in governing their closed twenty-four-hour community is a radical one in the context of maritime history and tradition. The military character of the shipboard organization was historically a necessary response to the internal threat of mutiny and the external threats of piracy and the elements. Methods of recruitment, which often meant that many seafarers were not on board by free choice, underscored the need for coercive authority. This militaristic tradition continued, being relaxed only by degrees, into the modern era.

Several factors caused a break with this tradition in recent decades. First, the expectations of seafarers and the philosophies of management in shipping companies were influenced by the societal trends toward workplace participation in the countries studied. Second, during the manpower shortage a few shipowners fostered participation to help make seafaring more attractive. Third, when high labor costs became a competitive liability, participation was sometimes seen as part of a strategy to increase crew motivation and productivity and to improve operating decisions.

The trend to give ratings more voice proved to be very uneven among the eight countries. It mainly took the form of participation in the planning of work. Typically, officers and a rating representative decided in a strategic sense what work needed to be done on a voyage. Then ratings were involved in decisions about who would do what tasks and when and how. This participative process led to a blurring of other distinctions between the work of officers and ratings. The participation process usually extended beyond task planning to decision making about food, liquor, social activities, and other matters of vital concern to members of the ship community.

A researcher of the Oslo Work Research Institute, reporting on the Norwegian ship *Balao*, an early pioneer in shipboard participation, expressed the ideal spirit of this innovation.

> What we had at the end of 1976, after almost four years of development, primarily guided by the members of the ship's company themselves, was a completely new, more democratic form of organization based on full participation in work planning. Temporary autonomous groups changed from week to week depending

on tasks and training needs. Work duties and functions are not divided according to deck and machine
crews or between officers and crew as is typical on
conventional ships. Qualified members of the crew
cover a variety of duties across traditional functional
and status dividing lines. Work load, training needs
and safety considerations are the deciding factors in
allocating specific tasks to specific people . . . each
one had his special duty which demands special
qualifications, and in addition is competent for duties
overlapping others' competence.[23]

The techniques used to implement participation in work
planning can be illustrated by the practices of Shell B.V. Tankers.
Management developed a planning board system, and when it
proved effective, Shell made it available to other shipowners on a
commercial basis. The planning board itself was a mounted
Plexiglass sheet listing the tasks to be done during the voyage. The
ratings consulted the board during the day and checked off the jobs
they chose to do next. The system divided the ship into a number
of elements: cargo equipment, main engine, safety, and so on. For
each element there were prescribed tasks to be accomplished at
specific intervals. The programmed tasks were supplemented by a
listing of other tasks that could not be anticipated. The importance
of the technique was that it simultaneously promoted planning that
was economically rational and implementation decisions that were
participative.

Even in such progressive companies as Shell B.V. Tankers in
Holland and Hoegh in Norway, companies that had encouraged
participative patterns of shipboard management on their vessels,
actual practices often fell short of the policy ideal. For example, this
shortfall was observed on the Hoegh *Mallard* in 1979, years after the
company had begun to diffuse its shipboard innovations throughout its large fleet. The observations were made by several American
seafarers recruited by Robert Schrank for a study sponsored by the
Ford Foundation to observe the shipboard innovations.

The American journalist who accompanied the seafarers
reported:

I knew almost from the moment we sat down that this was not the kind of meeting I had expected. The only rank-and-file crew member present was the bosun [the foreman], and it was his job to make decisions about the work every day. The others around the table were all licensed men—the chief mate, the chief engineer, first engineer, and electrician. At the head of the table sat the captain, very much in charge. Clearly he was the leader and coordinator of the meeting. He was running the show, getting their ideas together, keeping the dialogue going.

The Norwegians discussed dozens of items concerning the ship's operational priorities: what had to be done, what was now being done, what must be done immediately, and what could be postponed. Throughout the meeting the bosun participated fully in the spirited give-and-take discussions. But we were always aware that none of the ordinary seamen were there.[24]

The American observers concluded that on this ship the total pattern of crew meetings had been "only moderately successful in engaging the men in planning the work."[25]

Just as ratings in many instances gained influence vis-à-vis ships' officers, the latter received more delegated responsibilities from shore superiors. The trend represented a break with recent maritime tradition and a return step to an earlier tradition.[26] In the days of the clipper ships, the master navigated the ship, stowed the cargo, purchased provisions, obtained much of the homebound cargo business, and had an equity stake in the bargain.

Shore organizations progressively increased their control over ships as vessels and fleets got bigger and more expensive and cargoes more complicated. Routes began to be controlled by shore units, and shipboard maintenance became the responsibility of a marine superintendent in company headquarters. A ship's officer complement was increasingly provided with detailed rules and asked to submit detailed reports. And the reports served to enable more decisions to be made centrally. As a result of these trends, ships' officers were sometimes characterized as expensive bus drivers and engine mechanics.

The head office staff was usually departmentalized into units specializing in marine (deck), chartering, accounting, personnel, engineering, purchasing, and so on. Even when head office departments channeled their contacts with the ship through the master, the separate requests they made to different senior officers were seldom a coherent set. Often the shore's uniform rules, procedures, or requests failed to take into account local circumstances. These, of course, are widely recognized limitations of centralized, functional organizations generally.

Understandably, in recent maritime history officers typically had not thought of themselves as managers in the sense of being responsible for the efficient and effective use of resources against given commercial objectives for their vessel. Rather, they had defined their accountability strictly in terms of discipline and professional technical standards, which has been called "command accountability."[27]

This traditional view of the occupation and a strong emotional attachment to it is reflected in the words of an American master seaman in reaction to his observations of the expanded managerial role of the master on a Norwegian vessel, the *Mallard*.

> . . .When I walk on a ship I do the best job I can. I am secure whether the chief mate likes me or not. I'm not there to make points with the chief mate, the company, or anyone else. They can't lay work on me that's out of my jurisdiction. They know that I have certificates showing my skills, I can do my job, and that I'm a member of my union. I am responsible to the job and also to my union. *I am my own man.*[28]

Beginning in the late 1960s, a growing interest developed in what was often referred to as "shipboard management teams." The idea was a familiar one in decentralization strategies: Those in charge of a unit were held responsible for results and given discretion on how to achieve them. It also emphasized the formation of a top officer team on board ship, typically built around the master and chief engineer. The officers were expected to collaborate in planning and controlling the use of resources, to meet commercial objectives, and to involve their subordinates in these activities. The enlarged responsibilities of the captain of the Hoegh *Mallard,* typical of this trend toward shipboard management, are nicely captured by the American seafarers after they had accompanied the vessel on a seven-week voyage from the west coast of the United States to Europe.

> Roar Johansen, captain of the *Mallard,* performed a variety of functions and assumed a number of different roles. We saw him as the humane and empathetic officer who played the guitar at a ship's party. We saw him as the confident and undisputed master of the *Mallard* when the ship was maneuvering into port or loading and unloading its cargo. We saw him as the chief executive officer of a floating enterprise, who labored long into the night to complete reports to the company and to make out the ship's budget. We saw him as the patient but controlling supervisor who ran meetings with a blend of cooperativeness and authority. And we saw him as the educator-dean who decided which crew members should receive further education and training based on their performance on the ship.[29]

The captain, along with other senior officers, had become accountable for actively managing events and people, rather than reacting to them.

Toward a Socially Integrated Crew. In view of the departmental structure, the way authority was exercised, and the temporary nature of relationships on board the traditional ship, it is not surprising that the social system was fragmented and stratified. The following statement captures a traditional view of the shipboard social structure in the British merchant marine.

> As things stand, officers and ratings eat in separate messrooms, use separate lounges, and are accommo-

> dated on different decks. Facilities such as games
> rooms are usually shared. Seafarers on British ships
> have so far rejected moves towards common messing
> or use of lounges and bars. The officers feel that
> authority will be undermined by any form of integra-
> tion. No one believes that the ship manager ashore sits
> down to dinner with the office porter. Why then
> should a shipmaster eat with a deck boy? [30]

The most fundamental social schism divided officers and
ratings. The two groups were strictly segregated during nonworking hours and were accorded markedly different privileges and
status. Both groups developed norms that restricted relationships
between them and often tended to maintain group solidarity by
expressing hostility toward the other group. [31]

Physical features of the ship promoted not only the social
distinctions between officers and ratings but finer distinctions as
well. Employees with the dirtiest and lowest jobs traditionally had
quarters in the dark, narrow, noisy space next to the engine room.
The higher the rank, the more spacious and better situated the
quarters. A Swedish union official offered some details of this
allocation of privileges.

> The higher up the cabins, the larger and lighter, the
> more the occupants are paid. For centuries in Sweden
> this class structure was a matter of law. As late as the
> 1960s the Seamen's Act stipulated the amount of space
> varied according to the function on board. Even the
> bunk size was determined by class; the captain by law
> was entitled to a far wider bed than anybody else. As
> late as the 1950s ships were still being built according
> to this rigid class structure. Everything was based on
> job status, down to the dining facilities. The captain
> ate either alone or with the chief engineer and had his
> own cabin attendant. The mate's dining room had a
> separate attendant. There were five levels and five
> dining facilities in the best tradition of the military. [32]

Similar practices characterized the maritime traditions of all of the countries studied.

Over the period studied, the eight countries experienced a general egalitarian trend in the workplace, which influenced practices in the shipping industry. In the late 1960s and early 1970s, shipowners responded to personnel shortages by upgrading the perks and privileges of ratings.

Apart from either of these reasons for upgrading the shipboard lives of ratings, it became increasingly awkward to maintain different perks and social segregation as crews shrank in size. Under conventional staffing systems, with crew sizes of thirty or more, the ratio of officers to ratings is about 1 to 2. As crewing is reduced to between twenty and twenty-five, the officer-to-ratings ratio becomes about 1 to 1.5; and when the total crew size is eighteen or less, it becomes about 1 to 1. In this situation, the traditional distinctions between officers and ratings make little sense.[33] And with smaller crew sizes, shipowners began to treat loneliness as a practical problem. Some believed it would become necessary to break down social barriers in order to increase the number of persons with whom a seafarer could potentially socialize. Besides, with small crews the expense of maintaining a number of separate messes could not be justified.

To further social integration, shipping managers took four types of action. They (1) upgraded ratings' quarters and equalized perks for officers and ratings, (2) provided common mess and leisure-time facilities for ratings and officers, (3) scheduled common social activity for all ship personnel, and (4) designed new ship superstructures to promote crew interaction during working and nonworking time. Ambitious versions of the new organizational pattern usually included all four types of action. But the first two often were implemented independently of any other organizational changes. The first, upgraded quarters and perks for ratings, often was pursued strictly as a recruiting tactic. The second, common mess and other facilities, often was initiated by shipowners in order to save space and personnel in the steward's department.

Thus, a modern Norwegian vessel designed to promote social integration was equipped as follows, as seen by several American seafarers against the background of traditional conditions:

Each crew member had a private room, about twelve
by eighteen feet, with a large bunk in a curtained
nook. Each room contained a couch and two easy
chairs, a coffee table and a desk, rugs, framed pictures
on the imitation wood walls and a live potted plant.
Each room had a small refrigerator and a private
toilet, shower, and sink. The Americans were impressed. One said that he has seen first-class American
cruise ships with passenger cabins no better than those
set aside for sailors. . . .

The next stop was the cafeteria: the cretonne-
covered chairs, the tablecloths, and the pictures and
posters on the walls. The galley was spotless. Next to
the common mess room was a large coffee bar, used as
a general gathering place during breaks.

The dayroom, one flight up, was connected by
an open stairwell surrounded by a variety of plants.
Soft chairs and tables were decorated in shades of coral
and blue. There was wall-to-wall carpeting. A stereo
system had been installed in the lounge for off-duty
crew members. A library across the way included a
television cassette system and books and magazines.
Our biggest surprise was an indoor swimming pool,
which [we were told] would be filled when the ship
reached the tropical waters near Panama.

We also saw a sauna and a full-sized gymna-
sium available to officers and men. The ship's bar,
next on the tour, would be open three nights a week
after . . . [we] made for the open sea.[34]

Though such facilities were not always fully utilized by the
crew, for example, because of work loads, and though they did not
ensure easy interaction among crew members when they were used,
they did promote a more egalitarian ship community.

Implications of Work Innovations for Competitiveness

Over the period studied, effective implementation of the types of
work innovations described above became increasingly regarded by

shipowners and other industry groups as contributors to competitiveness.

The most apparent form of the economic benefit from the innovations, especially role flexibility, is their effect in decreasing the size of crews and lowering overall crew costs. These benefits were relatively easily calculated. Another easily calculated economic benefit came directly from social integration—the decrease in space and galley personnel required by fewer separate dining and lounge areas.

Another source of economic benefit came from the improved quality of shipboard decisions and the quality of their implementation by the crews, especially as a result of continuity of employment and assignment, participation, and delegation. While some shipowners in the countries studied claimed improved effectiveness and could provide examples, they had not attempted to quantify the gains. Of course, not all shipowners shared the same level of expectation that improved competence and commitment on the part of seafarers would result from these innovative changes and would translate into better performance.

Safety was still another concern with direct economic salience. On the basis of direct experience with a more flexible organization, many ships' officers claimed they felt much safer with a more competent, flexible, and cohesive crew. On the other hand, some union officials claimed that increased levels of stress accompanied the reduced crewing and increased the risk of accident. The actual safety records reported by governments, industry associations, and unions showed that there was either an improvement or no change in safety accompanying the several relevant trends occurring aboard ships, namely, smaller crews, revised organization, and technological changes.

Whatever practical advantages were associated with organizational changes in older ships staffed by crews in the twenty-five-to-forty range, these advantages became progressively more compelling with more technically advanced ships staffed by smaller crews.

Table 3-5 arrays many of the technological changes and their implications for the nature and size of the shipboard organization.

**Table 3-5. Technological Changes and Their Implications
for Shipboard Organization.**

Technological Innovations	Human Resources Policy Implications
Monitoring and Controls Engine-room remote sensing and control, automatic alarms, and record keeping of operating parameters	Eliminate need for round-the-clock watch keeping in engine spaces (leaving maintenance and repair as the main engineering responsibilities); and create an incentive for multiskilled officers to share bridge watches
Colocation of engine, fuel cargo, and navigation controls in the bridge	Eliminate officer manpower and better enable multiskilled officers to handle deck and engine functions
Maintenance Maintenance techniques: epoxy paints, sealed bearings, fewer cylinders	Decrease requirements for deck and engine-room ratings and supervision
Bridge Microprocessor-equipped position-finding and collision-avoidance devices	Decrease demands on deck officers
Mooring and Anchoring Mechanical innovations: self-stowing line baskets, constant-tension winches, communication equipment	Decrease size of mooring party and brute strength required
Cargo Operations Minimizing number and automation of hatches	Improve safety and convenience and decrease manpower requirements for both deck officers and ratings

Thus, the full benefit of the new technology depends on corollary innovations in work innovations.

The effect of a smaller crew size by itself increased the economic incentive to consider the work innovations. Several specific advantages were cited by shipowners. Flexibility to perform assignments across departments and across organizational levels

Figure 3-1. New Technologies, Smaller Crews, and Work Innovations.

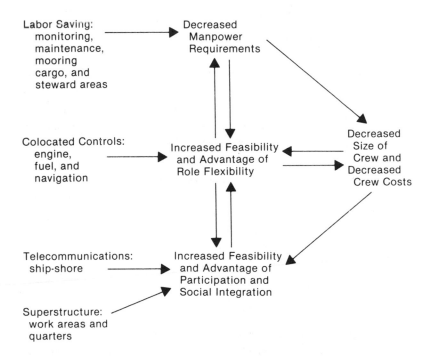

became operationally more advantageous as the number of individuals in a department shrank. Social integration, for example, in mess rooms offered more logistical advantages as the number of shipboard personnel decreased. The overall performance of the crew became more dependent on the competence and motivation of every crew member as the number of shipboard personnel decreased.

Many of the relationships among the three developments— new technologies, smaller crews, and work innovations—are summarized in Figure 3-1.

Thus, while some shipping companies achieved significant crew size reductions to the low twenties without work innovation, these companies were increasingly at a disadvantage in achieving further reductions in crew size compared with other firms that had already developed some versions of the flexible organization.

Summary

I have sketched features of the industry context and shown how work innovations were adaptive in the following ways:

- Economic cost pressures increased interest in role flexibility and smaller crews.
- Societal trends toward social equality, participation, and employment security changed the expectations of seafarers and employers about shipboard organizations.
- Shorter times in ports, often located away from the romantic cities, decreased the traditional appeal of seafaring.
- Specialized and technically sophisticated vessels made continuity of assignment more advantageous.
- Technological advances made broad and flexible roles more advantageous and easier to implement.
- Smaller crews made the advantage of flexibility, social integration, participation, and crew stability even more compelling.

Each of the four work innovations presented here is a discrete response to particular environmental trends. The potential relationships among them become more apparent in Chapter Four and are analyzed directly in Chapter Five. I emphasize the qualifier "potential" because sometimes these relationships were recognized and capitalized on and other times they were not.

Chapter 4

Assessing and Ranking Innovative Change in Eight Countries

The four work innovations—role flexibility, continuity in employment and assignment, delegation/participation, and social integration—were adaptive. The innovations were increasingly regarded by shipowners not only as desirable but also as ultimately necessary for high-wage countries to compete in the world shipping industry. Traditional organizations started to give way to versions of the flexible organization in almost all countries studied, in some more completely than others. This chapter ranks countries in terms of their record of innovation in the period from 1966 to 1983. An explanation of these differences is the main object of the analysis contained in the chapters that follow. (See Appendix, Some Notes on Research Design and Methods.)

The eight countries fell into three clusters. Norway, Holland, and Japan were high innovators; the United Kingdom, Sweden, and West Germany were moderate innovators; and Denmark and the United States were low innovators. The many differences in specific practices that add up to these overall judgments are discussed below and summarized in Table 4-1.

Table 4-1. Comparison of Specific Work-Innovation Practices.

Innovations	High Innovators			Moderate Innovators			Low Innovators	
	Holland	Norway	Japan	United Kingdom	Sweden	West Germany	Denmark	United States
1a Role flexibility (ratings)[a]	Extensive practice	Extensive practice	Extensive practice[b]	Limited practice	Limited practice	Limited practice	None	None
1b Role flexibility (officers)[a]	Significant trend	Experiments only	Significant trend	None	None	None	None	None
2a Employment continuity	Universal by law	Extensive practice	Universal practice (lifetime employment)	Extensive practice	Universal by law	Universal by law	Limited practice	Limited practice
2b Crew/vessel assignment continuity	Limited practice	Limited practice	Limited practice	Very limited practice	Very limited practice	Very limited practice	Very limited practice	Very limited practice
3a Participative work planning (ratings)	Limited practice	Limited practice	Limited practice	None, with few exceptions	None, with one exception	None, with one exception	No formal practice	No formal practice
3b Shipboard management delegation (officers)	Extensive practice	Extensive practice	None	Extensive practice	Limited practice	None	Limited practice	Limited practice
4 Social integration[a]	Limited practice	Extensive practice	Extensive practice	Very limited practice	Extensive practice	Limited practice	Extensive practice	Very limited practice

[a]Role flexibility is regarded as the cornerstone innovation in this study and is weighted more heavily than the other innovations. Social integration is given the lowest weight affecting the overall ranking of the eight countries.

[b]Rating role flexibility in Japan includes certification for watch standing, allowing ratings to take charge of a bridge watch even though they are not fully licensed officers.

Norway: A High Innovator and the Pioneer

In December 1983 the Norwegian fleet contained 529 ships. It was the fifth-largest fleet in the world in tonnage capacity. Several Norwegian companies are credited with pioneering the work innovations that subsequently diffused throughout a significant part of the Norwegian industry and to other shipping countries.

Most influential was a large and progressive shipowner, Leif Hoegh. Two Hoegh experimental ships in the early 1970s were to become the classic demonstration projects referred to throughout northwestern Europe over the next decade. (Hoegh and the pioneering companies in other countries are cited in Table 4-2.) During the 1960s Hoegh had attempted to utilize progressive managerial concepts employed in other sectors. One such concept was decentralization, in this case the delegation of managerial authority and responsibility to ships' officers. Another concept was interdepartmental flexibility of ratings.

In 1968 Hoegh began an experiment with interdepartmental flexibility on three ships. The results persuaded the planners that other changes were required to support role flexibility. Subsequently, Hoegh management carefully planned two successive experiments, with the assistance of social science researchers (Einar Thorsrud and his colleagues at the Oslo Work Research Institute) and the concurrence of a tripartite industry forum (the "contact group").

The experiment on board the Hoegh *Mistral* started in February 1970, when the ship left the construction site for her maiden voyage. She was a car/bulk carrier. The *Mistral* had the following experimental features: general-purpose ratings, crew involvement in work planning and supervision, common recreation room, delegation of new responsibilities to shipboard management, and a new personnel-planning and salary system designed to enhance crew continuity. *Mistral* confirmed the advantages of the above changes but also indicated the need to involve junior officers in a positive way.

The second project was conducted on board the Hoegh *Multina*, a liquified petroleum gas (LPG)/ammonia carrier. It started in 1971 and included all the features of the *Mistral* plus role

Table 4-2. Pioneering Efforts.

Country	Project Ships or Activities	Innovative Significance
Norway	Hoegh's *Mistral* (1970–) Hoegh's *Multina* (1971–) Klaveness' *Balao* (1973–)	Rating role flexibility, participation/delegation *Mistral* innovations plus officer flexibility *Multina* factors plus more participation and variable staffing
Holland	Shell B.V. Tankers. Several project ships Nedlloyd's *Loire* (1978–) Nedlloyd's *Colombo* (1983–)	Similar to Norway's project ships Rating flexibility Officer flexibility
Japan	Modernization committee; Mitsui O.S.K. Line and NYK Line among the pioneering companies	Industry program to transform the shipboard organization and to promote more relevant legislative reform and technological innovation
United Kingdom	Sealife Programme Denholm's *Arctic Troll* (1976–78) Bibby Brothers' *Dart Atlantic* (1977–79) Jebsens-U.K.'s *Sureness* (1976–) P.A.L.'s project ships (1981–)	Industry program supporting innovation Sealife project ship focused on ratings Sealife project ship focused on ratings Advanced staffing model, featured on German television Advanced model
Sweden	Salen's project ships (1975–) Brostrom's vessels (1978–)	Shipboard management teams and shore reorganization Transfer maintenance to shore-based crews; rating role flexibility, participation, delegation, and social integration
West Germany	Ship of the Future program Hapag Lloyd's project ships (1978–)	Industry program to develop technology and organization for a ship with a crew of twelve Similar to those of Brostrom of Sweden
Denmark	DFDS fleet	Well-developed system of shipboard management teams

flexibility for officers. Engineers were given nautical education, and mates were given additional technical training to enable them to operate and maintain all technical equipment on deck.

A third major Norwegian experiment occurred aboard the *Balao,* a new ship of the Torvald Klaveness company launched in March 1973, again with involvement with the Work Research Institute. It built on the two Hoegh experiments and emphasized the further development of participative work planning, as noted in connection with the researchers' account of this ship's experiences in Chapter Three. Officers and ratings had common dining and living rooms and similar individual cabins. Other features of the initial organization, decided by the crew during the first summer in 1973, were the conversion of the foreman position into that of a manager of training, application for approval of a fixed annual salary for all crew members, and variable staffing levels during the year around an agreed-on average staffing figure. These features were approved by the industry contact group for this experiment only, just as the Hoegh project ships' features had to be approved on an exception basis. The sanctioning role of the contact group, which included representatives of employers, seafarers' unions, and the government, is explored in more detail in a discussion of institutional forces in Chapter Eight.

Basically, by 1976 these three experiments had demonstrated the feasibility of almost all the elements of the most advanced crew concepts utilized in Norway eight years later. They also had been judged safe, socially effective, and economically effective. These early Norwegian experiments were primarily designed to improve shipowners' abilities to attract and retain qualified seafarers rather than to reduce costs. Hoegh estimated conservatively that their project ships had "comparable operating-cost experiences."

Demonstrating feasibility, even effectiveness, was one matter. Diffusing the new operational model was quite another. In 1972 when Hoegh management and the unions tried to extend the new concepts to two additional ships, the *Merit* and the *Mallard,* they encountered some difficulty.[1] The planners learned the source of their difficulty—too little participation by the new crews and, hence, too little identification with the new policies. Hoegh adjusted implementation practices to allow more participation and proceeded to diffuse the innovations gradually throughout the Hoegh fleet. In practice, as the study of the Hoegh *Mallard* discussed in Chapter Three suggested, implementation of the new concepts was less complete in some of the company's vessels than in others.

Hoegh made other changes to support the ship-by-ship diffusion of its new approach. Management introduced budgeting responsibility on all Hoegh vessels to enhance shipboard management accountability. It specified common mess rooms and recreational areas for all new-ship construction. It introduced a new personnel-planning system to provide more crew continuity. And it assigned senior officers to oversee construction of a new ship they would operate.

Hoegh was not unique in its use of new work concepts. In fact, another shipowner, Jebsens, was regarded by some industry observers as having gone the farthest in implementing advanced staffing concepts in Norway. By 1983 an influential one-third of the Norwegian shipping industry employed the model pioneered in the project ships, except for role flexibility at the officer level. Another one-third practiced increased role flexibility and employment continuity for ratings and some management accountability with its officers. The final one-third continued the traditional approach. Officials of the Norwegian shipowners' association summarized the following achievements in the Norwegian industry:

- Organizational methods and practices that motivate the whole crew to be more flexible in the execution and distribution of jobs and tasks have been widely implemented.
- Crew reductions by up to one-third of the rating complement of crews have been achieved.
- Relationships between ship and shore have been remarkably improved. Barriers between officers and ratings and between departments have broken down and are almost nonexistent in some ships. The crew works as a much closer team.
- Crew members, particularly the top officers, have been more cost minded.
- Messing and recreational facilities common to the whole crew continue to be implemented in a large part of the fleet.

The four Norwegian unions (representing ratings, deck officers, engineers, and masters) generally agreed with these assessments but were less enthusiastic about the crew reductions, which they felt sometimes overloaded the remaining personnel. The reforms necessary to train and certify officers capable of performing both navigational and engineering functions took effect in 1982, but a year later the officers' unions still had not signed an agreement to implement the concept.

A variety of other regulations and agreements dealt with staffing over the period of this study. A regulation in 1969 provided for the general-purpose (GP) rating and specified new minimum staffing levels.

An agreement reached between the shipowners' association and the unions in 1979 specified a set of terms by which a shipowner could reduce crew sizes. Shipowners who chose to operate under this agreement, the 1979 Frame Agreement, must provide regular employment and change crews after tours of no more three months of sea duty. Often the pattern under the Frame Agreement was three months at sea and three months of shore leave. The parties secured government permission to work overtime in excess of the fourteen-hour-a-week maximum prescribed by law. The companies guaranteed twenty hours of overtime.

Individual shipowners could continue to operate under the industry labor agreements and standard regulations or could agree with the ratings' unions to operate under the 1979 Frame Agreement. About 150 ships, 25 percent of the Norwegian fleet, were placed under the Frame Agreement. Although many seafarers were initially ambivalent about the Agreement, the maximum of three months away from home became especially popular with them and their families.

Early in 1983 the conservative government passed legislation that set new government staffing levels. The new low minimums were predicated on employing a ship's mechanic, a more highly trained version of the general-purpose rating. The new staffing levels were similar to those agreed to under the Frame Agreement. However, under the legislation, all Norwegian shipowners could secure approval for reduced crews without continuing any of the conditions that had been part of the labor-management deal in the

Frame Agreement, such as regular employment and the maximum
three months of sea time without shore leave.

The 1983 staffing levels, and especially the manner in which
the government imposed them, were vigorously opposed by the
unions. They charged that the conservative government elected the
previous year had listened only to the employers' concerns before
legislating the change. This violated the established practice of
tripartite discussion, in which the major negotiations occurred
between labor and management. The prospects for further change
in Norwegian shipping in 1983 were uncertain.

Holland: A High Innovator Gaining Momentum

Holland's fleet in 1983 comprised 448 ships. Work innovations in
Holland's shipping were pioneered by Shell B.V. Tankers, followed
by Nedlloyd Shipping Company. In 1983 Shell had thirty-one
tankers; Nedlloyd, ninety-six liners and bulkers. Each company
negotiated with the industry's two seafaring unions (one for officers
and one for ratings). The remainder of the industry was represented
by a shipowners' association in dealing with the unions. I will
explore the experiences of these major players in Holland's
shipping and their influence on the rest of the industry.

In 1968 Shell initiated two project ships with GP ratings and
within a year decided to extend the practice elsewhere in its fleet.
Over the next six years ratings, who were already company
employees, were cross-trained, cross-utilized, and increasingly
consulted about work planning and other ship matters. Several
billets were dropped from the staffing table, including two engine-
room specialties and the foremen for deck ratings. A single foreman
took responsibility for both engine-room and deck activities.

In 1976 Shell began another change program. Its earlier
effort to enhance the managerial orientation of its officers enabled
a major devolution of responsibility from shore to ship. Its earlier
efforts to develop the technical competence of ratings and their
participative skills permitted the complete removal of the foreman
layer of hierarchy. Its success with flexibility at the rating level
encouraged it to go still further, implementing role flexibility for
officers. By 1983 the company had trained sixty-five semi-integrated

officers, constituting 10 percent of its force, mostly junior officers, and had begun reducing the complement of officers on only three project ships. All new officers at Shell were to be cross-trained.

The Shell shore organization also had been transformed. The shipboard management team was delegated responsibility for the ship's husbandry (cost elements, spare parts, stores, voyage repairs, lube oil, and catering), and the team was given the authority to make purchase decisions. It met daily in the central administration room of the ship and consulted with junior officers and ratings.

A number of other changes were integral to the emerging Shell organization. Shell management perfected the planning board technique, mentioned in Chapter Three, for involving ratings in work planning on a daily basis. Masters were required to hold at least one consultation meeting involving the full crew every six weeks. Junior officer tasks were shifted to ratings in order to better utilize less costly personnel and to decrease the gap between ratings and officers. Ship continuity of 2.5 years, which included one maintenance trip to the dry dock, was established for members of the shipboard management team. The company intended to extend the stability of assignment to the junior officers. Two of Shell's thirty-one ships had common mess rooms, the standard for all new ships. Both officers and ratings were allowed to take their spouses on occasional trips.

Shell had studied the economic, safety, and social advantages of the new concepts. First, Shell attributed improvements in safety to crew stability and role flexibility. Second, crews on Shell tankers had declined steadily, from fifty seafarers in the 1960s to the low twenties in 1976, as a result of new technology and new organizational policies. Shell claimed these decreases had occurred without lowering maintenance standards. Third, crew members thought the jobs had improved. Despite initial resistance to new roles, neither the ratings nor the officers wanted to return to conventional roles. This was reflected in Shell's relatively low rate of turnover. For ratings who sailed for only five to eight years and then looked for work ashore, the GP experience equipped them with technical qualifications relevant to employment ashore.

Officer flexibility had not yet had its full effect, but it had already permitted watch duty to be spread more evenly among officers. Deck officers normally worked fifty-six-hour weeks, due to seven-day watch-keeping requirements for navigation. Engineers, on the other hand, were able to work a normal week of forty hours on ships with automation, which eliminated round-the-clock watch standing in the engine room. On these automated ships the different work weeks had produced different life-styles for the two departments. These differences had generated tension. The introduction of role flexibility balanced the work load and reduced the tension.

Nedlloyd's organizational changes were similar to Shell's but lagged them by several years. In 1977, Nedlloyd gained union concurrence to experiment with GP ratings and governmental permission to run with a crew smaller than was normally required by law. Nedlloyd agreed to provide increased training. A tripartite commission of government, employer, and union officials was established to oversee the experiments, which began with the Nedlloyd *Loire* and one other project ship. During the experimental period, from 1978 to 1983, Nedlloyd proceeded to introduce GP's on a total of fifteen vessels (eight multipurpose liners, six containerships, and one tanker). Plans in 1983 were to introduce GP's on fourteen more vessels in the near future.

The GP concept would not be completely implemented for many years, not until the GP's who were former deck ratings became technically competent in the engine room. In the meantime, the older seafarers who did not like the flexible roles could find a berth on Nedlloyd's ships that did not yet utilize GP's. As older ratings retired or returned to shore, the transformation of the fleet would continue.

Nedlloyd secured agreement in 1981 to experiment with semi-integrated officers on the Nedlloyd *Columbo* and by 1983 had declared its intention to recruit only cross-trained officers in the future. It also had begun delegating greater responsibility to shipboard management and stabilizing officer assignments to vessels.

Holland's third-largest shipowner began a project in 1978 along the lines of those of Shell and Nedlloyd, confirming the undeniable movement to transform the nature of shipboard organizations in Dutch shipping. By 1983 GP training had become the norm for new recruits to the rating ranks. Only a handful of ships could claim to effectively utilize semi-integrated officers, but the practice was gathering momentum among the larger shipowners. Moreover, the Dutch nautical colleges were in the process of designing a four-year program for semi-integrated officers. The shipboard management concept was now a widespread industry practice. Shell had achieved considerable assignment stability for officers and some for ratings; Nedlloyd and the others had achieved some for officers.

Participative work planning was practiced in Shell and elsewhere in the industry. A measure of social integration had occurred as an outcome of the other innovations. However, only a few direct measures had been taken to promote it. Common mess facilities were rare.

Holland was similar to Norway in many respects, especially in its rating innovations. Two differences are worth noting. First, Holland had made progress in implementing role flexibility at the officer level, and Norway had not. Second, Holland's overall pattern of innovation lagged Norway's in the earlier 1970s but was gaining momentum in the 1980s, whereas Norway's efforts appeared to have plateaued in the 1980s. Later in the book, I will attempt to explain these differences.

Japan: A High Innovator with the Most Momentum

Japan's fleet of 1,712 ships, with a capacity of 63,665,000 d.w.t., was ranked third in 1983, behind Liberia (a flag of convenience) and Greece. Japan started its innovation activity after Norway and Holland but by 1983 was clearly embarked on the most ambitious change program.

The collaboration between shipowners and the single union that represented all Japanese seafarers was an important aspect of this change program. It is significant that this collaboration had only developed during the mid to late 1970s. In 1972, in reaction to aggressive attempts by Japanese shipowners to cut crew sizes, the All-Japan Seaman's Union (AJSU) led Japanese seamen out for a major strike lasting more than ninety days.

Discussions of crew reorganization were begun by industry representatives in the mid 1970s and culminated in the establishment of a Committee for Modernization of the Seafarer's System in 1977. The Committee, composed of representatives of shipowners, the seafarers' union, the government, and the public, undertook two years of study, which included visits to Norway and other European countries. It supervised a program of project ships beginning in 1979, when an eighteen-man crew system was implemented on fourteen *A-stage* vessels. (The previous minimum crew in Japan had been twenty-four.) Among the fourteen A-stage ships were containerships, a tanker, a car carrier, and a bulk carrier. After three years six of these ships advanced to the B stage, a seventeen-man crew. At the end of 1983 sixty-five ships were in the program, and within a few years 150 ships were expected to be involved in the program.

The Committee was selective about the initial set of companies allowed to participate in the modernization program, but, with experience and success, the program was gradually opened to ships from any company ready to enter it. One of the pioneers was Mitsui O.S.K. Line (MOL), which operated thirty ships under the Japanese flag and another twenty under flags of convenience. All but one of the flags of convenience employed all-Japanese crews. Another pioneer was the large NYK Line, which operated a total of one hundred ships.

The A-stage vessels featured a number of technical advances, but the most noteworthy was the integration of engine and cargo controls centrally on the bridge, thereby facilitating the integration of the officers' responsibilities for the deck and engine room. The shipbuilding industry planned to use the experience with this design and other technical advances in their own project to develop a "highly advanced ultra rationalized ship capable of being operated by a crew of less than ten persons by the next decade."[2]

The concept of these smaller crews included GP ratings, integrated officers (initially junior officers), and ratings trained to perform some duties previously assigned only to officers. The third of these features was particularly noteworthy, because it was not among the achievements of Norway, Holland, or any other country studied. Ratings attended school for five months to earn a certificate permitting them to take charge of a bridge watch, previously performed only by fully licensed deck officers. By 1983 five hundred ratings had been certified. Also, by this date all three aspects of the trials were considered successful. An established industry commitment, subscribed to by all parties, was to continue with the diffusion of these innovations.

The parties also shared the objective of an all-officer crew, in which every member would be a highly skilled professional. The modernization ships had already started to eliminate distinctions between officers and ratings. They shared common mess and recreational facilities; they also had equal perks but different grades of cabins. Although conventional ships generally included forms of participation by ratings in planning and problem solving on board, the modernized vessels of some companies instituted more systematic forms of participation. Every morning the GP crew members on board ships in MOL Company met with the chief engineer and first mate to discuss the work to be done. These toolbox meetings, as they were called, lasted from fifteen minutes to an hour. They were regarded as highly successful. Each ship also had a friendly association, comprising two representatives for each of the three shipboard departments, which discussed the interest and concerns of the crew and represented them to the company and the union.

Japan's lifetime employment policies were the strongest form of employment continuity found in any country in our study. Lifetime employment was instituted by large companies before any other work innovations for crews on their oceangoing fleets. As a result of this policy, Japanese seafarers stayed in this employment until the normal retirement age of fifty-five, and they also stayed with their original employers unless the company went bankrupt. As a condition of the union's support for the other aspects of the modernization program, it had negotiated a strengthening of the employment assurances for its members, securing policy commitments that I will discuss in the chapter on economic incentives for change.

No initiative in the Japanese modernization effort was comparable to the delegation of management functions to the ships' officers found in Norway, Holland, and other European countries. Consultation of Japanese officers by the shore organization was not uncommon, but formal delegation of increased authority and responsibility to shipboard teams was not practiced or planned.

The program for modernizing the fleet included a major overhaul of Japanese laws in 1982, notably the Mariner's Law (covering ratings) and the Law for Ships' Officers. These laws simplified the classifications for both deck officers and engineers and specified the qualifications for officers who serve in both capacities. They indicated the special treatment of crew complements and qualifications for crew in the vessels formally participating in the modernization program. Similarly, in 1983 the educational and training institutions were being revamped to support the vision of the future shipboard organization—not only to provide the technical and interpersonal skills required but also to shape the attitudes needed to implement flexibility and participation effectively.

As already indicated, the stakeholders were generally satisfied with aspects of the emerging model, including the various forms of role flexibility, the toolbox meetings, and the diminished status distinctions. Seafarers reported an increase in work load but did not find this onerous. The modern ships were comparable to conventional ships in their rates of injury and illness.

United Kingdom: A Moderate Innovator and the Most Mixed Case

The U.K.-flag fleet contained 685 ships and was the world's sixth largest in capacity. By far the greatest innovative effort in the United Kingdom had been devoted to the development of shipboard management. This trend began in the late 1960s and gradually evolved to emphasize an openness in management style in addition to delegated accountability. Many companies also had attempted to streamline the shore staff and reorganize it to play support roles for the shipboard management team. Seventy-five percent of officers in the United Kingdom were company employees. The shipowners' association and government expressed an interest in role flexibility for officers and bridge watch-standing certificates for ratings, but no movement had occurred.

The history of work innovation for ratings began in 1967, when the seamen's union agreed to permit an oil company to cross-utilize deck and engine-room ratings. By 1983 approximately 15 percent of ratings were classified as GP. Some additional ratings were used in a more limited version of role flexibility. By and large, however, even the GP's had not actually been cross-utilized in a significant way, in part because the United Kingdom's industry had not upgraded the training and qualification requirements for GP's as had Norway and Holland. Casual hiring of seafarers was on the decline. In 1983 half of the ratings had permanent employment with a shipping company, and an additional 25 percent tended to stay with the same employer.

The differences in the perks for ratings and officers diminished somewhat during the 1970s. For example, officers alone could typically take their wives on an occasional voyage until the mid 1970s, when this privilege was often also extended to ratings. Shipowners advocated common mess facilities, but usually as an economy measure rather than an organizational change. These changes generated considerable controversy, vigorously supported by the seamen's union and opposed by the officers.

A tripartite program in organizational research and change—the Sealife Programme—began in 1974 and ended in December 1979. The Sealife staff had an ambitious agenda for reforms. Among other activities, they persuaded two U.K. shipping companies, Denholm and Bibby, to provide experimental ships to be patterned after the Norwegian project ships. The U.K. experimental ships were much less successful than their Norwegian predecessors, for reasons I will analyze later. To the great disappointment of the Sealife staff, the program failed to elicit broad company and union support and failed to influence practice in a substantial way. Nevertheless, it did stimulate major change in a handful of companies that became actively involved. It also generated change in the structures and programs of the ratings' union, the only one of the five seafaring unions in the United Kingdom to closely associate itself with the program.

In addition to the two companies that took part in the official Sealife projects, several others undertook comprehensive innovations similar to those developed in Hoegh of Norway and Shell of Holland. Jebsens-U.K. Ltd. had three stable crews assigned to two ships operating this way in 1983. One ship, Jebsens *Sureness,* had been shown on West German television as an example of innovative industrial practice. The company was considering a scheme for sharing the financial gains with the crew. Another company, P.A.L. Shipping Services, was formed in 1983 as a successor to the Panocean-Anco Ltd. The chairman of P.A.L. had served as chairman of the Sealife Programme. Not surprisingly, he and his staff were committed to continuing the diffusion of the innovations currently used on their ships. However, except for Jebsens-U.K., P.A.L., and a few other cases, new innovative efforts affecting the entire crew had virtually stopped by 1983.

The United Kingdom is the most complex case. On the one hand, employment continuity had spread widely for both ratings and officers, providing a potential foundation for other work innovations. In the few instances where shipwide change had occurred, it was systematic, bold, and successful. In addition, information about the experiments had been widely disseminated. Finally, there was a pattern of effective innovation in one area— shipboard management.

On the other hand, only a very small number of firms had attempted to change the way ratings were trained, utilized, and consulted on board ship. And less reduction in staffing had occurred in the United Kingdom than in any other country except the United States.

The U.K. case raises some particular questions, which I will address in subsequent chapters. Why the strong record in shipboard management in the United Kingdom, comparable to that of Norway and Holland, in contrast to the little change in other areas? Why did the interest in ratings' innovations peak in the 1970s and virtually disappear by 1983?

Sweden: A Moderate Innovator

The Swedish fleet comprised 216 ships at the end of 1983. A discussion of the policies and practices that characterized the Swedish shipping industry as a whole will be followed by a report on the exceptional case of Brostrom's, a company that generated much interest between 1978 and 1983.

Companies had been required by legislation since the early 1970s to provide regular employment to seafarers. The amount of stability in assignments of crew to vessels varied from company to company. Some companies tried to change 50 percent of the crew on a ship at a time and to reassign individual crew members back to the same ship after leave. In some cases a company would allow two individuals to share a billet and determine their own work/ leave schedules. These arrangements were aided by the common pattern in Sweden of providing equal leave and sea time.

GP ratings were introduced by some companies in the early 1970s and over the next decade came to represent perhaps a quarter of the work force. Typically, a Swedish ship used a combination of specialized deck and engine ratings and GP's rather than attempting to convert completely to GP ratings. Shipowners and representatives of the navigation officers' and engineers' unions said that the GP system had never worked as intended. The GP's who had started with deck experience lacked engine-room skills and therefore tended to be used by engineers for only the most routine tasks available. The GP's came disproportionately from the ranks of deck ratings, in part because many engine-room ratings could not meet the eyesight requirement for deck duty.

Status distinctions had decreased and social integration had increased. Both officers and ratings could bring wives on board. While the agreements of officers' unions still provided for separate messing, the industry norm had become single mess rooms. Nevertheless, officers and ratings tended to sit apart, sometimes separated by a carefully placed row of potted plants. Shipowners said that it was not unusual for the Swedish officers and their unions to indicate acceptance of common mess rooms, but for the ratings to express concern about being "supervised" during meals.

Consultation was required by Swedish law, but according to an official of the seamen's union, rating participation in work planning was generally not practiced in Swedish ocean shipping. Several Swedish firms did attempt to implement delegated authority to shipboard management teams. One company, Salen, had initial success on trial ships in the mid 1970s but failed in its attempt to extend it throughout its fleet. Other companies, committed to more gradual change than Salen had attempted, were implementing shipboard management teams in 1983.

Other areas where Sweden's shipowners had pressed for change included reduction in the number of mates and engineering officers. An agreement in the early 1980s with the navigation officers' union allowed—on the basis of ship-by-ship considerations—a reduction from three to two mates, normally requiring an increase in watch standing from eight to twelve hours a day. In 1983, twenty ships had this arrangement. No provisions existed for flexibility between deck and engine-room officers, however, despite its advantage for sharing the additional load of deck watch standing.

In an interesting trend, many officers spent some of their six months of yearly leave as *part rederi,* part owners in smaller ships typically engaged in coastal trade. Other officers who left the employ of the large shipping firms when operations were curtailed entered this growing segment of the industry. Often they mortgaged their houses and invested their life savings in order to buy into a vessel.

Shipowners' association representatives stated emphatically that in Sweden's case a financial stake was required to create highly motivated and effective crews. Similarly, the president of the seamen's union said his union would like to see more *part rederi* operating in the industry. He also believed profit sharing would eventually be introduced into the industry.

The most dramatic work innovation in recent history in the Swedish shipping industry was developed by Brostrom and implemented on six new vessels, three delivered in 1978 and three in 1979. Before signing the contract with a Japanese shipyard for the six ships, the company negotiated the staffing policies with the deck officers, engineers, and seamen's unions and then secured approval for these policies from the Swedish authorities. The total crew was sixteen, rather than the twenty-two or twenty-three normally required for this class of ship. The crew organization included six general-purpose ratings, called "ships' operators," and no foreman-level position.

All members of the crews for these ships were selected from volunteer applicants among Brostrom's employees. The selected crews were highly experienced. Two complete crews were assigned to a ship, each on duty about six to nine weeks followed by six to nine weeks of leave. The ships' operators carried higher qualification requirements than the normal Swedish GP rating. Deckhands had to spend nine months in the engine room, and engine-room ratings a comparable amount of time on deck. Crew members received additional training for the new equipment and the new organization on these vessels.

A work-planning committee included the master, the chief engineer, and a representative of the six ships' operators. A single cafeteria-style mess served all members of the crew. All accommodations were raised to a level previously reserved for officers.

The crew size and roles were carefully planned in relation to advanced developments in automation, ergonomic design of the bridge, and maintenance programs. One of the most important elements of Brostrom's strategy was to reduce the maintenance done by the ship's normal crew and to engage shore-based crews to perform much of the required maintenance. Brostrom possessed both the shore-based facilities and the experience to make its strategy feasible.

After four years the pattern had become standard operating procedure. Interestingly, a Brostrom's official acknowledged that they still had not completely erased the deck and engine-room orientations of the ships' operators. Despite the limited role flexibility achieved, management judged the new crew organization to be safe, cost-effective, and socially effective. Crew members preferred assignments on the new vessels. The unions were also pleased. In fact, the president of the seamen's union said he wished other companies would pursue similar innovations.

The Swedish record can be summarized as follows: While Swedish law had established employment continuity, and company policies had produced considerable assignment continuity, these forms of continuity were not used as a foundation for other work innovations. GP's constituted an estimated one-fourth of the ratings' force, but this overstated the actual amount of flexibility practiced. Only one company had implemented participation in work-planning mechanisms. No role flexibility between navigation officers and engineers was permitted. Swedish shipowners had shown some interest in shipboard management, but less than did those in Norway, Holland, and the United Kingdom. Finally, Sweden had its exceptional case in Brostrom, which implemented changes similar to those of the pioneers in Norway, Holland, and the United Kingdom, although Brostrom's changes were somewhat less ambitious in participative work planning and role flexibility.

Comparing the Swedish case and others raises a number of questions. Why had not more change in policies affecting ratings occurred? Why had there not been a move toward integrated officers, especially given the owners' interest in reduced officer billets? Why had there been little or no emulation of Brostrom's comprehensive model, which was successful and approved by management, employees, and all three unions? Again, I will address these questions in subsequent chapters of this book.

West Germany: A Moderate Innovator

In 1983 437 ships sailed under the West German flag. West Germany's innovation record was similar to Sweden's in many respects but slightly weaker. It too had regularized employment for seafarers by legislation enacted in the early 1970s and had achieved some continuity in crew assignment. In both countries legislation required formal consultation at the company level, but participation in planning shipboard work was not practiced (with a single major exception in each country, Brostrom in Sweden and Hapag Lloyd in West Germany). Differences in status and perks had decreased, and social integration between officers and ratings had increased in West Germany although less than in Sweden. The pattern reported in Sweden of acceptance by officers and ambivalence of ratings toward common mess arrangements also was cited in West Germany. Finally, like Sweden, West Germany had not made progress in breaking down the departmental boundaries between deck officers and engineers (although, according to government officials, some West German shipowners expressed interest in the development). Shipboard management was not practiced in West Germany. Officials of the officers' union said they were impressed with the practices on the Jebsens-U.K. ship, which had been reported on West German television. They favored delegation in order to promote professional interest and greater career mobility, especially for deck officers.

The most innovative activity in West Germany was devoted to the development of the GP practice. Although the practice had not yet diffused widely by 1983, it was expected to become the industry norm in the future.

The Hapag Lloyd Company was the first to utilize GP's in 1972, as a part of a crew concept that allowed it to reduce crews from thirty-three to twenty-five. The company reduced the number of ratings and replaced three departmental foremen with one general foreman who reported to both engine and deck officers. Direct negotiations with the ratings' union secured union approval, awarded GP's a premium over regular rating pay, and provided GP's additional company training. The concept worked sufficiently well to be adopted by Hapag Lloyd in the rest of its container fleet.

Despite Hapag Lloyd's overall satisfaction, the GP concept was not picked up by many other companies. Older seamen found it difficult to work as integrated ratings. By 1983, only about fifty ships in the West German fleet utilized GP's. Nevertheless, shipowners, union officials, and government officials all agreed that further reductions in crew sizes would make GP's necessary. In June 1983 the authorities had received applications from an additional seventy ships to employ GP ratings and the reduced staffing scales that applied when GP's were used. They planned that by 1988 the only entry-level training available for ratings would be for GP certification.

The leading innovation in the early 1980s conducted on four Hapag Lloyd ships was similar in many respects to Brostrom's in Sweden. It was based on transferring maintenance from shipboard crews to land-based crews, it broke new ground in the industry with reduced crew size (from twenty-five to eighteen), and it increased the commitment to cross-train ratings for a new ship's mechanic classification. Hapag Lloyd was also similar to Brostrom in seeking volunteers from existing ratings and officers. However, work planning involved only the deck foreman. To achieve assignment continuity, Hapag Lloyd formed six complete crews to man the four ships. (Brostrom had a ratio of two crews per ship because of the more generous leave provisions in Sweden.)

The Hapag Lloyd ships in this experiment were converted containerships, not new construction. The three-year project, which started in 1980, was sponsored by the shipowners' association and agreed to by the two seafaring unions, one representing primarily ratings and the other officers. It should be noted that the ratings' union also included a small number of officers, which injected an additional element of rivalry between the two unions. In 1981, a year after the project began, the officers' union withdrew support and involvement, when the company refused the union's request to add a third engineer and another engine-room rating to the crew. The officers' union claimed that the staffing created too much stress for the engineers. The project was monitored and approved by several other groups, which included shipowners, government, and ratings' union representatives. Thus, all except the officers' union judged the crew concept safe and operationally effective.

Although the shipowners' association indicated that there was general industry interest in the Hapag Lloyd model, the interest was not shared by a second major shipowner, Hamburg Sud. Both companies were important members of the industry, Hapag Lloyd with forty ships and Hamburg Sud with seventeen under the West German flag. Hamburg Sud executives were opposed to making the GP the industry standard for education and certification. They were committed to a conventional staffing strategy on all but a few of their ships, which already employed GP's.

Unlike Hapag Lloyd, which had routes that brought its ships back to West German ports with reasonable frequency, Hamburg Sud ships were largely cross-traders on long routes to Australia, New Zealand, South America, and North America. Both the time ships spent away from West Germany and the mild weather on their routes made more on-board maintenance desirable. Moreover, because the company planned to make part of its profits by selling and replacing ships whenever a favorable opportunity presented itself, it had higher standards of maintenance, particularly regarding cosmetic painting, than did Hapag Lloyd. Hamburg Sud management believed these ships required larger crews and could work equally well with deck and engine specialties. Thus, Hamburg Sud did not want to pay a premium for GP's and provide additional cross-training on their ships when the company would not benefit much from the flexibility.

Concerned about its competitiveness, the West German industry established a major program called Ship of the Future, involving the unions, shipowners, and academic researchers. The project sought a fuel-efficient oceangoing vessel with technology and organization for a twelve-man crew. At the time the project was conceived, Hapag Lloyd and Hamburg Sud agreed to purchase West German–built ships incorporating the program's findings, but depressed economic conditions in the industry forced these plans to be postponed indefinitely. It was unclear when the findings of the project would be put into practice.

In summary, West Germany resembled Sweden in many respects. It differed most from Sweden in the complete absence of shipboard management delegation. Also, although this is perhaps a subtle difference between the two leading-innovation firms, Hapag Lloyd reflected less commitment to participation in particular and to crew motivation in general than did Sweden's Brostrom.

Denmark: A Low Innovator with a Notable Exception

The Denmark story can be told in few words, because markedly less organizational change had occurred in Denmark's fleet of 261 ships than in that of any other European country included in the study. The exception in the Danish industry was DFDS, a relatively small shipowner that was one of the first European firms to implement shipboard management teams.[3]

Why is Denmark judged a low innovator? First, overall employee continuity in Danish shipping was relatively low. Most Danish officers had employment contracts, but only 10 percent of engine-room ratings and no deck ratings did. There was at best a modest effort to ensure ship assignment continuity. Second, role flexibility was not practiced. Among ratings, firemen and cooks could not help tie up the vessel, and deck ratings would not work at any time in the engine room. Government authorities had approved the request of one company to utilize GP's on newly constructed ships, but the deck-ratings' union refused. Third, there was no formal participative work planning for ratings and only one instance of delegated management accountability to ships' officers.

Social integration in Denmark's shipping did not appear to be significantly different from that in Sweden. It included a trend toward one mess room equipped with flexible dividers, which could be used to divide the room into separate messes. Feelings about this issue were reported to be similar to those expressed in West Germany and Sweden. Although on-board relations in Denmark's fleet were similar to those of its nearest neighbors, there was somewhat more tension between the seven unions that represented Danish seafarers and between some of these unions and shipowners.

The DFDS case of shipboard delegation was impressive in several respects. It had been in practice for many years, had led to a simpler shore structure and had been credited with producing tangible commercial benefits, was greatly appreciated by the senior ship officers and served as an advantage to DFDS in attracting officers to its employ, and had been sold by the company as a packaged management system to three foreign shipowners. DFDS's success had not led other Danish firms to develop shipboard management, although a larger shipping company, which had recently acquired DFDS, was considering promoting this concept in its other divisions.

The question raised by the Danish case is most obvious. Why was Denmark less advanced in shipboard organization than the other Scandinavian countries, with which it presumably shared social and cultural traditions?

United States: A Low Innovator with the Least Staffing Change

In December 1983 the U.S-flag fleet comprised 538 oceangoing ships, with a capacity that ranked eighth largest in the world. Slightly less than half of the U.S. fleet of oceangoing vessels was engaged in foreign trade. The rest was employed in domestic trade, including routes along the coasts and with Hawaii, Alaska, and Puerto Rico.

The innovation record of the U.S.-flag fleet is remarkably similar to Denmark's but slightly weaker. The United States, like Denmark, could claim some instances of delegating shipboard management to officers. Neither country practiced rating participation. The United States was marked by even less interest than found in Denmark in shipboard social integration. The trend toward equalizing perks and using common facilities was slower in the U.S. fleet than in the Japanese and most of the six European fleets.

The United States also lagged Denmark in movement toward role flexibility. Whereas Danish shipowners had sought and the government had approved the dual-rating classification, U.S. companies had made no comparable effort. Similarly, U.S. operators had made no serious attempt to achieve flexibility at the officer level. This is particularly interesting, inasmuch as U.S. maritime academies graduated some officers who had earned dual licenses certifying them for both engine and deck assignments. U.S. legislation (the so-called crossover law) precluded an individual from working in both capacities on the same voyage.

The traditional rotary system of employment had continued to be more significant in the United States than in any other country studied. Each seafarers' union—and there were eleven of them—operated its own hiring hall, where union members came to get their next voyage assignment. According to an observer of the U.S. shipping industry, the unions have "promoted the system of casual employment even to the point of ensuring that there was continuous movement among ships."[4]

A major difference between the United States and Denmark is in their record of noninnovative change in staffing practices. Whereas Denmark had managed to decrease its crew levels only somewhat less than its more innovative neighbors, the United States had lagged far, far behind other countries in our sample, including the United Kingdom, in reducing crews. The lag is shown in the following comparisons of typical crew sizes:[5]

	Newer U.S. Vessels	*Advanced European and Japanese Vessels*
Modern large containership	34	18–25
Roll-on/roll-off cargo vessels	34	16–24
Tanker	21–23	20

There were many reasons for this poor record of noninnovative change, which I will explore at various points as the story unfolds, including the older average age of the U.S. fleet. However, it is significant that shipowners continued to staff ships traditionally during extended "proof" periods, even diesel-powered ships with automation that permitted the engine room to be left unattended.[6]

While the average crew sizes in the United States were high, a few agreements were struck in the 1980s between shipowners and unions for major decreases in the size of the crew for specific ships, invariably newly constructed vessels. For example, one company had secured an agreement covering several new ships on order from a Japanese shipyard for crews in the low twenties. No plan existed to implement work innovations in these ships.

Summary Ranking of Countries

The innovative activities and results for each of our eight countries can be summarized. Their records place them into high-, moderate-, and low-innovator categories. The countries' records can be compared in each of the four areas of innovation, in some cases also distinguishing the application of the innovative concept to ratings and officers. Table 4-1 summarizes these comparisons.

The four types of innovations are not treated equally in the overall rendering of the clustering. Role flexibility is double weighted, because it has the most direct economic benefit and therefore the most plausible relationship to competitiveness. Moreover, the rationale for the other innovations was more often to support role flexibility than the other way around. Social integration is given a half weight, because it has the least direct relationship to competitiveness.

1. *Role flexibility:* Role flexibility for ratings was more extensive in Norway, Holland, and Japan than in Sweden, West Germany, and the United Kingdom. It had not been introduced in Denmark and the United States.

Role flexibility for officers had been implemented only by Holland and Japan, although Norway had experimented with it and was making progress toward introducing it. These three countries also had achieved more flexibility than the other countries in their ability to have some tasks performed at either the rating or the officer level.

2. *Continuity policies:* Japan's lifetime employment policies provided by far the most employment certainty. In Sweden, West Germany, and Holland employment relationships between seafarers and shipping firms were required by law. In Norway and the United Kingdom a number of companies had, either by company policy or agreement with labor, managed to achieve employment continuity, especially with officers. In Denmark continuity existed for officers and a small portion of engine ratings; all deck ratings were still hired on a casual basis. The United States relied the most on casual employment.

Stability in the composition of crews from one voyage to the next was dependent first on employment continuity and then on management's staffing strategies and procedures. The most change toward crew stability occurred in Japan, Holland, and Norway. Crew stability was policy for many Swedish and a few U.K. firms. Crew stability was still less prevalent in West Germany, Denmark, and the United States. In all cases more assignment continuity applied to senior officers than to junior officers and more to junior officers than to ratings.

3. *Influence sharing:* Participation by ratings in work planning was more prevalent in Holland, Norway, and Japan than in the other five countries. In the United Kingdom it was a part of several experimental ships and continued as policy in these ships after the trials were concluded. In both Sweden and West Germany some formal participation had been implemented in one of the country's progressive and influential shipping firms. In Denmark and the United States participation was virtually nonexistent as either a policy or a practice.

Delegation of management accountability to ships' officers was developed to the greatest degree in Holland, where it was policy for all of the larger shipping companies, which together accounted for a major portion of the Dutch maritime fleet. It also was policy for many leading companies in Norway and the United Kingdom. Only a few Swedish companies pursued the practice. A single Danish firm, DFDS, had successfully developed this concept, and another Danish firm, which acquired DFDS, was currently exploring it. There was some practice in the United States but no reported instances in West Germany and Japan.

4. *Social integration:* The countries also differed in their practices directly affecting social status and social interaction. Japan, Norway, Sweden, and Denmark, in that order, had changed more than the other four countries. Holland and West Germany had changed less, and the United States still less. The United Kingdom was significantly different from the other countries. Many of the substantive policies, for example, in equalizing perks, may not have been very different from those in the other northwestern European countries, but status consciousness and social distance appeared to have decreased much less than elsewhere.

In summary, Japanese, Dutch, and Norwegian shipping industries had achieved the most change toward the many specific innovations we analyzed. They were high innovators across most of the policy areas. Sweden and West Germany are relatively easily placed in the middle cluster. They had achieved measures of rating role flexibility, employment stability, and assignment continuity but little formal consultation. The United Kingdom had achieved only slightly less in these respects. In other respects, the United Kingdom was the most mixed case—generally advanced in shipboard management and laggard in social integration. Denmark and the United States had innovated the least. Denmark had made little or no change toward any of the innovative policies except one isolated program to increase shipboard management teams and a general trend toward more social integration. The United States could only claim some practices in shipboard management teams.

The rankings are presented in a form that will be used throughout the book in Table 4-3.

The ranking changes in only one important respect when instead of innovation one considers the amount of noninnovative change in staffing practices, particularly decreases in crew sizes. The United Kingdom and Denmark switch places. The United Kingdom drops out of the middle cluster and into the lower cluster, which still includes the United States. Denmark joins the middle cluster.

The challenge presented by the particular ranking set forth in this chapter is all the more intriguing because the records of

Table 4-3. Innovation Rankings of Countries Studied.

Country	Innovation Records (Ranking)
Norway	2.0
Holland	2.0
Japan	2.0
United Kingdom	5.0
Sweden	5.0
West Germany	5.0
Denmark	7.5
United States	7.5

innovation do not fit any of the generalizations commonly used when comparing the countries in this sample. Consider two common generalizations.

First, Japan, with its highly adaptive approach and its impressive economic performance, is often appropriately placed at one end of a spectrum, and the European countries, with their more structured approach and social welfare orientation, at the other end, allowing the United States to fall in an intermediate position. The records of adaptive work innovations studied here do not fit this pattern. Japan is only one among three of the more impressive performers, and the United States is one of two of the poorer performers.

Second, when European countries are compared, the Scandinavian countries—Norway, Sweden, and Denmark—often are lumped together, with the implicit assumption that they will be more similar to each other than to their neighbors in northwestern Europe. But this does not hold true in the endeavor studied here. One Scandinavian country is in the cluster of high innovators, a second in the cluster of moderate innovators, and the third among the low innovators.

The many differences observed in this chapter offer opportunities for several types of comparative analysis, all aimed at general insight into the determinants of innovations and their diffusion. The most obvious analysis is accounting for the high, moderate, and low innovation records of the eight countries. This will be the major task of Chapters Five through Nine. Other interesting differences have been revealed by the foregoing analysis. For example, role flexibility diffused more widely among ratings than officers, but continuity was more prevalent among officers than ratings. Why? Consider two innovations targeted at officers: Delegation was more prevalent than role flexibility. In contrast, when these two innovations were targeted at ratings, participating was less common than role flexibility. Explaining these and other differences will be a secondary analytical task for later chapters.

PART THREE

Using the Innovation Framework

Why Are Changes Made or Not Made?

The chapters in Part Three treat in turn each of the basic components of the capacity for innovative change—guiding models, social context, economic necessity, institutional forms, and individual competence in the innovation process.

Each chapter addresses a number of questions: (1) What conceptually is the role of a component, say, institutional forms? (2) What specific aspects of the component determine whether it supports or weakens innovative change? For example, both the internal structure of institutions and the mechanisms that link them are influential. (3) How are these conceptual dimensions of a component made operational in the social systems being investigated? For example, the structural unity of the seafaring union movement in a particular country may be assessed by noting the number of separate seafaring unions that comprise it. (4) Is there evidence suggesting that the factor in question is influenced by or influences another factor? (5) Finally, how important is the element in this setting?

These questions are relevant to any setting. Moreover, they apply whether the framework is used as theory or as an action tool. Therefore, each chapter has two broad purposes. The primary purpose, signaled by the question "Why were the changes made— or not made?" is to test the ability of one of the five basic theoretical propositions to explain the ranking of the innovation records of the eight countries presented in Chapter Four. The secondary purpose of each chapter is to demonstrate an analytic method for diagnosing how a component, say, institutions, is facilitating and hindering innovative change. Diagnosis, in turn, yields ideas about constructive policies and actions. Each chapter ends with two concluding discussions: the first is about the component's significance in explaining the innovation records, and the second is about the general implications of the analysis for practice.

A rationale could be advanced for discussing the components in several different orders because the models that emerge to guide activity, the motivations that drive and restrain it, and the innovation processes that enable or hinder it are potentially interrelated in many different ways.

The guiding model is considered first, in Chapter Five, because it is the element most clearly dependent on the others. As noted in Chapter Two, a guiding model emerges to reflect the interplay of social and economic motivations; it also results from some process choices.

The motivational forces are considered next, in Chapters Six and Seven, in order to provide a background for analysis of the innovation process. Differences in the incentives and disincentives for change clarify the difficulty of managing the process, especially the difficulty of engineering consensus. The chapter on social forces precedes the one on economic incentives, departing from the pattern followed elsewhere in the book. Economic necessity is usually considered first because by definition the organizational innovations of interest are ones that enhance economic performance. The sequence is reversed in the chapter outline, primarily for reasons of continuity and hence reading efficiency. The internal organization of the social context chapter continues a pattern (of analyzing each of the four specific innovations) used in earlier but not subsequent chapters. Moreover, the findings in Chapter Seven, Economic Necessity, provide the best transition to the discussion of institutions that follows.

Institutions (Chapter Eight) and Competence (Chapter Nine) are taken up in this order because the institutions provide the structural context in which the process is managed. We need first to understand the institutional constraints to the process and the institutional levers for facilitating the process in order fully to appreciate the role of individual skill and knowledge in managing the process.

The influence of a given element is indicated primarily by examining the amount of correspondence between the ranking of the eight countries on the element (for example, the strength of economic necessity) and the ranking of their overall innovation records. The more correspondence, the greater the influence. The way specific conditions, say, modernization of a country's fleet, affect the rate of work innovation is also clarified by examining the experiences of specific countries. Some specific conditions turn out to be of limited value in explaining the overall ranking of innovation records but nevertheless contribute importantly to an understanding of the strength or weakness of a specific country.

Chapter 5

Guiding Model for Innovation

When the Oslo Work Research Institute (WRI) was asked to assist the Norwegian shipping industry in dealing with the manpower shortage problem in the late 1960s, the WRI researchers agreed to help provided several conditions were met, including

> First, that no single element in the organization of a ship could be understood or changed . . . unless it was seen as part of the total system on board (as a sociotechnical system). We were particularly concerned about adapting the status structure and departmental segmentation with the requirements of new technology, higher level of education, and other societal changes.
>
> Second, that the ship must be seen as a twenty-four-hour society and not only as a workplace. If changes were to take place in the work system, corresponding changes were necessary in the physical lay-out and social interaction during leisure time, meal time, etc. Changes in the work system of the ship must also be viewed in the context of a changing career system.[1]

Before commenting on the content of their stipulations, I want to emphasize and endorse the Norwegians' strong concern about the quality of the concepts that guide innovation activity.

When existing organizational patterns are judged inadequate to the requirements placed on them, and after some relatively undirected adaptations are tried, a broad conception—a vision—of a better organization usually develops and gets translated into more specifically defined models. The GM/Toyota organization in Fremont, California, and the GM Saturn organization, cited in Chapter One, illustrate a model resulting from such a process.

The purpose of this chapter is to explore the validity of Proposition One, which states that the capacity for innovative change depends on the strength of the model that guides it. The proposition is summarized in Figure 5-1. Note that the idea that some types of organizational innovations are inherently stronger than others employs two criteria.

First, the changes should ensure alignment among different elements and policy areas—task technology, job design, structure, reward systems, management style, training selection criteria, employment assurances, and so on. Simply stated, the organization will be more robust and effective when interdependent policies reinforce each other and send the same messages to members. Both of the Norwegian conditions quoted above stipulated this notion that the innovations should be systemic, taking account of the interrelationship of task roles and social roles and the interdependencies among elements of the task organization.

Second, the organization design should not only address task requirements but should also meet the human needs of its members—for autonomy, development, career opportunities, recognition, sense of accomplishment, social support, and the like. This attribute influences the energy, cooperation, initiative, and commitment that can be elicited by the organization. Thus, the organization will be more robust and effective when the design of tasks, structures, rewards, and so on permit the simultaneous satisfaction of human needs and business requirements.

I deduced four general models from the countries' innovation records described in Chapter Four. One of these models involved change within the spirit of the traditional shipboard organization. It involved crew reductions permitted by increased work loads and

Figure 5-1. The Role of Guiding Models in Innovative Change.

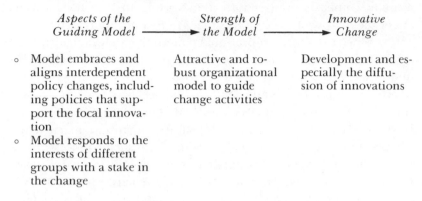

Aspects of the Guiding Model	→	Strength of the Model	→	Innovative Change
o Model embraces and aligns interdependent policy changes, including policies that support the focal innovation o Model responds to the interests of different groups with a stake in the change		Attractive and robust organizational model to guide change activities		Development and especially the diffusion of innovations

laborsaving technology. The other models each involved some combination of work innovations. One innovative approach featured role flexibility and employment continuity for ratings. Another involved delegation of authority to ships' officers and continuity in their employment and their vessel assignments. Still another innovative model, the most comprehensive, incorporated all the changes of the other approaches plus further supporting changes. For each country, one or two of these models emerged to guide the shipping industry's change activities.

After identifying differences in the strengths of these various approaches, I will explore whether the strength was an important asset in diffusion.

Related Policies and Many Stakes

Chapter Three treated each type of innovation—role flexibility, continuity policies, delegation and participation, and social integration—as responsive to some particular economic, technological, or social trend. To establish that the criterion of policy alignment applies to the shipboard innovations studied, it must be demonstrated that the four types of innovations are more than parallel responses to environmental changes, that they are closely interdependent.[2] To establish that the strength of the model is affected by how well it integrates the interests of different groups, it must be shown that the four innovations affect employee well-being as well as serve shipowners' interests.

The Traditional Model: Sound in Its Historical Context. As implied in Chapter Three, the traditional organization was sound in its historical context. Its various elements were consistent with each other, and it met important needs of the groups affected. We can understand how and why this was the case by an analysis that begins with the practice that most strongly influenced all other aspects of shipboard organization—the practice of assigning crew members to ships based on the coincidental availability of voyages and crew members. Under this practice, no effort was made to reassign crew members to the same ships after shore leaves. I call this practice instability of crews and lack of continuity.

In countries where regular employment of seafarers was not required by law, casual employment enabled a shipowner to keep the crew costs totally variable. Even when seafarers were regular employees, assignment based on availability had an immediate cost advantage for shipowners. If every person with the same certificate could be regarded as interchangeable with the others holding that certificate, there were few constraints. In contrast, if the personnel manager of the shipowner must coordinate the assignments of a given group of seafarers to some or most billets on a vessel, additional costs would be incurred, in extra travel of seafarers from their homes to a particular port and in extra pay for time not on shipboard duty. The coordinated assignment of many individuals to the same vessel was further complicated by turnover, which often ran at high rates in this industry.

Instability also satisfactorily met the needs of the individual seafarers. They associated seafaring with variety—in the vessels they worked, people they met, and places they visited. The idea of seafarers seeking variety was directly related to the reason many of them went to sea, to seek adventure or escape. These seafarers favored temporary relationships with bosses and peers as well as voyages on different types of vessels and different routes. Junior officers often needed to work on a variety of vessels and routes to help them in their promotion to higher ranks.

Crew instability not only satisfactorily met the needs of owners and seafarers but also aligned with the other three policies of the shipboard organization, hierarchical control, narrow roles, and the maintenance of social distances among ranks. The major types of implications of these four policies for each other are designated by the arrows in Figure 5-2. For example, each of the three arrows emanating from crew instability refers to what this policy directly implied for the other three elements in the traditional organization.

1. Crew instability made it necessary to structure jobs sufficiently narrow in scope so that each new incumbent could be held immediately responsible for satisfactory performance of the job. It also limited the time perspective of job holders because crew members could not be expected to assume responsibility for the vessel and its condition beyond the length of their tour of duty.

2. Instability also influenced shipboard relations. Crew members usually emphasized being sociable with each other, but their contacts tended to be of a superficial nature. They protected themselves against strong interpersonal attachments.

3. Crew instability strengthened the need for persons in leadership positions to be vested with clearly prescribed authority and to exercise strong hierarchical control. The absence of ongoing relationships precluded more complex forms of participation and influence within the crew.

4. Hierarchical control, in turn, reinforced the narrow job policy. Individuals who were subject to strong controls preferred narrow jobs, which placed boundaries on the exercise of control by superiors. Narrow, clearly delineated job requirements not only limited what the incumbent could be asked to do but also clarified for both parties the minimum performance requirements.

5. Control-oriented organizations also encouraged officers to keep their distance from ratings socially. Seafarers willingly collaborated in many ways to maintain social distance in order to limit their surveillance by officers.

Other interdependencies among these four policies could be traced, but these should be sufficient to make the point. The traditional model was internally consistent, and the four policies

Figure 5-2. Policies in the Traditional Organization.

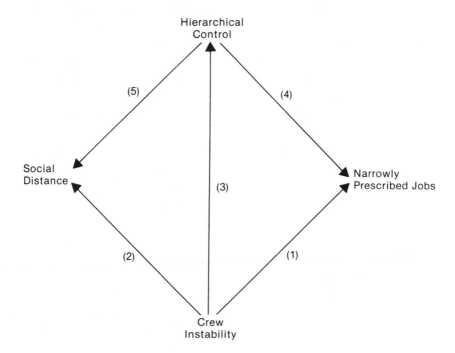

served the interests of both shipowners and seafarers as they defined these interests.

The Innovations: Interdependent and of Concern to Multiple Stakeholders. There are, as indicated earlier, several different new organizational patterns, each incorporating a distinct combination of changes in the four types of policies. To set the stage for assessing the strength of each of these patterns, I will analyze the relationships among the four policy changes.

I start with broader roles, the change most common to all the efforts studied. To achieve better performance, especially with the technological advances and smaller crews described in Chapter Three, many shipping companies defined broader roles for crew members, both in scope, for example, interdepartmental flexibility, and in time perspective. They expected crew members, especially officers, to develop a sense of responsibility for performance that extended well beyond the duration of a specific tour of duty. The broader responsibilities, including the challenges that accompany them, were a source of growth and satisfaction for seafarers and increased the seafarers' attachment to the company. However, realizing these potential benefits depended on making coordinated changes in other policies toward crew stability, shared influence, and social integration (see Figure 5-3).

1. Broader job scope required training and on-the-job development of new capabilities, which paid off for the company only when the seafarer stayed with the company. Indeed, without continuity of employment, neither the companies nor the seafarers had any incentive to invest in training and other change activities required to increase role flexibility or delegation. The company would be constantly bled of newly acquired knowledge, skills, and attitudes. Similarly, a seafarer whose next assignment was likely to be on a conventional ship had little incentive to make the personal investment to acquire new skills and change attitudes. These investments to develop broader capabilities paid off most when crew members returned to the same crew and vessel. Similarly, longer time perspectives only developed and paid dividends for the company when crew members stayed with the same vessel.

2. Broader job responsibilities, if they were to be actually accepted by job incumbents, had to be matched by greater influence. With power went responsibility and vice versa. Each helped to legitimate the other. Thus, shore management developed a greater sense of responsibility by officers for the commercial performance of the ship when it expanded the officers' sphere of influence. Similarly, officers only elicited more responsibility by ratings when they involved ratings in a broader range of matters affecting themselves and the ship's performance. Role flexibility of ratings or junior officers was resented by these seafarers when it simply meant they could be directed to work first in one area and then in another. Therefore, role flexibility was more effective when accompanied by mechanisms allowing the crew members, under normal circumstances, to influence their own assignments.

Figure 5-3. Policies in the Innovative Organization.

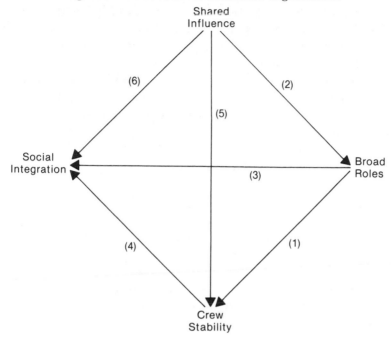

3. Broad roles also affected the type of social relations sought. With a structure of broader roles some jobs could be performed by either ratings or officers, and others could be performed by most crew members at the same organizational level. This redundant capability created more potential flexibility, but taking good advantage of this potential required good communication, which depended upon trust. Trust in turn was assisted by the reduction of social distance across ranks and the development of closer interpersonal relations among peers.

4. A socially integrated ship community depended on achieving crew stability. It took time to develop the necessary familiarity and trust.

5. Shared influence—delegation and participation—was made possible by social integration, which helped the parties with the necessary trust and communication.

6. Shared influence was also assisted by crew stability, which gave superiors time to expand progressively the involvement of

subordinates as they found they could make this involvement mutually productive. Conversely, greater employment stability reinforced employees' desire for participation. In brief, if one lowered the employees' "exit" option, one sharpened the employees' desire for voice.

These four types of policy innovations had many interdependencies and many implications for both shipowners' and seafarers' interests. I expect the models that better recognize these facts to be the more viable.

Alternate Models

In responding to pressure for change, some countries relied more exclusively on traditional methods; hence, the *base case model,* which involved change without innovation. Where the response was to innovate, the patterns or models were similar in direction—they reached for more responsibility and flexibility. They differed in two respects—whether they focused on ratings' or officers' roles and whether they involved fewer or more coordinated policy changes.

Change Without Work Innovation. In all countries some shipowners responded to economic pressures with changes in staffing practices that did not involve work innovation. In the 1970s and early 1980s, shipowners cut crew sizes by introducing laborsaving technology or increasing the standard for effort required. "Salami method" was the label given by the industry to this approach of successively slicing the number of seafarers in crew complements (see Figure 5-4). The shipowners wanted to become more cost-effective without sacrificing safety. These changes did not affect the internal consistency of the organization or the way it related to members' needs. Therefore, they were not expected to alter the viability of the traditional organization, except that by each reduction in crew size, the need for innovation would become more urgent.

In 1983 this model still provided the dominant vision for activity in the United States and Denmark and guided at least some of the activities in most of the other countries.

Figure 5-4. Traditional Approach to Crew Reduction.

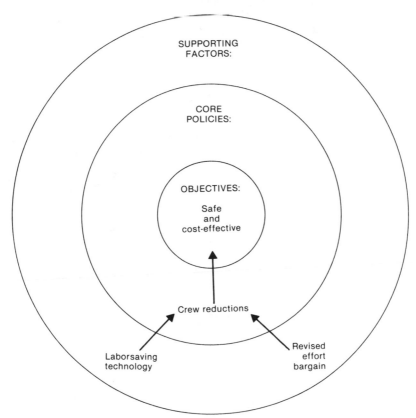

Limited Officer Model: Delegation and Vessel Continuity.
One approach focused on officers, broadening the management
responsibilities of the top officers of the ship (see Figure 5-5). This
approach, which is called the *limited officer model,* involved
control over more aspects of the ship's operations and decisions
made with a longer time horizon. For delegation to work, the
master, chief engineer, and other members of the management team
must work together for a period of time. For the team to accept full
responsibility for the state of repair of a vessel, they must stay with
it over a long period of time. Hence, the need for a policy of
continuity in vessel assignment, extended to the officers involved in

Figure 5-5. Assignment Officer Delegation and Continuity.

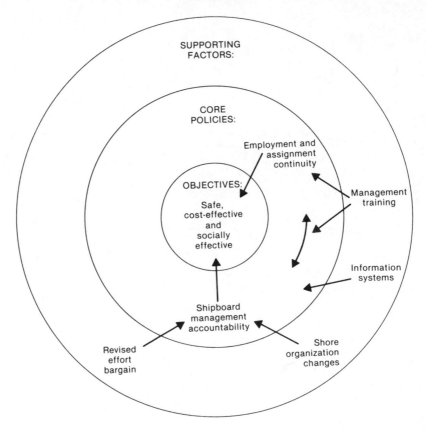

the team effort. The limited officer model recognized the need to support delegation by other changes as well—by additional company training, different information and control systems, and coordinated changes in roles and attitudes of shore personnel.

The model satisfied the two criteria set forth earlier. It included the redesign of related policies covering roles, structures, information systems, and educational systems and the redesign of both levels of the hierarchy directly affected—ships' officers and shore staff. It created as well an integrated set of objectives embracing not only economic performance but also satisfaction and development of officers. Therefore, I judge the approach viable in theory and expect to find it viable in practice.

This model was a prominent one in U.K. industry and was used by individual shipowners in some other countries.

Limited Rating Model: Role Flexibility and Employment Continuity. Another approach, which I will call the *limited rating model,* incorporated two innovations, role flexibility and continuity of employment for ratings. It also recognized the need for certain other changes—cross-training of existing deckhands and engine-room ratings, multipurpose training for new seafarers, and additional pay. The objective was to go beyond labor reductions resulting from technical change and increased effort and to become more efficient and effective in the use of human resources—without sacrificing safety, of course (see Figure 5-6).

I judge this approach too limited in scope to be viable. Although it embraced a set of coordinated expansions in job content, training, and pay, it did not include an expansion in worker influence over work plans. Although it provided for continuity of company employment, it did not recognize the importance of stability in the composition of crews. Moreover, the model focused exclusively on changes at the lower level of the shipboard organization; it did not provide for coordinated changes at the officer level to ensure proper implementation. Finally, on its face, it did not offer improvements in both cost-effectiveness and social effectiveness.

The limited rating model guided innovation activity in West Germany and Sweden and much of the innovation in the United Kingdom. The West German case was the one most completely captured by it. During the interviews with groups in the West German shipping industry, it became clear that the overall industry vision and the evaluation of discrete innovations emphasized industrial-engineering concepts of efficiency and did not include motivational effects on economic performance. The vision and evaluation emphasized the very limited social implications of the innovations, in the form of stress induced by work loads; they did not include concerns about boredom, autonomy, or human development. I encountered less recognition by West Germany's

Figure 5-6. Role Flexibility for Ratings.

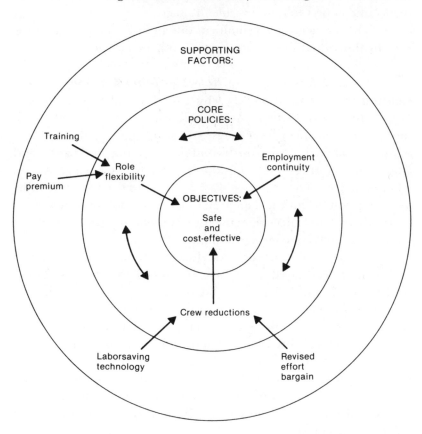

shipowners and government officials than by those in any other country that boredom on ship was a problem, and that officers might welcome delegated management responsibility and in turn contribute more if given the responsibility. The formal industry agreement covering the Hapag Lloyd project ships was prefaced: "The endeavor to make the German marine more efficient in international competition and at the same time keep *bearable* working and living conditions for seamen . . ." (emphasis added). Elsewhere the document spoke of "satisfaction," but the limited social concepts of bearable working conditions and satisfaction can be contrasted with the more ambitious themes of the Norwegians,

Dutch, and Japanese, who referred to greater competence, meaning-ful jobs, and career development.

In Sweden the actual practice closely approximated this limited model, but discussions with industry participants suggested a somewhat more complex vision. The editor of a Swedish shipping publication emphasized that a highly motivated crew was the key ingredient, echoing similar comments by many shipowners and labor officials. Many persons interviewed in Sweden emphasized the role of ownership and other economic incentives, and a few referred to the motivational effect of broader job design and expanded employee influence, indicating an appreciation of motivation as a mediator of economic performance.

In the United Kingdom the most positive industry model focused on officers. However, to the extent that there was a vision related to ratings, it approximated the limited one. An address by Menzies-Wilson, the president of the International Shipping Federation (ISF), a shipowners' association, is interesting for what was emphasized and what was not mentioned. His thoughts were reported by a journalist:

> He highlighted four areas in which he felt the UK was lagging seriously behind its competitors. Firstly, there is technological change.
>
> Second . . . he sees little progress towards the integration of jobs . . . some progress had been made with "general purpose" ratings but noted that there was "not much movement yet on the officers' side."
>
> . . . for his third point, Menzies-Wilson suggested valuable money would be saved by return of management responsibilities to ship's masters.
>
> Finally, there is the thorny old problem of social change aboard ship, especially communal messing. Menzies-Wilson and many other shipowners feel that the cost savings are important—at least £60,000 some would say—but that the division caused by the two-tier social facility on the projected 18- to 24-man complements was potentially even more damaging. He predicted a lot of lonely men on board

so sparsely manned ships of tomorrow if change, so fiercely resisted on both sides of the fence, is not brought about.[3]

The treatment of the fourth point, communal messing, and the absence of references to participation are the most revealing. The lessons of the Sealife Programme, which clearly point toward a more comprehensive model, were not reflected in the ISF president's change agenda. Communal messing was advocated not only as a source of a direct economic benefit but also as a factor promoting social integration. However, the former reason— economic benefit—is the more credible reason advanced by the ISF president. During the early 1980s shipowner after shipowner in the United Kingdom had attempted to introduce common physical facilities without the other organizational changes that would facilitate social integration, such as upgrading the quality of ratings, increasing task interdependence, and power sharing. Menzies-Wilson did not mention rating participation, which had figured so importantly in facilitating role flexibility and use of common physical facilities in Norway, the country he characterized as "the sacred cow to which all U.K. owners bow their heads in admiration."

Although a few British companies developed remarkably ambitious and successful changes, the U.K. shipping industry as a whole had great difficulty grasping the idea that the same set of innovations could serve many objectives and the interests of multiple stakeholders.

The review of the shortcomings of this limited model in West Germany, Sweden, and the United Kingdom has anticipated the advantages of the *comprehensive model,* discussed next.

Comprehensive Flexible Model. Another approach, called the *comprehensive model,* incorporated all the policies of the two limited models, thus addressing in a coordinated way the interdependent roles and activities of ratings and officers. In addition, it went well beyond the combined features of the two limited models, including participation by ratings in work planning and provision of common facilities for ratings and officers (see Figure 5-7). The

Figure 5-7. Comprehensive Flexible Model.

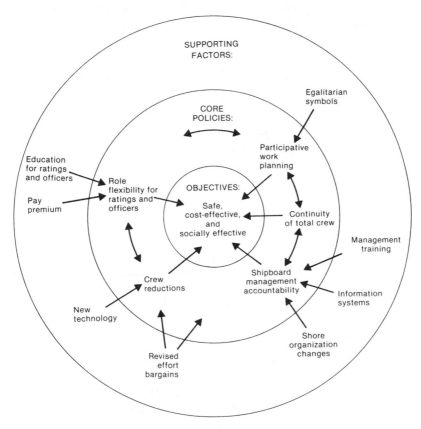

approach assumed and encouraged better social relationships. Most important, it attempted in numerous ways to integrate safety, cost-effectiveness, and social effectiveness.

Regarding the potential integration of stakeholders' interests, Moreby commented on the following irony:

> Employers, in so far as they have to defend their actions before their sources of finance, claim to be most concerned about labor costs; unsaid and deeper down is their drive toward securing a captive labor force. Employees, on the other hand, as articulated by

their trade union representatives, are most concerned
about the remuneration; unsaid and deeper down are
their concerns about career development, job security,
and satisfaction. It is a sad reflection on our political
systems that both employers and employees have a
common goal of needing a captive or committed labor
force, yet are prevented from reaching it.[4]

On theoretical grounds, I expect the comprehensive model to
be the most viable, assuming it can be implemented. The question
of implementation cannot be taken lightly. If one focuses on the
innovation process and not on the merits of the innovation model
itself, one would predict that the comprehensive approach would
not succeed as well as the limited one for ratings.[5] Specifically, it
is plausible to expect that with more complex models, more
difficulty would be encountered in gaining acceptance, implementation, and communicating the model for diffusion purposes. I will
consider these and related issues in Chapters Eight and Nine.

For now, considering the inherent qualities of the comprehensive model when compared with the limited rating model, I
expect it to be more robust, more self-maintaining, rewarding for
more groups, and thus likely to be diffused more widely in the long
run.

Comprehensive models guided change in the shipping
industries in Norway, Holland, and Japan and a few individual
companies in other countries. The models in the three countries
were similar in their focus on flexibility and provision for many
policies to support it, but they differed somewhat in form and in
their emphasis on integrating commercial and social objectives.
Norway's and Holland's were the most similar in form. While
Norway had not begun to implement role flexibility for officers, it
was included in the vision shared by shipowners, the government,
and maritime academies. The cases differed more in the historical
evolution of underlying objectives.

In Norway's case, when the new comprehensive staffing
models were first being developed, social objectives received as
much attention as did economic objectives. In fact, meeting
manpower shortages was as much a social as an economic

challenge, in the sense that it involved recruiting and retaining better qualified seafarers and improving their capabilities and motivation. Thus, a research article documenting the *Balao* experiment in the mid 1970s was totally concerned with the implications of this work system for human development and made no mention at all of economic criteria.[6] Similarly, a Hoegh company document reporting on the *Mistral* and *Multina* project ships reflected a vision containing the following elements: "decentralization—both in connection with the head office and on board ship," "an organization where people in their jobs could feel responsibility, be independent and have the chance to learn," "an organization which is able to compete with the shorebased industry when recruiting young well educated people," "reduction in number of crew," "new techniques because of automation," and "more variation and learning in the work."[7] In Hoegh, a smaller crew was a part of the vision but certainly not featured as the point of it all. By the late 1970s, the Hoegh vision and the Norwegian industry vision had placed more emphasis on economic benefits. In fact, representatives of the Norwegian shipowners' association said they believed they would have promoted more diffusion of the innovations earlier if they had attended more to its economic advantages. Similarly, a Norwegian ministry official said he had regarded the new model at first as an "interesting intellectual exercise" but, in 1983, "as an idea floating on the wave of commercial interest."

Holland's pioneer, Shell, emphasized the commercial objectives from the outset but also acknowledged the social benefits of the shipboard changes. When the new pattern of practices received industrywide endorsement, the government in particular advocated them on both economic and social grounds.

Japan's model was formulated explicitly to meet both types of objectives. It was the most ambitious in several policy areas and the most comprehensive overall. It provided for interdepartmental integration at both officer and rating levels and the additional flexibility of ratings standing watch in lieu of officers. It included immediate decreases in status differentials comparable to practices in Norway and Holland, but more significantly, it offered a shared vision of an all-officer crew in the future. It also incorporated the strongest policy for employment continuity—lifetime employment. It provided for rating participation comparable to that in Norway and Holland. Only in failing to envision increased delegation of formal authority to ships' officers was the Japanese model less ambitious than others.

Summary and Conclusions

Explaining Innovation Records by the Strength of Models. The review of models and countries that relied on them provides striking support for the proposition about the importance of models that align policies and serve multiple interests (see Table 5-1).

The noninnovation model—laborsaving technology and revised effort requirements—guided Denmark's staffing practices except for one firm. If any vision of change existed in the United States, this was it. A lack of innovation did not necessarily mean a lack of change. The traditional approach was adequate to achieve reductions from crew sizes in the high thirties to the mid twenties. This is illustrated by Denmark's industry and by parts of the industries in Sweden, West Germany, and the United Kingdom. It was widely believed, even in these countries, that further reductions would become increasingly difficult without innovations, especially role flexibility.

The limited officer model, judged to include a sufficient set of relevant policies and to integrate the interests of shipowners and officers, was in practice viable. The cluster of policies—delegation to officers, continuity of assignments for officers, and directly supporting changes—proved to be effective not only as integral elements of a more comprehensive set of changes in Norway and Holland but also as a stand-alone cluster of changes, which it was in one Danish company, a few Swedish and U.S. companies, and many British companies. In West Germany, where there were no reported instances of shipboard management accountability, a union official observed, "In Germany the captain of the ship is really only the pilot of the ship. He is supposed to just drive it." He saw no evidence of change in the centralized character of West German shipping companies. In Japan there was consultation of officers but not formal delegation of authority to them.

**Table 5-1. Comparison of Innovation Records
to Innovation Model Strengths.**

Country	Innovation Records (Ranking)	Strength of Innovation Models (Ranking)
Norway	2.0	2.0
Holland	2.0	2.0
Japan	2.0	2.0
United Kingdom	5.0	5.0
Sweden	5.0	5.0
West Germany	5.0	5.0
Denmark	7.5	Not Applicable
United States	7.5	Not Applicable

The limited rating model, judged to be both too limited in scope and too singly focused on shipowners' interests to be viable, guided almost all the innovative activities targeted at ratings in Sweden, West Germany, and the United Kingdom. The results in practice had been disappointing, as expected, helping to place these three countries into the moderate-innovator category.

I judged the comprehensive approach highly viable and expected innovators guided by models of this kind to be relatively successful. The findings strongly support these ideas. It is characteristic of the trends in Norway, Holland, and Japan. It guided change in one firm in Sweden, one firm in West Germany, and several firms in the United Kingdom.

Holland, Norway, and Japan made the most progress in changing actual practice in rating role flexibility, widely regarded as the work innovation with the most direct economic benefit. They were able to achieve progress in this innovation in part because they did not focus on it exclusively. They viewed changes in crew flexibility and employment continuity as necessary but not sufficient. They understood, for example, that unless they supported role flexibility with participation, they would not achieve effective flexibility. In contrast, the shipping industries in Sweden, West Germany, and the United Kingdom evidently still saw the more limited set of policy changes as sufficient in 1983. Therein lies the most critical difference in the visions that guided industry-level decision making and change initiatives. This difference helps explain why Holland, Norway, and Japan achieved more flexibility for ratings than did Sweden, West Germany, and the United Kingdom. In the exceptional cases in the United Kingdom, Sweden, and West Germany, where companies reached for more comprehensive innovations, the results tended to confirm the conclusion that participation is required to make role flexibility work.

I argued strongly on theoretical grounds that the comprehensive approach would be more successful than the one focused more narrowly on rating role flexibility, and indeed the findings are precisely consistent with this theory. This places considerable importance on determining why different approaches evolved in different countries. In the next chapter I explore how a country's social attitudes toward some of these discrete innovations may help explain why that country gravitated toward one model and shied away from others. In subsequent chapters I examine how economic forces, institutions, and competence may have affected whether the simpler or more comprehensive innovations were pursued.

Implications for Diagnosis and Action. Taken by itself, this chapter suggests that the capacity for innovative change is no stronger than the models that guide change activity. Thus, the findings in this chapter underscore the practical importance for policymakers to apply the two criteria for sound models to work innovations they are considering and to use the type of analysis employed here.

Even in work-reform activities in the American manufacturing sector, where activity has steadily increased over the past fifteen years, managers and labor leaders are only slowly coming to appreciate what is required for work innovation to be effective and robust. For example, quality circles are still frequently introduced without the other changes in management structure, systems, training, and attitudes required to support them. Only a minority of industry leaders show evidence they recognize that, to effect permanent change, the models guiding them must be broad in scope and integrative of the interests of the groups affected.

When considering organizational innovations with less history, such as new long-term relationships between automobile manufacturers and their suppliers and mechanisms to implement just-in-time inventory systems, it becomes even more important to have systematic ways for assessing the soundness of alternative models.

Chapter 6

Social Context
for Innovative Change

According to a British researcher, writing in 1979:

> The social integration issue remains problematic. It is
> the most immediately identified aspect of the Scandi-
> navian projects, and carries such emotional overtones
> that it discolours opinion about the experiments as a
> whole, particularly concerning the far more signifi-
> cant changes in work organization. The ratings in the
> U.K. projects saw social integration as a highly
> desirable feature of the experiment, whilst the officers
> saw it as the most undesirable.[1]

Social attitudes, such as the ones reported here, can hasten or slow
down the rate of adaptive change. In extreme cases social beliefs and
attitudes can even defeat the change.

The general proposition is that the capacity for innovative
change is strengthened when the social context supports the
particular innovations in question. Social context includes social
values, beliefs, and attitudes about the particular innovation in

question held by members of the stakeholder groups. It includes politically motivated assessments of these innovations made by leaders of the groups. It also includes other factors that may influence these assessments, such as training practices in the industry and work reforms in other industrial sectors.

The social context affects the amount of innovative change by two routes: by affecting the overall level of motivation for proposed change and by helping shape the direction of the change, the models that guide it. Chapter Five found that the countries that diffused rating role flexibility more successfully supported it by also implementing continuity policies, participative mechanisms, and social integration. But the analysis did not explain why these countries—Japan, Holland, and Norway—pursued more comprehensive organization change models, and why others relied on more limited ones. Perhaps different models emerged because of differences in the social contexts.

The purpose of this chapter is to explore whether these ideas, contained in Proposition Three of the theory and summarized in Figure 6-1, help explain the innovation records.

By itself, role flexibility affected only social habits and related attitudes. However, the other three policy reforms required to support role flexibility raised basic value issues. Contrasting values were embodied in the traditional shipboard policies and in work-innovation policies of continuity, power sharing, and social integration.

First, the two sets of policies promote different amounts of mutual commitment in the employer-employee relationship. The traditional rotary hiring system, which often is run by the union, emphasizes the seafarer's attachment to his profession and his union rather than to a company. The innovative policies—employment continuity accompanied by broader responsibilities for the commercial interests of the shipowner—emphasize the seafarer's attachment to the company. Reciprocally, when casualism is replaced by permanent employment, shipowners must enlarge their obligations to seafarers. Shipowners must not only provide more assurance of employment continuity and due process when employment is interrupted but must also assume more responsibility for maintaining seafarers' skills and knowledge.

Figure 6-1. The Role of Social Context in Innovative Change.

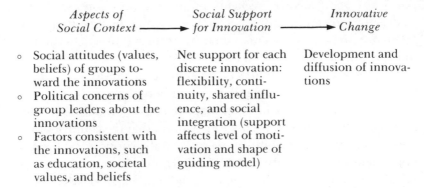

Aspects of Social Context ⟶	*Social Support for Innovation* ⟶	*Innovative Change*
o Social attitudes (values, beliefs) of groups toward the innovations o Political concerns of group leaders about the innovations o Factors consistent with the innovations, such as education, societal values, and beliefs	Net support for each discrete innovation: flexibility, continuity, shared influence, and social integration (support affects level of motivation and shape of guiding model)	Development and diffusion of innovations

Second, the traditional and innovative approaches are guided by different beliefs about how power and control should be distributed. The steep hierarchy and unilateral style of direction in the traditional shipboard organization emphasize the need for unchallenged authority and unity of command. Consultation with subordinates and the removal of layers of the hierarchy reflect a belief that sharing influence will enhance the legitimacy of superiors and their effectiveness.

Third, the policies of the two approaches are shaped by contrasting ideas about social structure. The privileges of rank and segregation of activities in the traditional policies reflect a belief in steep social stratification. Policies that equalize perks for ratings and officers and promote common social activities reflect egalitarian values and a belief in the efficacy of an integrated ship community.

These differences in beliefs and social values were salient for all stakeholders, including seafarers, shore staff, employers, and union officials. However, the attitudes of employers and union officials toward a proposed innovation were influenced by additional factors, namely, the political implications these innovations had for them in their institutional roles. For example, for employers company attachment meant increased control over human resources. For unions employment continuity could mean a loss of control over members, who become more attached to the company; in addition, role flexibility could result in loss of union members and the loss of a separate institutional identity. These potential losses caused some union officials to view the innovations as inimical to the social role of the union.

Certain types of social beliefs play other roles influencing innovation records. Social beliefs shape the institutional forms examined in Chapter Eight, for example, adversarial versus collaborative structures among labor, management, and government; and they influence the action strategies used in the innovation process treated in Chapter Nine, for example, directive versus participative methods for introducing shipboard change. I will defer consideration of these types of social beliefs, although they may be related to the values that affect the motivation toward the innovations considered here, until I focus the analysis on the innovation process.

Social Context in the Shipping Industry

Some significant differences in the social views of groups within a country and across countries were reported to me by informed members of the industry, and others were cited in the literature on shipping. The analysis of country differences in this chapter goes beyond these relatively direct indications of the social values or social attributes toward the innovations held by groups in the shipping industry. It includes an assessment of country differences in the broader social context, differences that made the social climate in the industry either more supportive or more hostile toward the shipboard innovations.

Individuals working in the shipping industry developed their own values and beliefs about work organizations, influenced by forces operating at each of three levels: trends in the national society, general practice in the industry, and the culture of a particular company.

Societal values influenced expectations that individuals brought to the shipping industry. Chapter Three noted several social trends affecting all eight countries during the period from the mid 1960s to the mid 1980s. The trends, sometimes codified into law, covered the three value dimensions identified above. Employers were expected to accept more obligations for employment continuity, to provide more employees with more voice over more issues, and to diminish differences in rank and privileges at work. The rate of these value changes appeared to accelerate during the 1970s and then to slow down during the early 1980s.

While all industries in a given country will partly reflect the society's values, industry differences may exist due to their unique histories, technologies, work-force characteristics, and market conditions. The maritime industry in each country did have a set of values somewhat differentiated from the norms of most shore industries. Moreover, inherited practice in this sector was an especially powerful force. Individuals made decisions to go to sea based on their perceptions of past practices. They were trained and socialized in academies that reflected industry practices. As in professional programs for doctors and lawyers, maritime training programs were powerful shapers of attitudes and beliefs. The traditional high mobility of seafarers among vessels owned by different companies, the need for uniform roles, and the expectation of unquestioning acceptance of directions from persons in authority had made industrywide socialization especially important.

The trend was, however, for both the individual company and the larger society to become more important socializing forces. Two developments were responsible for this trend. First, when several countries legislated permanent employment for seafarers in the early 1970s, independent of any other movement toward flexible staffing, the employing company immediately became a more significant shaper of seafarers' beliefs and attitudes. Some companies reinforced the industry norm; others offered deviant attitudes and beliefs. Second, as leave times lengthened and seafarers spent more time at home, they became more aware of societal trends and the practices in other industries. Thus, together company employment and long leave times diminished the influence of inherited practice and enhanced the influence of both company policies and societal trends.

An individual's social values and the forces that shaped them were important because they in turn influenced initial reactions to a proposed innovation. I refer here to the individual's social reaction, acknowledging that his or her overall reactions were also influenced by economic interests.

While initial reactions influenced the innovation and early diffusion results, subsequent assessments based on direct experience with the innovation determined its effectiveness and diffusion over the longer term. Sometimes participants' initial skepticism or resistance was replaced by enthusiastic support, a phenomenon also observed in many other industrial settings when similar organizational changes were implemented. In shipping, this generally was true for the more comprehensive versions of the innovations but not for the simpler version of rating flexibility.

Social Support for Specific Work Innovations

How do variations in social values and other aspects of the social climate help explain the strength of support for or opposition to each of the innovative policies?

Role Flexibility. The concerns of employers and seafarers about role flexibility were primarily economic, not social. Role flexibility usually offered an economic advantage to the employer. It could be an economic advantage or disadvantage to seafarers, depending on the trade-offs involved in eliminating billets per ship in order to preserve ships in the national fleet. Seafarers also could favor or oppose the revised effort/wage bargain implicit in the flexible roles.

Apart from any implications for jobs and pay, individuals directly affected were mildly opposed to role flexibility on social grounds, at least initially. Both ratings and officers had psychological attachment to the separate traditions of the deck and engine departments. The reactions of ratings to role flexibility were slightly less negative in Norway, West Germany, and Japan because their maritime traditions included some informal helping out between departments. Also, slightly more resistance existed among seafarers in the United Kingdom, the United States, and Denmark because strong jurisdictional demarcations were much more the norm in these countries as a whole than in any of the other countries. However, these were subtle differences, and I can only infer slight differences in the initial social attitudes toward role flexibility.

The subsequent assessments by general-purpose (GP) ratings based on experience in these roles did differ across countries. In Sweden, West Germany, and the United Kingdom assessments continued to be negative. In contrast, in Norway, Holland, and Japan they became more positive with experience. As reported earlier, only in the second cluster of countries did shipowners tend to include challenging work in the assignments to both departments and to give ratings more say in their assignments.

Role flexibility had two types of political implications for unions in some countries, but both are similar to major effects analyzed in subsequent chapters.

Where separate unions represented the deck and engine-room ratings—in Denmark and the United States—the proposal for a single general-purpose rating was threatening to the ratings' unions because it affected their survival as separate entities. The separate deck-officers' and engineering-officers' unions in Norway, Sweden, the United States, and Denmark were similarly threatened by any proposal for an integrated officer. Because the multiple-union structure is a more general institutional factor with similar adverse effects on the innovative process, this effect will be treated in Chapter Eight, Institutions.

Role flexibility had a second political implication for the unions. On the one hand, by reducing crews, it decreased union membership and union power. On the other hand, crew reductions also made the fleet more competitive and in that way tended to make jobs and membership rolls more secure. Because these mixed concerns of union officials about role flexibility directly paralleled the mixed economic interests of seafarers, which are treated as a major aspect of the analysis of economic necessity, they will be covered in Chapter Seven.

Continuity of Employment and Vessel Assignment. Shipowners had a stronger economic rationale for providing continuity of employment and vessel assignment to officers, to whom they gave more responsibility, than to ratings. The greater application of continuity policies for officers reflected these economic considerations, not social concerns.

I will focus on differences in continuity practices for ratings, where both the practices and the attitudes toward them differed among countries. The legislation of permanent employment in Holland, Sweden, and West Germany indicated societal support for companies to take on more obligations to their employees. Some shipowners in most of the other countries also appreciated the control and company attachment that were yielded by regular employment. Japan's policy of lifetime employment reflected by far the strongest beliefs in the value of company attachment.

Ratings generally preferred the stability and certainty continuity of employment provided, although some did not want to give up being "free birds of the sea." Ratings' unions in several countries had been concerned about the employment relationship strengthening seafarers' bonds with the company and weakening ties with the union, but in only one European case did a union hold out against this practice—the deck-ratings' union in Denmark. The ratings' unions in the United States were even more opposed to permanent employment than their Danish counterparts, but they had not been as directly tested by shipowners' attempts to offer it.

What about continuity of vessel assignment? Although a small minority of seafarers preferred varied experience with different types of vessels and/or preferred not to be a part of stable social relations, all stakeholders predominantly favored vessel continuity. In the small twenty-four-hour community of a ship at sea, turnover offered a useful escape valve for interpersonal resentments and other social antagonisms. Thus, the degree of social support for continuity increased when the organization of work was improved and an integrated shipboard community developed. The practical limiting factor was the shipowners' judgment about what it was worth in terms of supporting other innovations and about what it would cost.

Delegation to Ships' Officers. The primary stakeholders in this innovation were senior officers, who were delegated more responsibility and authority; shore staff, who usually were reduced in number, realigned, and urged to be less directive regarding ships' activities; and top company executives, who decided whether it would make economic and social sense for the company and who took the initiative for change. Some implications for these stakeholders are shown in an example of a medium-sized Norwegian company. A third-generation shipowner and ex-president of the shipowners' association recalled how his company decentralized some ten years ago: "I was very much afraid that unless we had this change, this shift of mentality prepared properly, we would experience a boomerang effect. But the people onboard seized the opportunity eagerly." The shipowner spent a long time preparing for the changeover from centralized, shore-based operations to decentralization, including changing his own attitudes. He admitted, "I was very bad at delegating, so they told me."[2]

Officers generally wanted more responsibility for managing the ship. The large majority saw it as a way of relieving the boredom resulting from specialization of ships and automation. They regarded the practice as developmental, increasing their future career mobility on shore. However, individual differences existed in all countries. For example, some Swedish officers in one company concluded they did not want the additional responsibility. A similar reaction was also observed in a U.K. case, where the officers were concerned about the increased visibility of their performances.[3]

When authority was delegated from shore to ship, shore staff invariably opposed it. A terse item in a U.K. company's report on its implementation of management-team accountability is indicative of the problem. It noted that "traditionally steeped shore personnel find the team system unacceptable and will undoubtedly either leave or be asked to leave." Then it added pointedly, "This situation cannot be ignored by committed management."[4]

What about companies? The views of top managers varied widely across the eight countries. Shipowners might have two possible economic reasons for this innovation: to enhance the officers' jobs and therefore attract better talent and to increase the officers' willingness and ability to improve the ships' commercial effectiveness. The social beliefs of a given shipowner would determine whether it expected these potential benefits to occur. In West Germany shipowners' beliefs were uniformly pessimistic; in Denmark, Sweden, and the United States a few shipowners were optimistic; and in the United Kingdom, Holland, and Norway shipowners' beliefs were generally optimistic. In Japan it had not become an issue.

Industry observers in several countries offered explanations for some of these differences in shipowners' beliefs. Norwegian officers had always taken more responsibility for the commercial interests of the vessel, thus predisposing all groups in this industry to be more receptive to this innovation. In contrast, Swedish and West German officers had traditionally received training with a heavy technical orientation and virtually no managerial content, perhaps making them appear to be less capable of handling management responsibilities.

Participative Work Planning. Social values related to participation were more important than economic considerations in the initial reaction to this organizational innovation. Initially, officers were opposed, and ratings were receptive or ambivalent. The officer tended to see it as a loss of power and authority and a complication of his job. The rating tended to see it as a potential gain in influence but expressed skepticism about the likelihood of realizing the potential.

Ambivalence by some ratings toward work planning and related changes in their role was noted in the Norwegian and Dutch pioneer projects, but it was more common in those of the United Kingdom. The majority of ratings on the Sealife project ships responded favorably to greater involvement in work planning. However, some ratings on each project ship rejected the combined implications of participative work planning and continuity of assignment. Clearly, this minority did not welcome the additional responsibility that was implied by influence and the additional commitment that was implied by continuity.[5]

Shipowners were another stakeholder group. In addition, they could influence the seafarers' values through their espoused philosophy and actual company practices. Critical here were top management's social beliefs about the relationship between participation and effectiveness. Shell of Holland, Hoegh of Norway, and P.A.L. of the United Kingdom each had a socially oriented philosophy, which had created a company setting relatively favorable to participation by ratings. However, these specific instances provide no basis for characterizing the beliefs about participation held by shipowners as a group in a particular country prior to their involvement in work innovations.

Because work-planning initiatives were largely absent in all but Holland, Norway, Japan, and the United Kingdom, I cannot make an eight-way comparison of the direct attitudes of any of the stakeholders toward this innovation. However, looking at some of the underlying forces that shape such attitudes (societal trends, industry practices, and company philosophies) may help explain the differences.

The general trend was to give employees more voice in economic institutions. The specific trends throughout the eight countries studied took several forms: codetermination (having worker representatives on company boards), worker councils (representative mechanisms that allow workers a voice regarding the management of major units of the enterprise), and, to a lesser extent, shop-floor participation (mechanisms that enable workers to influence the content of their jobs and decisions that directly affect them). Participative work planning aboard ship was an instance of this third form.

A comparison of various forms of industrial democracy in European countries, including shop-floor participation in our six northeastern European countries, was published by the American Center for the Quality of Work Life (ACQWL) in 1978, a date that reflects the social context midway through the period covered by the study.

Sweden was far ahead of every other European country in terms of quantity and quality of shop-floor work-restructuring projects. All of Sweden's major companies—for example, Volvo, Saab-Scania, Husqvarna, Orrefors, ASEA, and Trelleborg Rubber— had made highly visible, large-scale advances. According to the ACQWL report, "employee pressures on Swedish management to modify traditional hierarchical and authoritarian management structures seems relentless."[6]

Norway had conducted the pioneering shop-floor experiments in the early 1960s, conceived at that time as a more promising form of industrial democracy than the codetermination mechanism, which was spreading throughout Europe. The results of early experiments initiated by Einar Thorsrud and the Work Research Institute in a pulp-and-paper mill, a fertilizer plant, and an electrical-appliance factory received considerable attention within Norwegian industry in the 1960s and throughout Europe in the early 1970s. The leading experiments in shore industries, like the subsequent projects in shipping, had been conducted within a tripartite framework. Shop-floor participation continued to make slow, steady progress in Norway, although more slowly than might have been expected and much more slowly than in Sweden.[7]

In Denmark, like Sweden, interest in shop-floor participation developed about 1970, often under the joint sponsorship of employers and unions. A number of experiments showed excellent results in both job satisfaction and productivity, but the momentum faded somewhat with the economic recession. In addition, evidently some union suspicion developed about changes imposed by management.[8]

Shop-floor participation in Holland's industry occurred early but did not lead to any general trend. Philips Lamps began a major program in the early 1960s. With the encouragement of the Dutch government, other managements began to sponsor shop-floor experiments in work redesign and worker participation, sometimes with and sometimes without the unions' involvement. The unions became increasingly skeptical for at least two reasons: workers' high expectations were disappointed, and there was a tendency for many managements to keep tight control over the programs, "unilaterally terminating them when they no longer seemed to serve a useful purpose."[9] The unions grew more strongly in favor of other participative mechanisms where powers and rights were legally guaranteed, for example, works councils. Nevertheless, the government continued to encourage shop-floor experiments, not as a substitute but as an additional mechanism for participation.

In West Germany, where the idea of codetermination was pioneered, and where the works councils had become the most powerful institutions of their kind in western Europe,[10] there had been little or no attention paid to individual workers or to the quality of working life at the shop floor. An important event occurred in October 1973, raising the level of consciousness in West German industry about the design of work and its human implications. It was a local but highly significant "humanization-of-work" strike by members of the metalworkers' union, which lasted two weeks and resulted in understandings about the organization of work. For example, management agreed to minimum task time cycles for moving assembly lines and increased worker control over group organization. The next year the government launched the most comprehensive and ambitious program to promote "humanization of work" in Europe. Within two years it had funded nearly two hundred research projects, demonstration projects, and in-company experiments.[11] As ambitious as this German humanization-of-work development was, it is not exactly in the spirit of shop-floor participation being surveyed here. These German projects were characterized by a stronger emphasis on reengineering work, for example, by allowing workers a more varied pace rather than by using participative mechanisms in day-to-day shop-floor activities.

The United Kingdom lagged behind the other countries, despite the fact that its experiments as early as 1952 had inspired much of the subsequent activity in other countries. In 1975 the British Research Institute was established in the Department of Employment to spread information on work restructuring and sponsor experiments in British companies. Its budget was small compared to the West German government's support for humanization of work. Moreover, despite the fact that this program was supervised by a tripartite body, the vast majority of union leaders and managers continued to concentrate attention on pay and job security.

How do Japan and the United States compare with the European countries? Japan dominates the field, as evidenced by the widely publicized diffusion of quality circles throughout many of its major corporations. The idea of self-management was a key idea that had been strategically employed by a large number of major Japanese corporations engaged in the export of manufactured goods, including autos, steel, ships, machine tools, and electronics products. Although the concept of the quality circle in particular and participation in general had been taken by Japanese industrialists from American literature recommending such practices, the Japanese perfected the techniques, and more importantly, they developed organizational cultures to support them.

Activity in the United States was comparable to that in Sweden in many respects, although union sponsorship for this type of change developed more slowly in the United States. Pioneering experiments in work restructuring were started in the late 1960s. One of the most publicized projects was a General Foods pet-food plant in Topeka, Kansas, started in 1969. It played a role in establishing a prototype for the future comparable to Volvo's Kalmar plant in Sweden and Hoegh's project ship *Mistral* in Norway. The trend toward shop-floor participation gained support when it became perceived as a constructive response to the malaise among workers in the early 1970s. General Motors (GM) and the United Automobile Workers (UAW) pioneered the idea of joint union-management sponsorship of quality-of-work-life (QWL) programs, a joint program that I cited several times in Chapter One. At first GM viewed participation as reducing absenteeism, then as increasing product quality, and by the 1980s as improving the quality of decisions and their implementation. Although GM was one of the more visible companies implementing shop-floor participation throughout the 1970s, by 1978 most major American corporations had initiated programs to promote participation in some of their facilities.

In general, the trend toward participation involved all eight societies, although as I have just noted, the strength of the trend varied. Seafarers in Europe participated fully in this shift of attitudes, according to David Moreby, dean of maritime studies at Plymouth Polytechnic in Britain.[12] He emphasized the importance of age in his interpretation of the shift in attitudes of European seafarers toward authority and participation. Unlike the United States and Japan, where seafarers typically made a commitment to the sea for their working lives, seafaring in the northwestern European countries was a young person's profession. Seafarers were recruited in their late teens or early twenties; most of them left the sea for shore jobs by their later twenties or early thirties. Even though young seafarers continued to defer to authority, it did not mean they accepted prevailing conditions, warned Moreby. He also noted that most personnel managers and shipping executives were over forty-five years of age and out of touch with the attitudes, aspirations, and ideals of the young recruits.

Age was a theme echoed by Einar Thorsrud, the researcher who has influenced European shipboard work practices the most. He observed that many Norwegian shipping companies elected to go slowly in introducing participation and similar changes out of deference to the older captains, who had problems adjusting to the new ways.[13] Shipowners in every northeastern European country confirmed that their older seafarers were less receptive to all of the innovations than were their younger colleagues. Older seafarers are, on the average, less ready to make a major investment in training, to yield perks and share power (as officers), to accept more responsibility (as ratings), and to change social habits aboard ship.

The idea of a correlation of ages and social values introduces some interesting possibilities. The average age of seafarers rises in a declining industry, and the innovations needed to revitalize the industry are more difficult to implement when the average age of seafarers rises. Thus, the age of seafarers may reinforce either a downward or an upward industry trend that is based on other, more fundamental forces. A case in point was reported by one Swedish firm: The average age of crew members on its vessels rose from thirty-two to forty-nine years within a few years, as the fleet was more than halved.

If age indicates less receptivity to the work innovations, including not only participation but also role flexibility, continuity, and social integration, then the United States was at a distinct disadvantage, because the average age of its seafarers was fifty-four years in 1983—more than fifteen years older than European seafarers and more than ten years older than Japanese seafarers.

Factors other than age also influenced the prevailing hierarchical and authoritarian attitudes in shipping. According to Moreby, former colonial powers, especially Britain and Holland, were more conscious of class differences than were the Scandinavian countries. West Germany was the most conscious of traditional authority relations.

The Norwegian and Swedish maritime trades were less authoritarian, due in part to the fact that a common entry system ensured that all officers had been ratings. However, the president of the Swedish seamen's union cautioned against simply assuming that, because all officers "go through the hawspipe," they would be similar to the ratings they supervise. He believed that ratings who become officers and those who are content to remain ratings probably tend to come from different backgrounds.

A related pattern should be noted here. In two countries, Holland and the United Kingdom, the entry and certification requirements for ratings were relatively low. This had depressed the quality of the talent at the rating level. Equally importantly, this created pessimism about the ability of ratings to assume a more responsible role and inhibited more social integration aboard ship. In Holland, for example, young men and women could enter the industry from three levels of education. The officers entered from the third level, whereas ratings entered from the first level. No seafarers entered from the second level. This gap made it virtually impossible for ratings to become officers. It also was a barrier that had to be overcome in delegating officers' work to ratings, in giving ratings voice in work planning, and in narrowing social-status differences. In contrast, Japanese ratings were among the best educated and trained in the world.

Whatever their initial attitudes toward work planning, with actual experience direct participants tended to become moderately to strongly positive. Even most officers who developed the necessary skills in listening and running meetings[14] had come to accept that participation promoted a more congenial, more effective, and safer ship. The seafaring unions had tended not to make an issue of work-planning participation, neither advocating nor opposing it.

Social Integration. Social values played an important role in determining whether industry stakeholders supported or opposed equalized perks and social integration aboard ship. Ratings' social attitudes and beliefs were generally favorably disposed to both developments, but they were reportedly ambivalent about common messing in particular. The views expressed by a chief electrician on the Hoegh *Mallard* are consistent with what was reported by shipowners in other Scandinavian countries, Holland, and West Germany:

Just to sit down for roughly twenty to twenty-five
minutes—and out—you have your food, but it is not
cozy, it is not pleasant. Eating should be a pleasure;
you should have peace, good talks with other people;
we have peace only because we have more or less
separated ourselves so we who are sitting together talk
about things we like, but we do not mix. The
company's intention was that we should mix. When
we came aboard the ship it was said that everybody
should change seats for every meal. Everybody was
supposed to mix. But you can see that every person has
a rigid and fixed place.[15]

It is difficult to make a case that ratings' attitudes were significantly
more favorable in one country than in another, except in the United
Kingdom, where the change had special symbolic value for ratings
and their union as an attack on social-class differences.

Generally, officers were initially unhappy about narrowing
the difference between ratings and themselves in perks, accommodations, and other status symbols and were either negative or
ambivalent about more social interaction. For example, the
Japanese junior officers were troubled at first because they had to
make their own beds and stand in a cafeteria line, but subsequently
they felt that the loss of these perks was more than offset by the
benefits they gained from increased harmony within the crew. The
attitudes of Norwegian and Swedish officers followed a similar
pattern. They were mildly opposed to these changes initially and
were relatively relaxed about the issues in 1983.

The U.K. officers were the most opposed to these developments. They were very upset by the equalizing of perks in the early
1970s and were strongly resistant to social integration in the late
1970s. Because common messing removes the perk of being served
in an officers' dining room, U.K. officers also regarded it as a
diminishment of their total reimbursement package.[16] And because
their labor agreements specified such matters as separate messes,
officers' unions were able to slow the rate at which these steps were
implemented.

Despite the care taken by Sealife leaders in the United Kingdom to inform participants that social integration was not a primary objective and would merely occur in time as a natural consequence of the other changes in the organization, it did become one of the most controversial issues in the projects, as the opening quotation in this chapter testifies.[17]

Some change efforts in the United Kingdom met with more success. P.A.L.'s experiments, which involved comprehensive and successful change, integrated meals but preserved separate bars. Social mixing occurred "spontaneously"; it was "not forced." The positive trend toward social integration was attributed by participants to the fact that the P.A.L. ratings were better trained and better utilized. The inference drawn was that ratings' status in the United Kingdom would only improve with changes in training and work practices.

Companies that sponsored comprehensive work innovations generally believed strongly in the efficacy of an integrated ship community. Other shipowners supported more comparable perks and common facilities, based on such economic considerations as attracting seafarers, saving space, and reducing steward personnel. In the latter circumstances little genuine social integration occurred.

Summary and Conclusions

Explaining Innovation Records by Social Context. To summarize the effects of social attitudes in each of the four policy areas:

In the area of role flexibility, social attitudes played little or no role in explaining differences in amount of innovation. In general, ratings and officers were initially opposed to role flexibility, less because it raised fundamental value issues than because it disturbed social habits and identities. There were no significant country differences in these initial social attitudes. With experience ratings became positive in Holland, Norway, and Japan. However, these changes in attitudes were attributable more to a parallel implementation of work planning than to a reevaluation of role flexibility itself.

In a second policy area, continuity of employment and vessel assignment, values played only a moderate role in the eight-country sample. In general, the social attitudes of ratings, officers, and shipowners were favorable to both continuity policies. In Japan the attitudes were very favorable. In the other countries where employment was not required by law—Norway, the United Kingdom, Denmark, and the United States—Norwegian and British shipowners offered more employment stability, but I cannot attribute this to social as opposed to economic considerations. However, in two countries some unions were opposed to continuity policies on social grounds. The leaders of the ratings' unions in both Denmark and the United States opposed regular company employment arrangements because they eliminated the role of the union hiring halls and appeared to threaten the seafarers' attachment to the union.

The delegation of shipboard management appeared to be influenced by social values, or more accurately, by the social beliefs of shipping executives. The officers in every country where shipboard management was practiced liked it, and in almost every country where it was not, officers said they would like it. The shore staff invariably resisted it. Thus, on the face of it, shipowners faced reasonably similar attitudes. Recall that in Holland, Norway, and the United Kingdom they had made this practice almost an industry norm; that in Sweden, Denmark, and the United States there had been modest interest; and that in West Germany and Japan there had been none. In most instances these practices reflected different beliefs about the way officers would respond to broadened responsibilities.

The countries with the more favorable social contexts for rating participation and social integration were Japan, Norway, and Sweden. They were characterized by relatively strong trends toward participation in their manufacturing industries. Common recruitment for ratings and officers in Norway and Sweden and the high level of qualification requirements for ratings in Japan further strengthened their social climates for these practices.

The country with the least hospitable climate for participation and social integration was the United Kingdom. Only slightly more hospitable were the social climates of Holland and West

Germany. All three had less extensive movements toward shop-floor participation (despite the strong company-level participation mechanisms in Holland and West Germany). The three were former colonial powers. Residual class consciousness was especially strong in the United Kingdom. In Holland and the United Kingdom a big difference between the educations of entering ratings and entering officers created a relatively wide social gap to bridge and hence discouraged both participation and social integration. (Holland's actual social attitudes toward participation had become more favorable by 1983, but I regard them more as the result of extensive change than as a cause of it.)

The United States and Denmark were intermediate in terms of social conditions favorable to these practices. The U.S. shipping industry was favored by an active societal trend toward workplace participation but was handicapped by an older seafaring work force.

This ordering of predispositions helps explain the participative planning on Norwegian and Japanese ships but fails most notably to explain two observations: the absence of participation on Swedish ships and its prevalence on Dutch ships. I will return to these observations later.

Considering the social support for employment continuity for ratings, delegation for officers, rating participation, and social integration produces the composite ranking of social contexts shown in Table 6-1. It can be compared with the overall records of innovation.

Taken as a whole, there is some correspondence between the two rankings, but it is not remarkably strong. The correspondence is reflected in the very favorable social contexts of Norway and Japan, which could help explain their ability to develop a comprehensive model and to diffuse role flexibility more widely throughout their shipping industries.

Interestingly, the United Kingdom and West Germany switch places with Denmark and the United States, as one considers first one ranking and then the other. West Germany and the United Kingdom are in the middle-innovation cluster, despite possessing the two least favorable social climates for shipboard innovations. In

Table 6-1. Comparison of Innovation Records to Social-Support Rankings.

Country	Innovation Record	Social Support for Innovations
Norway	2.0	1.0
Holland	2.0	4.0
Japan	2.0	2.5
United Kingdom	5.0	7.5
Sweden	5.0	2.5
West Germany	5.0	7.5
Denmark	7.5	5.5
United States	7.5	5.5

contrast, Denmark and the United States are low innovators, even though they had intermediate social climates.

Also higher in both ranks, Holland and Sweden switch places. Holland's innovation performance is stronger than its social context would forecast, and Sweden's positions are just the opposite.

Let us review the findings on social context, with particular attention to whether they help explain the emergence of different models.

Why did no innovation models of any type emerge in the Danish and American shipping industries? The explanations are not primarily social. First, social attitudes were found to be of little importance compared with economic motivation in considering proposals for role flexibility. Second, the social contexts in these countries were intermediate in general and would have been moderately amenable to participation in particular.

Why did Sweden, the United Kingdom, and West Germany rely on the limited rating model rather than evolve a comprehensive model? Perhaps the attitudes toward participation in particular played a gate-keeping role in the development of the comprehensive model. It is significant that the limited model combined the two specific policies that were less sensitive to social values (role flexibility and continuity) and avoided those that were more sensitive (participation and social integration). This line of reasoning helps explain why the United Kingdom and West Germany, with their less favorable social contexts, would be attracted to the limited model. But by the same reasoning, Sweden, with its more positive context, should have entertained a model incorporating participation.

Why did the comprehensive model evolve in Norway, Japan, and Holland? Both Japan's and Norway's choices are readily supported by reference to social contexts. Holland's choice, however, is not. It had less favorable dispositions toward participation and social integration in particular and only a moderately favorable social context for the innovations as a whole.

Thus, to return to earlier observations, a few anomalies emerge from the analysis of social contexts and innovation records. The first is why Holland was a high innovator (with a comprehensive model) and why Sweden was not. The second anomaly is why the United Kingdom and West Germany were moderate innovators and why the United States and Denmark were not. The examination of economic incentives in Chapter Seven and of institutions in Chapter Eight will help.

Implications for Diagnosis and Action. Although social factors did not appear to play a decisive role in influencing the innovation records in shipping, they clearly were acting to either assist or resist the other forces that were more dominant in promoting innovative change.

The analysis in this chapter suggests a number of questions that should be used to diagnose the role of social conditions in relation to other organizational innovations, such as cooperative research and development in the U.S. computer industry or the American machine-tool industry.

1. Do the prevailing social beliefs tend to support or oppose the innovations? Knowing this determines whether the beliefs will be (1) part of the driving force and therefore need to be accompanied by only a moderately strong economic rationale in order to bring about change or (2) a source of resistance and therefore likely to complicate the process of managing consensus.

2. Do the potential concerns of the leaders merely give additional impetus to the social attitudes and economic interests of their groups' members, or do they confound the motivational forces

at work? Knowing this will help define the arenas in which change must be effected.

3. Do each of the several specific innovations that may be combined in practice elicit different attitudes? Such differences may influence the sequence in which specific innovations are introduced or emphasized.

4. Do attitudes change with experience, thus influencing the initial implementation in one way but the longer-term effectiveness of the innovation in another way? If the attitudes toward some innovations shift only when they are supported by another policy, then attitudes toward the gate-keeping practice become especially important targets of attitude-change interventions (as illustrated in shipping, where the attitudes toward role flexibility depended on whether role flexibility was accompanied by participation).

5. What aspects of society or the industry—for example, laws, educational systems, and institutional forms—influence attitudes toward the innovation? Which of them can be modified by individuals associated with the industry or company in question?

The answers to these diagnostic questions have implications that can be illustrated by focusing on several specific findings. The study confirms that while broader social forces, such as the societal trend toward participation, helped promote work innovations, other relevant aspects of the social context were subject to influence from within the industry. Several types of actions illustrate conditions that either were influenced or could have been influenced by the shipping industry itself:

- extending legislating or negotiating regular employment for the shipping sectors, which would cause a shift in attitudes as well as behavior
- changing the recruitment system for ratings to tap groups with more education and upgrading the training system for ratings, both of which would increase the receptivity of officers to participation and social integration
- including in the maritime curriculum for officers more commercial and organizational subjects, which would increase receptivity in the industry to delegation and participation

The first of these three examples of manageable changes in the social context, legislated regular employment for shipping, did occur and probably was partly influenced by shipping-industry institutions, particularly seafaring unions. The other two are cited as conditions that played important roles in shipping attitudes and beliefs, and that were *potentially* (if not actually) targets of strategic change initiations, targets of metacompetence.

A finding with important practical importance and broad application is the tendency for social assessments of innovations to become more favorable on the basis of direct experience when the innovations were soundly conceived but not when the models were too limited in scope or focused too exclusively on the interests of one group.

This suggests that if the other factors—economic, institutional, and competence—are sufficiently favorable to produce action, and if the action is guided by a sound model, then the action itself may well modify the social context such that it also drives rather than resists the innovative change.

Chapter 7

Economic Necessity for Innovation and Change

U.K. shipowners have put their cards clearly on the table, showing all concerned that they feel the progress of efficient manning to be of monumental concern. . . . Without it he [the president of the shipping association] foresees the final disappearance of an effective U.K. deep-sea fleet.[1]

This urgent message about competitive threat mandating change was reported by a journalist covering a meeting of a British-based shipping association.

What is the role of economic necessity, assessed to be very high in this view of the British shipping industry, in the overall capability of a social system for innovative change? The general argument is that economic factors force management and labor to consider change, and that the incentive to achieve a more secure competitive position provides the rationale for adopting particular innovations. If the argument is generally valid, how far can the logic embedded in it be extended? For example, does the strength of economic pressure beyond a threshold level continue to increase a company's or an industry's ability to innovate? At some point does additional pressure discourage innovation? Still other specific questions are raised by the proposition that economic necessity influences the capacity for innovative change. How much of the net necessity for change derives from market forces (such as comparative wage levels), and how much can result from government policies affecting employers (such as subsidies) and from employer policies affecting labor (such as employment security)? If economic necessity is to play an important role in producing change, how important is it for labor as well as management to feel similar pressures to change? How important to the capacity for innovative change is the construction of new facilities or similar conditions that provide uniquely favorable cost/benefit opportunities for implementing innovations?

Answers to these questions have important implications for making policies and taking actions designed to promote a favorable economic context for innovation. In addition, of course, the answers will help refine the general theory of innovative change and, in particular, Proposition Two. My current understanding of the role of economic factors is summarized in Figure 7-1.

To continue the approach employed in Chapters Five and Six, the primary device for exploring the role of economic necessity in this chapter is to assess whether differences in economic necessity help explain the innovation records of the eight shipping countries. Chapter Six showed that while the trend in social values in the shipping industry was in a direction favorable to the innovations, this meant on balance less resistance to rather than greater demand for them. At best, positive attitudes and beliefs played a supporting, but certainly not the lead, role in producing change. Moreover, differences in social values among countries were only moderately helpful in explaining their innovation records. These observations heighten the importance of assessing the role of economic motivation.

The shipboard innovations in question used human resources more efficiently and therefore offered economic advantage, an advantage that grew as automation permitted fewer people to operate ships. However, this notion is complicated in two ways. First, the innovations involved costs as well as benefits. They often

Figure 7-1. The Role of Economic Factors in Innovative Change.

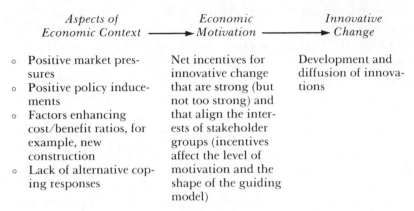

Aspects of Economic Context →	Economic Motivation →	Innovative Change
o Positive market pressures o Positive policy inducements o Factors enhancing cost/benefit ratios, for example, new construction o Lack of alternative coping responses	Net incentives for innovative change that are strong (but not too strong) and that align the interests of stakeholder groups (incentives affect the level of motivation and the shape of the guiding model)	Development and diffusion of innovations

required more effort and caused labor dislocations. Employers incurred costs in retraining experienced seafarers, attracting higher-caliber recruits and training them, and investing the time and effort required to implement the changes. Second, the argument for economic advantage was premised on the shipping sector as a whole, including shipowners, shore staff, seafarers, their unions, government agencies, and the public. The fact is that some of these groups derived more of the economic gains of the innovation, while others absorbed more of the economic costs. These two conditions— the mix of incentives and disincentives and the uneven distribution of these among industry stakeholders—provide the grist for most of the analysis in this chapter.

After characterizing the general economic interests of each of several groups, I will examine the potential effects of two forms of economic necessity for shipowners—pressures from a tight manpower market and competitive pressures on labor costs. When faced with these pressures, shipowners had many options available to them, including work innovations. Thus, the strength of the connection between economic pressure and innovation depended partly on the availability and attractiveness of other options, such as registering ships under flags of convenience.

Seafarers were threatened by many of the shipowners' methods for coping with cost pressures. The severity of the employment threats and any inducements the shipowners or the government offered for labor to cooperate in change influenced the overall incentives and disincentives for labor to accept change.

The economic necessity of shipowners and the incentives for seafarers to accept change are given equal weight in the total assessment of a country's shipping sector. The need to consider the economic interests of seafarers as part of an analysis of the capacity for innovative change is based on the assumption that the agreement of the seafarers' union was required to implement the innovations, and/or that the cooperation of seafarers was required to do so effectively. These conditions gave the seafarers and their unions power.

The seafaring unions were strong in all the countries studied, in contrast to some of the emerging maritime countries with which they competed, such as Taiwan and South Korea, which had no significant seafaring unions. I could not differentiate among the countries studied in terms of power wielded by their seafaring unions. The way they used this power, however, did differ according to whether their particular orientation toward ship- owners was adversarial or cooperative, and this factor enters importantly into the analysis of the difficulty of achieving institutional consensus in Chapter Eight.

Economic Necessity and Major Stakeholders

Three groups in the countries studied had economic stakes in the flexible work innovations: (1) shipowners and their associations, (2) seafarers and their unions, and (3) governments in behalf of the national economy.

The economic stakes of shipowners have already been suggested. On the one hand, innovations could yield smaller, more competent, and more highly motivated crews and therefore safer and more cost-effective ships. On the other hand, costs were incurred in the transition, and some costs, such as training and pay, were higher on an ongoing basis. The interests of shipowners' associations reflected both those of their constituent members and the position of the industry as a whole.

Table 7-1. Percentage of National Unemployment from 1965 to 1982.

Country	1965	1967	1969	1971	1973	1975	1977	1979	1981	1982
Denmark	1.2	1.2	1.1	1.1	0.9	4.9	7.3	6.0	10.3	11.0
West Germany	0.5	1.7	0.7	0.7	1.0	4.0	3.9	3.3	4.6	6.7
Holland	—	—	—	—	—	5.2	5.3	5.4	8.6	11.4
Japan	0.9	1.2	1.1	1.3	1.3	1.9	2.1	2.1	2.3	2.4
Norway	0.9	0.7	1.0	—	1.5	2.3	1.5	2.0	2.0	2.6
Sweden	1.2	2.1	1.9	2.5	2.5	1.6	1.8	2.1	2.5	3.1
United Kingdom	1.2	2.0	2.0	2.8	2.2	3.2	5.2	4.7	9.0	10.4
United States	4.4	3.7	3.4	5.8	4.8	8.3	6.9	5.7	7.5	9.5

Source: OECD, 1985, pp. 467–497.

The economic stakes of seafarers included, on the one hand, the certain loss sooner or later of some jobs per ship and, on the other hand, the potential preservation (or addition) of ships and therefore total jobs in the national fleet. The stakes also included the higher wage rates warranted by multiskilled jobs and other improved benefits (for example, leave time) accruing to crew members when they became more valuable to operations. They also included the additional investment seafarers made in being trained more broadly, training that also increased their mobility for shore work. Unions' stakes reflected the economic gains or losses of their members. Unions were also concerned about the total number of jobs, because this affected the size of their memberships.

A government's economic stakes reflected the interests of both shipowners and seafaring citizens. A government had other concerns as well. It had an interest in preserving jobs for nationals and in keeping the shipping sector healthy so that it could pay taxes, support other national industries, and bring in foreign exchange.

Manpower Shortage, 1966–73

During the period from 1966 to 1973, a tight labor market provided an economic stimulus for work innovations. Flexibility could reduce the demand for labor, while regular employment and participation could be used to attract a greater supply of recruits. The analysis of shortages focuses on the European countries, where all the innovation occurred during this earlier period.[2] The question pursued is whether the innovative developments were linked to the severity of shortages, and the brief analysis shows that they were not.

The shortage of seafarers was due to the growth in shipping and shifts in the expectations of youth entering the labor market. With rising living standards, more extensive education, and the lost allure of the seafaring life, described in Chapter Three, seafaring became attractive to a diminishing proportion of the labor force.[3] Moreover, shore jobs were plentiful in all of the countries. Unemployment was low throughout the region, ranging from 1 to 3 percent (see Table 7-1).

Shipowners acted in a number of noninnovative ways to decrease their demand for labor and increase its supply (see Figure 7-2). First, shipowners took actions that cut their demand for labor. They replaced small vessels with larger ones, attempting to preserve their share of seaborne trade with smaller work forces, and they introduced laborsaving technology. However, shipowners did not reduce crew sizes during this period by as much as the new technology would have permitted because they were reluctant to drive a hard bargain over work loads at a time when they were trying in other ways to attract seafarers. Changes in the size and structure of the fleet and the introduction of technology eased total labor demand by varying amounts in the six northwestern European countries (see Tables 7-2 and 7-3), but in no country did the reductions in total demand eliminate the shortage.

Second, shipowners strengthened their position in the tight domestic labor market by agreeing to improvements in maritime wages, benefits, perks, and physical working conditions. During the late 1960s union-and-management agreements in all of the European countries brought the wages and benefits of seafarers up to or above the level of shore-based workers who did similar work. Shipowners in three countries—Holland, West Germany, and Denmark—also increased the supply of seafarers by hiring more foreign labor (see Table 7-3).

The net effect of declining employment and changes in the use of foreign labor decreased requirements for domestic seafarers by 15 percent in Denmark, 16 percent in Sweden, 25 percent in Norway, 30 percent in West Germany, and 52 percent in Holland (see Table 7-3). Exact data were not available for the United Kingdom. The effect of smaller decreases in demand for domestic labor was to promote the persistence of manpower shortage. Thus, Denmark and Sweden had stronger incentives to take other steps, such as work innovations, to address shortages, and Holland and West Germany had weaker incentives.

This rendering of the relative strength of economic incentives for work innovations in the European countries during this period does not correspond to the innovation records. As reported in Chapter Three, by 1973 Norway and Holland had already forged ahead in shipboard work reform, experimenting with more

Figure 7-2. Manpower Shortages: Causes and Coping Responses.

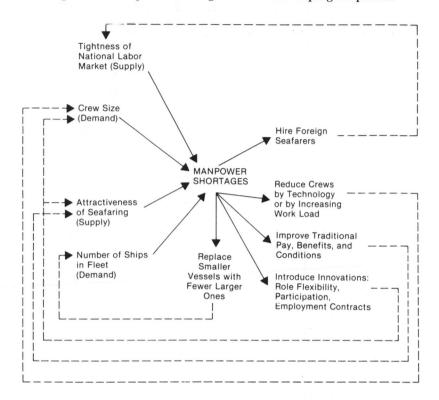

comprehensive changes, including participative work planning. Sweden, the United Kingdom, and West Germany had introduced general-purpose (GP) roles. Denmark had not introduced any of the innovations.

In summary, while the manpower shortage did indeed stimulate the innovation that occurred in this period, differences in the severity of the shortage do not help explain the innovation records. Therefore, we must look to other factors to explain these early differences.

Cost Pressures on Shipowners, 1973–83

With the slowdown in the growth of world seaborne trade from 1975 to 1979 and the absolute decline from 1979 to 1983 (see Table 3-1),

Table 7-2. Nationalities of Personnel Employed in Shipping.

Countries	Total	Own Nationals		Others	
		Number	Percentage of Total	Number	Percentage of Total
1968					
Denmark	18,145	15,817	87	2,328	13
West Germany	44,161	38,202	86	5,959	14
Holland	25,570	16,671	65	8,899	35
Japan	NA	NA	NA	NA	NA
Norway	57,504	43,413	75	14,091	25
Sweden	17,160	11,036	64	6,124	36
United Kingdom	90,000[a]	NA	NA	NA	NA
United States	54,535	54,535	100	—	—
1973					
Denmark	16,786	13,483	80	3,303	20
West Germany	34,996	26,831	77	8,165	23
Holland	14,860	8,033	54	6,827	46
Japan	118,258	118,258	100	—	—
Norway	41,462	33,249	80	8,213	20

Sweden	13,997	9,285	66	4,712	34
United Kingdom[b]	112,721	88,721	79	24,000[c]	21
United States	25,245	25,245	100	—	—

1983

Denmark	13,246	11,527	87	1,719	13
West Germany	23,143	18,006	78	5,137	22
Holland	15,628	10,417	67	5,211	33
Japan[d]	106,991	106,991	100	—	—
Norway	33,501	26,879	80	6,622	20
Sweden	11,661	9,894	85	1,767	15
United Kingdom	45,832	40,006	87	5,826	13
United States	25,000[e]	25,000[e]	100	—	—

[a]Estimate based on size of fleet and staffing practices during this period.
[b]1974 figure.
[c]Estimate.
[d]1984 figures.
[e]Estimate. The figures available for the United States are not comparable. The number of jobs (billets) declined to 14,216, but the number of active seafarers did not decline significantly due to job sharing and the lag in permanent shift out of the seafaring work force.

Source: OECD, 1969, p. 147; 1974, p. 138; 1984, p. 183.

Table 7-3. Percentage Increase or Decrease in Employment.

Country	Total Employment 1968-73	1973-83	Own Nationals Employment 1968-73	1973-83
Denmark	-8	-21	-15	-14
West Germany	-21	-34	-30	-33
Holland	-42	+5	-52	+30
Japan	NA	-10[a]	NA	-10[a]
Norway	-28	-19	-25	-21
Sweden	-19	-17	-16	-7
United Kingdom	-25[b]	-59	NA	-55
United States	-54	0	-54	0

[a]1973-84.

[b]Estimate based on change in size of fleet and staffing practices during this period.

Source: Table 7-2.

the overcapacity in the industry, and the continued emergence of new low-wage competitors, there can be no doubt that shipowners in the industrialized maritime countries were feeling strong competitive pressure to reduce their costs, including labor. Yet, reducing labor costs was difficult for employers in most of these countries because of the higher wage and benefit patterns established in the early 1970s.

Pressures to reduce labor costs and ways used to cope with them are shown in Figure 7-3. Differences in costs and the nature of government actions affected the pressures felt by shipowners. Shipowners responded in different ways—reregistering ships under flags of convenience, phasing out of shipping, modernizing their fleets, reducing crew costs through traditional methods, and innovating. Each response relieved one or more of the forces on shipowners and affected the pressures on other stakeholders. An examination of the pressures to reduce labor costs, the nature of government assistance, and shipowner responses is required to determine the residual necessity for shipowners to innovate in each country.

Figure 7-3. Cost Pressures: Sources and Coping Responses.

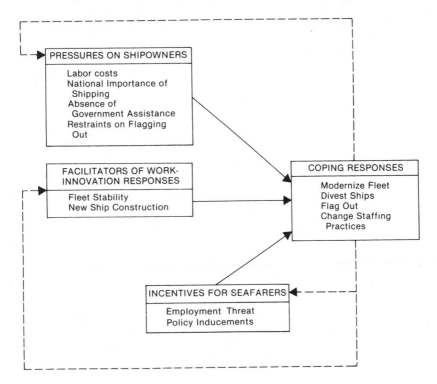

Staffing Costs. Labor cost pressures on shipowners resulted from the level of pay and benefits and the size of the crew. All eight countries had, by world standards, very high pay and benefit rates. The level of pay and benefits for ratings ranked from highest to lowest is listed in the left-hand column of Table 7-4.[4] The pay of the Japanese rating was twice that of the British rating. Officers' pay fell into a slightly different pattern. The pay of American officers was the highest (almost double that paid to Japanese and Swedish officers).

Taking into account the effect of different crew sizes on total labor costs to operate a vessel, particularly between a country clearly more efficient—Norway—and those clearly less efficient—the

Table 7-4. Rankings of Rating Pay and Total Crew Costs.

Ranking by Pay Rates for Ratings	Ranking by Total Crew Costs (Pay rates and crew sizes)
Japan	United States
United States	Japan
Sweden	Sweden
West Germany and Norway	West Germany
Denmark and Holland	Norway
United Kingdom	Denmark, Holland, United Kingdom

United Kingdom and the United States—I adjust this ranking slightly, as shown in the right-hand column of Table 7-4.[5] Combining the relatively high maritime labor rates in the United States and its largest crew sizes, which typically were one-quarter to one-half larger than the crews of comparable ships in the more progressive fleets, U.S. shipowners' crew costs were highest, and by a wide margin. Annual crew wages for a representative modern U.S. containership were estimated at $3,780,000 in 1983, 2.5 times those of European crews and over six times those of Third World crews.[6] The United Kingdom's lower pay and larger crews brought that nation's total crew costs more in line with those of Denmark and Holland.

National Importance of the Shipping Sector. Labor costs impinged on shipowners, who must ultimately implement most of the innovations considered. Greater importance of shipping to the national economy increased the pressure on the government bodies responsible for national economic policy and also indirectly on shipowners. Shipping made an important contribution to the economic strength of most of the countries in our sample, although by different amounts.

The importance of shipping had both objective and policy interpretations. Objective aspects of the national importance were indicated by two comparisons of the magnitude of economic activities in shipping to aspects of the national economy: (1) the size of the flag fleet compared to the country's gross national product (GNP) (see Table 7-5) and (2) the percentage of the country's oceanborne trade carried by the country's own ships (see Table 7-5).

The comparisons showed that in 1977 shipping was more important to Norway than to any other country. It had the smallest GNP and the second-largest fleet in the sample. Despite the fact that 92 percent of Norway's fleet was engaged in cross-trading (routes between two other countries), the fleet still carried a high percentage, 37 percent, of the country's own seaborne trade. Shipping provided 22 percent of Norway's foreign earnings in 1979. It also provided important employment, particularly for coastal districts where other job opportunities were limited. Most Norwegians had a close family connection with someone who was in seafaring or had been to sea. Finally, seafaring had a central place in Norwegian history. Throughout the period of the study, Norway remained number one, not only in the objective importance of shipping to its economy but also in the policy importance it attached to the industry.

After Norway, the national importance of shipping was highest for Japan and the United Kingdom. Japan ranked with Norway in carrying its own seaborne trade, and it ranked third considering the relative size of its fleets and GNP. There was an appreciation by Japanese, both inside the industry and in government, that shipping was vital to Japan's economy. The United Kingdom ranked second and third in the indexes of the national importance of shipping in 1977. However, the perceived importance of this sector in the United Kingdom was not commensurate with its objective importance at that time, and its position in world shipping continued to decline steadily through 1983.

The United States ranked lowest, just behind Holland. The capacity of the U.S.-flag fleet was small compared with its GNP, and it carried a mere 4 percent of its own seaborne international trade. The other three countries—Denmark, West Germany, and Sweden—were in the middle of the spectrum.

Government Assistance. Governments assisted their shipping industries in varying forms and to varying degrees. All eight countries utilized many forms of subsidies over the period studied,

Table 7-5. National Economic Importance of Shipping (1977 to 1978).

Country	GNP		Tonnage Capacity of Fleet		Size of Fleet Relative to GNP		National Fleet and National Trade	
	Col. A Amount ($ billion)[a]	Col. B Percentage of Eight-Country Sample	Col. C D.W.T.[b] (thousands)	Col. D Percentage of Sample	Col. D less Col. B	Rank Importance of Shipping to GNP	Percentage of Oceanborne Trade Carried on Flagships[a]	Rank Importance of Shipping to Country's Trade
Denmark	46.5	1.2	8,468	3.9	+2.7	4.5	11	6
West Germany	529.4	13.6	14,281	6.5	-7.1	7	17	4.5
Holland	106.9	2.8	7,651	3.5	+.7	6	4	7.5
Japan	737.2	18.9	59,925	27.3	+8.4	3	39	1.5
Norway	34.6	.9	49,843	22.7	+21.8	1	37	1.5
Sweden	77.2	2.0	10,819	4.9	+2.9	4.5	20	4.5
United Kingdom	254.1	6.5	46,412	21.1	+14.7	2	32	3
United States	2,108.0	54.1	21,926	10.0	-44.1	8	4	7.5
Sample Total	3,893.9	100.0	219,325	100.0				

[a]U.S. Department of Commerce, 1981a, pp. 36, 56, 92, 113, 120, 152, 166, 170.
[b]U.S. Department of Commerce, 1979, p. 7.

including accelerated depreciation on ships, construction subsidies, lowered interest rates and loan guarantees, lowered tax rates for industry revenue and seafarer wages, and research and development funds for industry projects. Shipowners in Norway and the United Kingdom received the least financial support.[7] Those in West Germany and Sweden received slightly more assistance. The shipping sectors in Denmark and Holland received the most government support of any in northwestern Europe, a factor that may help explain why their fleets were more stable throughout the period. Government support for Japan's shipping industry was similar in form to that found in Europe and slightly more generous than those of Holland and Denmark. Finally, the U.S.-flag fleet was unquestionably supported more generously than any other fleet. The U.S. assistance was significantly more powerful in alleviating the pressure on shipowners because of its form as well as its amount. In addition to the types of assistance just listed, the U.S. government provided operating differential subsidies, designed to make up the difference between high operating costs of U.S.-flag vessels and the lower costs of foreign vessels on designated routes.[8]

U.S. operators could take advantage of other government policies that insulated them from foreign competition. Cargo preference provisions gave preference to U.S.-flag ships for government-owned or government-financed cargo. In addition, a provision in the Jones Act reserved domestic coastal routes for U.S.-flag ships. To qualify for subsidies and preferences, the ships must have been purchased from American shipyards. This last requirement was temporarily modified in 1982, at the end of the period studied, with limited effect. All U.S.-flag vessels were required to employ American crews.

Apart from the generosity of the government support, there was the question of how well this assistance encouraged adaptation by the industry. Most governments supported their shipping industries by maritime training, education, research, and technical assistance. These subsidies were sometimes used to influence shipowners' and unions' responses to labor cost pressures. For example, government training, education, and research and technical assistance were occasionally designed to support work innovations. This aspect of government assistance was indicative of

Table 7-6. Flagging Out (1978, 1981, 1984).

	Controlled Fleet (Combined Total of Flag and FOCᵃ Fleets)	Number of Ships in Flag Fleetᵇ	Number of FOCᶜ Ships	Percentage FOC Represents of Combined Total
1978				
Denmark	387	338	49	15.9
West Germany	916	590	326	35.6
Holland	519	441	78	15.0
Japan	2,442	1,778	664	27.2
Norway	947	876	71	7.5
Sweden	265	265	NA	NA
United Kingdom	1,331	1,210	121	9.1
United States	1,694	879	815	48.1
1981				
Denmark	329	275	54	16.4
West Germany	781	473	308	39.4
Holland	561	444	117	20.9
Japan	2,647	1,762	885	33.4
Norway	763	616	147	19.3
Sweden	265	232	33	12.5
United Kingdom	1,197	1,056	141	11.8
United States	1,461	578	883	60.4
1984				
Denmark	320	261	59	18.4
West Germany	796	437	359	45.1
Holland	541	448	93	17.2
Japan	2,876	1,712	1,164	40.5
Norway	743	529	214	28.9
Sweden	257	216	41	15.9
United Kingdom	906	685	221	24.4
United States	1,252	538	714	57.0

ᵃFOC (flag of convenience) refers to those ships that fly the flag of another country but are "beneficially owned" by the countries listed in this table. The beneficial owner is the person, company, or organization that gains the pecuniary benefits from the shipping operations.

ᵇU.S. Department of Commerce, 1979, p. 7; 1981c, pp. 2–3; 1985a, pp. 5–6.

ᶜUNCTAD 1979, p. 11; 1982, p. 8; 1985, p. 10.

the institutional relationships that will be reviewed in Chapter Eight.

Flagging Out. Shipowners could respond to labor cost pressures in various ways. One option was to flag out, that is, to register new ships or transfer existing vessels under a flag of convenience (FOC). Liberia, Panama, the Bahamas, Bermuda, and Cyprus maintained open registries. By flagging out, shipowners could save labor costs and taxes, but they would forego any government assistance reserved for flag-fleet vessels. Governments wanted ships under their national flag for reasons of taxes, employment, national prestige, and national security. However, countries usually preferred that shipowners flag out rather than divest from shipping completely so that the country would continue to derive some revenue and employment benefits.

Shipowners in all countries in our sample had flagged out, some making greater use of this option than others (see Table 7-6). In 1981 FOC ships represented the following percentages of the total *controlled fleet*, that is, the combined flag fleet and FOC fleet owned by a country's shipowners:

Sweden (12%), United Kingdom (12%), and Denmark (16%)
Norway (19%) and Holland (21%)
Japan (33%)
West German (40%)
United States (60%)

Interpreted in terms of the present analysis, flagging out had provided relatively little relief for shipowners in the United Kingdom, Sweden, and Denmark. By the same reasoning, the FOC option had provided greater help to shipowners in the United States and West Germany in moderating their need to take other steps to reduce labor costs.

Changes in Fleet Size. Shipowners also divested—phased completely out of shipping—at significant rates during this period, as shown in Tables 7-7 and 7-8. While data on the divestitures themselves were not available, the changes in tonnage capacity of

Table 7-7. National Fleets (1966 to 1973).

Country	December 1966		December 1973		Changes from 1966 to 1973			
					Number of Ships		d.w.t	
	Number of Ships/ Percentage of World Fleet	d.w.t./ Percentage of World Fleet	Number of Ships/ Percentage of World Fleet	d.w.t./ Percentage of World Fleet	Absolute	Percent Change	Absolute	Percent Change
Denmark	342 (1.9)	3,878 (1.7)	299 (1.4)	6,553 (1.5)	-43	-12.6	+2,675	+68.9
West Germany	860 (4.7)	7,712 (3.3)	702 (3.3)	11,417 (2.6)	-158	-18.3	+3,705	+48.0
Holland	469 (2.5)	6,123 (2.6)	434 (2.0)	6,708 (1.5)	-35	-7.5	+585	+9.6
Japan	1,406 (7.6)	20,576 (8.6)	2,145 (9.9)	57,280 (12.8)	+739	+52.6	+36,704	+178.4
Norway	1,356 (7.9)	25,402 (10.9)	1,102 (5.1)	40,781 (9.1)	-254	-18.7	+15,379	+60.5
Sweden	433 (2.4)	6,118 (2.6)	322 (1.5)	5,647 (1.3)	-111	-25.6	-471	-7.7
United Kingdom	1,985 (10.8)	26,759 (11.5)	1,596 (7.4)	47,783 (10.7)	-389	-19.6	+21,024	+78.6
United States	965 (5.2)	14,961 (6.4)	596 (2.8)	13,717 (3.1)	-369	-38.2	-1,244	-8.3
Total world fleet	18,423 (100.0)	232,197 (100.0)	21,600 (100.0)	446,370 (100.0)	+3,177	+17.2	+214,173	+92.2

Source: U.S. Department of Congress, 1967, pp. 6–7; 1974, pp. 2–3.

Table 7-8. National Fleets (1973 to 1983).

Country	December 1973		December 1983		Changes from 1973 to 1983			
					Number of Ships		d.w.t	
	Number of Ships/ Percentage of World Fleet	d.w.t./ Percentage of World Fleet	Number of Ships/ Percentage of World Fleet	d.w.t./ Percentage of World Fleet	Absolute	Percent Change	Absolute	Percent Change
Denmark	299 (1.4)	6,553 (1.5)	261 (1.0)	7,444 (1.1)	-38	-12.7	+891	+13.6
West Germany	702 (3.3)	11,417 (2.6)	437 (1.7)	8,869 (1.3)	-265	-37.7	-2,548	-22.3
Holland	434 (2.0)	6,708 (1.5)	448 (1.8)	7,040 (1.3)	+14	+3.2	+332	+4.9
Japan	2,145 (9.9)	57,280 (12.8)	1,712 (6.7)	61,191 (9.2)	-433	-20.2	+3,911	+6.8
Norway	1,102 (5.1)	40,781 (9.1)	529 (2.1)	32,470 (4.9)	-575	-52.2	-8,311	-20.4
Sweden	322 (1.5)	5,647 (1.3)	216 (.8)	4,688 (.7)	-106	-32.9	-959	-18.8
United Kingdom	1,596 (7.4)	47,783 (10.7)	685 (2.7)	27,251 (4.1)	-911	-57.6	-20,522	-42.9
United States	596 (2.8)	13,717 (3.1)	538 (2.1)	21,569 (3.3)	-59	-9.7	+7,852	+57.2
Total world fleet	21,600 (100.0)	446,370 (100.0)	25,579 (100.0)	666,404 (100.0)	+3,979	+18.4	+220,034	+49.3

Source: U.S. Department of Congress, 1974, pp. 2–3; U.S. Department of Transportation, 1984, pp. 5–6.

the fleets reflect the combined effect of flagging out and divestment. From 1973 to 1983, the changes in the capacity of national
flag for fleets were

United Kingdom (-43%)
West Germany (-22%), Norway (-20%), and Sweden (-19%)
Holland (+5%), Japan (+7%), and Denmark (+14%)
United States (+57%)

These figures had dual implications for economic necessity,
each implication canceling the other in our rankings. On the one
hand, more drastic declines were an index of greater threat to
shipowners and hence greater pressure to change. On the other
hand, more drastic declines were an index of the uncertainty for
shipowners and hence shorter planning perspectives; shorter
planning horizons discouraged investments in innovation.

Thus, the situation in the United Kingdom, which suffered
the greatest decline, was the most urgent. At the same time
shipowners and observers in the United Kingdom stated repeatedly
that pessimism in the industry by 1983 had all but eliminated new
innovations targeted at the rating work force. A cluster of three
countries—West Germany, Norway, and Sweden—experienced
moderate declines, moderate urgency, and moderately favorable
planning conditions. Holland, Japan, and Denmark, which grew
slightly, experienced low urgency but had a relatively certain
environment for investing in change. The protected U.S. fleet
capacity expanded significantly. The U.S. industry experienced the
least threat from actual declines but was marked by the most certain
conditions for investing in innovation activity.

Modernization. Shipowners' responses to cost pressures were
also influenced by the rate of modernization of the fleets because
new construction improved the cost/benefit ratio from innovation
initiatives.

During this period the eight countries modernized their fleets
in varying degrees and in varying directions. In all cases the fleets
changed their mix of general-cargo ships, bulkers, and tankers, but
I could neither propose nor find a pattern to those changes related

to work innovations. More important than changes in mix was the fact that within each category, especially in tankers and general-cargo vessels, the newly acquired ships were more specialized and more technologically sophisticated. This increased the salience of a more skilled and more committed crew and hence the incentive for work innovations. The more automated ships required fewer crew members, which increased the advantages of role flexibility and social integration.

Moreover, new construction created a uniquely favorable opportunity for introducing work innovations. First, when a shipowner proposed reforms to the union for newly constructed ships, they were more favorably received than when the same change proposals were applied to existing ships. Second, the new ship's technology could be tailored to reinforce the changes in the size, composition, and organization of the crew. Third, the ship's superstructure could be designed to foster social integration by providing common spaces and similarly sized quarters. Fourth, by sending the officers designated to operate the new ship to the shipyard to oversee construction, shipowners could reinforce the commitment of the ship's management team.

New construction thus represented an important opportunity to introduce work innovations. The following percentages of the flag fleets in 1983 had been built in the past ten years. (See Table 7-9 for a detailed breakdown of the age of national fleets.)

Denmark, West Germany, Norway, and Sweden	68–77%
United Kingdom, Holland, and Japan	57–60%
United States	39%

The average age of ships for all but the United States ranged from 7 to 10 years; the U.S. average was seventeen years. Thus, the U.S. fleet was by far the oldest, considering both the average age of its ships and the percentage of tonnage in the fleet built more than ten years earlier. Japan, the United Kingdom, and Holland had somewhat less favorable opportunities to introduce innovations than did the other four European countries.

For four countries, over two-thirds of the tonnage in their fleets had been built within the past ten years, and their average ship

Table 7-9. Ages of Fleets (mid 1983).

Country	Tonnage Built in Different Periods (percent)[a]				Average Age (years) of Vessel (Jan. 1, 1984)[b]
	Under 5 Years	5–10 Years	10–15 Years	Over 15 Years	
Denmark	22	55	14	9	7
West Germany	25	44	18	13	7
Holland	26	33	19	22	8
Japan	28	32	35	5	7
Norway	20	48	27	5	8
Sweden	20	52	19	9	9
United Kingdom	14	43	29	14	10
United States	16	23	16	45	17

[a]Lloyd's Register of Shipping Tables, 1984, p. 177.
[b]U.S. Department of Commerce, 1985b, p. vii.

was less than ten years old. Considering how important green-field plants were during the same period in providing U.S. manufacturing with opportunities to implement radically new work organizations, I view these rates of new-ship construction as having presented these four countries with unusually favorable opportunities for social as well as technical innovation.

Summary of Economic Context for Shipowners. I have examined a number of factors that influence whether a favorable economic context existed for innovative change by shipowners. Table 7-10 summarizes how each country ranked on five factors.

The economic context for shipowners in Sweden and Norway was relatively favorable for innovation. The context was considerably unfavorable for Holland, in the sense that the incentives were relatively weak. The U.S. context provided very weak incentives, except for one item, high labor costs. Intermediate economic contexts existed for the other four countries—the United Kingdom, Japan, West Germany, and Denmark.

Pressures on Seafarers, 1973–83

Although shipowners typically initiated consideration of innovations and implemented them, they needed union agreement for

Table 7-10. Ranking of Countries in Overall Economic Context for Shipowners and Five Subfactors.

Country	Overall Economic Incentives for Shipowners (Ranking)	Labor Costs	National Importance of Shipping	Absence of Subsidies	Absence of Flagging Out	New Construction
Norway	1.5	5.0	1.0	1.5	4.0	2.5
Sweden	1.5	3.0	4.0	3.5	1.5	2.5
United Kingdom	3.0	7.0	2.5	1.5	1.5	6.0
Japan	5.0	2.0	2.5	7.0	6.0	6.0
West Germany	5.0	4.0	6.0	3.5	7.0	2.5
Denmark	5.0	7.0	5.0	5.5	3.0	2.5
Holland	7.0	7.0	7.0	5.5	5.0	6.0
United States	8.0	1.0	8.0	8.0	8.0	8.0

certain changes, including role flexibility and common mess arrangements. The shipowners also wanted seafarer cooperation for these and other changes. Therefore, an analysis of economic necessity must take into account whether it was in labor's economic interest to accept the changes.

Two general conditions sometimes existed during this period to encourage labor to accept change. One was the threat to employment represented by declines in the fleet, which was a market pressure. The other was the incentive that shipowners or the government provided labor to accept change, which was a policy inducement.

Employment Threats. The eight countries varied widely in the extent to which concerns about the maintenance of seafaring jobs generated pressures and incentives for labor to change. The loss of ships from the fleet, due to divestment or reregistration to FOC's, translated directly into the loss of jobs. (Minor exceptions occurred when some officers continued to work on vessels reregistered under a flag of convenience.) Therefore, when labor assumed that the rate of loss of ships from the fleet could be slowed or reversed by staffing changes, they had an incentive to accept change. Their incentives related to employment were mixed, of course, because they had to agree to changes that would result in a decrease in the size of crews and hope to realize a more than offsetting benefit in preserving jobs in the overall fleet.

Acknowledging this ambivalence and the differences in degree of concern between ratings and officers, I can nevertheless gauge the differences among countries in the pressures on labor for change. Three interrelated trends during the period from 1973 to 1983 were threatening to labor. The first was the actual shrinkage in the size of the fleet—the net losses of ships. The second was the decline in the total number of seafarers employed in the fleet. The third was the decline in the number of nationals employed.

The magnitude of these trends is set forth in Table 7-11 and summarized in the following three clusters of countries, beginning with those under the most employment threat: (1) higher threat: the United Kingdom, West Germany, and Norway; (2) intermediate threat: Sweden, Denmark, and Japan; and (3) lower threat: the

Table 7-11. Declines in Ships, Total Seafarers Employed,
and Total Domestic Seafarers Employed (1973 to 1983).

Country	Overall Employment Threat (Ranking)	Percentage Change in Number of Ships[a]	Percentage Change in Number of Seafarers Employed[b]	Percentage Change in Number of Domestic Seafarers Employed[b]
United Kingdom	2.0	−58	−59	−55
West Germany	2.0	−38	−34	−33
Norway	2.0	−52	−19	−21
Sweden	5.0	−33	−17	−7
Denmark	5.0	−13	−21	−14
Japan	5.0	−20	−10	−10
United States	7.5	−10	0	0
Holland	7.5	+3	−5	+30

[a]Table 7-8.
[b]Tables 7-2 and 7-3.

United States and Holland. The United Kingdom, West Germany, and Norway lost from 38 to 58 percent of their 1973 fleets, suffering steeper declines than the other countries. They also lost relatively more employment for national seafarers, ranging from 21 to 55 percent. Finally, their overall employment declined more than that in the other countries, with the minor exception of Denmark, which lost two percentage points more than Norway.

Sweden, Denmark, and Japan all experienced smaller losses, but their losses were still of a sufficient magnitude to cause considerable concern on the part of labor. I rate the urgency for labor in these three countries as intermediate (see Table 7-11).

Labor in Holland and the United States was the most exempt from the pressures that generated high urgency in the other countries. Holland's fleet maintained its size, and the U.S. fleet lost only 10 percent of its vessels over the decade. In the United States the number of seafarers employed did not change materially, and in Holland employment for all seafarers increased, as did employment of nationals (see Table 7-11).

The raw market forces that acted on labor to produce change are only half the story. The other half deals with whether industry practices offered labor relief from these forces, and then whether this relief was made contingent on labor's acceptance of change.

Policy Inducements. One practice that helped relieve employment hardships preserved jobs for nationals at the expense of foreign seafarers (see Table 7-11). Sweden and Denmark displaced foreign seafarers more rapidly than nationals between 1973 and 1983. Sweden's total seafaring employment dropped 17 percent, but employment of nationals declined only 7 percent. Denmark's employment totals shrank by 21 percent, but national employment by only 14 percent. Holland displaced foreigners while expanding the employment of nationals.

A second practice moderated the impact of losses of ships on total employment. In Norway, Japan, and Sweden, the declines in employment from 1973 to 1983 were proportionately less than the declines in the number of vessels in the fleet (see Table 7-11). During this period the number of vessels per fleet for Norway, Japan, and Sweden dropped by 52, 20, and 33 percent, respectively, while employment for these countries dropped by 20, 10, and 17 percent, respectively. Shipowners agreed to increase shore leave relative to sea duty. For example, in Sweden the practice of two months of shore leave for every three months of sea duty was revised to three months leave for three months at sea. This type of change was made for various reasons, but its effect, increased employment, was clear. Before the change a Swedish shipowner needed 1.5 seafarers for every billet in its fleet (or 1.5 crews for every vessel); after the change the shipowners employed two seafarers for every billet (two full crews for every ship). Increased leave was significant in Norway, Japan, and Sweden because in all three cases it more than offset the decline in crews (billets per ship).

The practice of spreading employment was also significant in the United States, where the number of seafarers in active employment remained relatively constant, while the fleet was declining slightly, by 10 percent. However, in the United States, where casualism was still practiced, the longer leaves were not agreed-on policy by shipowners. Rather, they resulted from union hiring-hall policies to spread the available work among their members by increasing the time between their sailings. U.S.

seafarers' high pay scales enabled them to accept decreases in the number of months worked per year and yet earn more than they could in alternative shore employment.

The union practice of spreading the work was reinforced by large unfunded pension liabilities in the U.S. shipping industry, which inhibited innovation. As the number of seafarers reaching retirement age expanded, the gap between resources and obligations of the plans grew dramatically. Any actions that reduced the active work force, and therefore contributions to the funds, compounded the problem, especially if the unemployed were eligible for some immediate benefits. Thus, shipowners as well as seafaring unions were inhibited in considering steps that exacerbated the problem. For example, permanent employment provided full-time employment for fewer seafarers and reduced contributions without decreasing the obligations.

Considered by themselves, these two practices (displacing foreigners and increasing the number of seafarers per billet) tended to relieve the hardship imposed on a country's seafarers and their unions (see Table 7-12). The next question is whether these forms of relief were made contingent on labor's acceptance of work innovations.

When a country's industry used one of these two practices to cushion the employment effects and made it contingent on labor's acceptance of change, this sharpened labor's incentives to change. When an industry used one of these practices and did not make it contingent on the acceptance of change, the practice blunted the effect of employment threats; it acted to insulate labor from market pressure to change. When the industry employed neither practice to cushion employment effects, I refer to the industry's practices as neutral in their effect on the market forces.

Table 7-13 indicates the policy choices in each country and their implications for labor's incentives to change.

Japanese policy inducements involving employment assurances were the most impressive. Prior to the modernization program, the companies' policies already assured seafarers jobs until retirement unless the employing company went bankrupt. Under modernization, companies also committed themselves to consulting with the union in advance about any plans they had to

Table 7-12. The Nature and Conditionality of Practices
That Cushion Employment Effects.

Countries	Did country have significant practices that maintain total employment by increasing ratio of seafarers to billets?[a]	Did country have practices that maintain domestic employment at expense of foreign seafarers?[b]	Were practices made generally conditional on labor's acceptance of change?
Holland	No	Yes	Yes
Norway	Yes	No	Yes
Japan	Yes	No	Yes
United Kingdom	No	No	Not Applicable
West Germany	No	No	Not Applicable
Denmark	No	Yes	No
United States	Yes	No	No
Sweden	Yes	Yes	No

[a]Reflected by total employment declines that are smaller than fleet declines (see Table 7-11, first two columns).

[b]Reflected by declines in employment of nationals that are smaller than declines in total employment (see Table 7-11, second and third columns).

Table 7-13. Policy Choices by Country and Implications
for Labor's Incentives to Change.

Country	Did the country use practices to cushion employment effects?	Were the practices made conditional on labor's acceptance of change?	What were the implications for labor's incentives to change?
Holland	Yes	Yes	Sharpen
Japan	Yes	Yes	Sharpen
Norway	Yes	Yes	Sharpen
United Kingdom	No	Not Applicable	Neutral
West Germany	No	Not Applicable	Neutral
Denmark	Yes	No	Blunt
United States	Yes	No	Blunt
Sweden	Yes	No	Blunt

retire a ship or reregister it under a flag of convenience. The agreed-on objective was that a modernized ship would replace each ship retired from the company's flag fleet. They also agreed that no members would lose their jobs as a result of the modernization program. The lifetime employment commitment by companies to seafarers took many forms. Ratings who no longer claimed a billet on a flag ship were reassigned to an FOC vessel owned by the employer at the same rate paid on a Japanese ship. Steward personnel were reassigned to shore jobs with the company at the same rate of pay they received at sea.

The Japanese modernization program included many other provisions that seafarers saw as beneficial. Ratings could upgrade themselves by attaining watch-officer and/or dual-rating qualification. Officers would receive dual training and more responsibility. For the first time, engineering officers could aspire to the top position aboard ship, a position to be retitled from "master" to "general manager." In all cases upgrading yielded pay increases. Ratings also began to see more opportunity to advance step by step to qualify as officers on one of the flag-of-convenience ships owned by their employer.

In Holland, the understandings that permitted seafaring unions to cooperate with work reforms involved the government as well as shipowners. The government approved changes in staffing practice requested by shipowners, shipowners agreed to reduce the number of foreign seafarers in favor of employing more Dutch seafarers, and labor agreed to the staffing reforms.

Most features of Norway's 1979 Frame Agreement related to compensating practices, for example, a maximum of three months of continuous sea duty and longer leave time. However, one feature, permanent employment, had the type of employment effects considered here. Also, through 1982, management and labor sought to preserve a cooperative spirit by compromising on the nature and rate of change.

Japan, Holland, and Norway provided stronger policy inducements for labor to join in the change in staffing practices. In effect, they pursued policies that sharpened labor's incentives to change. In Denmark, the United States, and Sweden, one or both of the relief practices was followed by but not contingent on any

Table 7-14. Ranking, by Country, of Labor's Interest in Work Innovations, Overall and by Factors.

Country	Overall Economic Incentives for Labor (Ranking)	Employment Threat	Policy Inducements
Norway	1.0	2.0	2.0 (Sharpen)
Japan	3.0	5.0 ·	2.0 (Sharpen)
United Kingdom	3.0	2.0	4.5 (Neutral)
West Germany	3.0	2.0	4.5 (Neutral)
Holland	5.0	7.5	2.0 (Sharpen)
Sweden	6.5	5.0	6.0 (Blunt)
Denmark	6.5	5.0	6.0 (Blunt)
United States	8.0	7.5	6.0 (Blunt)

adaptive change by labor. This unconditional protection of jobs blunted the incentives for labor to change.

In two countries neither form of relief was practiced. The United Kingdom's loss of 58 percent of its vessels from 1973 to 1983 was fully reflected in the 59 percent loss of total employment and the 55 percent loss of seafaring employment for nationals. Germany lost 38 percent of its fleet and experienced comparable rates of loss in total employment and employment of nationals. I view this condition as neutral, neither sharpening market incentives for change nor blunting them.

Summary of Economic Incentives for Labor. The general economic context affecting labor's interest in work innovation was composed of (1) employment threats, which imparted to labor a sense of urgency about the competitiveness of the national fleet; and (2) employment policies, which depending on their context either added an inducement for labor to change, blunted the effect of employment concerns, or had no effect on the basic threats to employment. Table 7-14 summarizes how each country ranked on these two factors.

Summary and Conclusions

Explaining Innovation Records by Economic Necessity. The chapter began by exploring the effects of manpower shortages.

While there can be no doubt that the innovative efforts were triggered by the shortages, the safest conclusion I could draw from the analysis was that the severity of personnel shortages played no significant role in determining which countries were more innovative prior to 1973.

The primary focus of the analysis in this chapter was on the economic necessity for innovative change for shipowners and seafarers after 1973. Based on analysis of many factors comprising the relevant contexts for shipowners and seafarers (see Table 7-15), I conclude the following ranking (Table 7-16). The reasoning for this ordering will be summarized by first examining three pairs of northwestern European countries: Norway and the United Kingdom, Sweden and West Germany, and Denmark and Holland. Each had striking similarities, particularly in the incentives for shipowners. I will conclude the examination with Japan and the United States, a pair that had some particularly instructive similarities and differences.

Norway and the United Kingdom. Norway and the United Kingdom, ranked first and second in economic necessity, had many similarities that strengthened incentives for the shipowner: high objective importance of shipping yet low government assistance and dramatic declines in tonnage yet a restrained use of the flagging-out option. Seafarers in both countries faced serious threats of loss of employment. Hence, both countries had some strong, symmetrical incentives. Two factors were less favorable for innovation: labor costs in both countries were lower than the average of the eight countries, and the steep declines in their fleets hampered planning. Norway and the United Kingdom differed in two respects that favored innovation in the Norwegian industry. Norway had the higher rate of new construction, and shipowners had developed employment policies that sharpened labor's incentives to support innovations.

The economic situations of Norway and the United Kingdom differed in a direction consistent with their records of change and innovation. However, Norway's economic incentives scored as only moderately more favorable than those of the United Kingdom, whereas its actual record of innovation was significantly better, and

Table 7-15. Economic Conditions Favorable to Innovation from 1973 to 1983.

	Norway	Holland	Japan	United Kingdom	Sweden	West Germany	Denmark	United States
Factors for Shipowners								
Labor costs	Low (5)	Lower (7)	Higher (2)	Lower (7)	High (3)	Intermediate (4)	Lower (7)	Highest (1)
National importance of shipping	Highest (1)	Lower (7)	Higher (2.5)	Higher (2.5)	High (4)	Low (6)	Intermediate (5)	Lowest (8)
Autonomy: Rely on market vs. subsidies	Higher (1.5)	Intermediate (5.5)	Lower (7)	Higher (1.5)	High (3.5)	High (3.5)	Intermediate (5.5)	Lowest (8)
Restrained use of flagging-out practice	High[a] (4)	Intermediate (5)	Low (6)	Higher (1.5)	Higher (1.5)	Lower (7)	High (3)	Lowest (8)
New construction	Higher (2.5)	Intermediate (6)	Intermediate (6)	High (3)	Higher (2.5)	Higher (2.5)	Higher (2.5)	Lower (8)
Summary (shipowners)	Higher (1.5)	Lower (7)	Intermediate (5)	Intermediate (6)	Higher (1.5)	Intermediate (5)	Intermediate (5)	Lowest (8)
Factors for Seafarers								
Urgency about employment effects	Higher (2)	Lower (7)	Intermediate (5)	Higher (2)	Intermediate (5)	Higher (2)	Intermediate (5)	Lower (7)
Employment policy inducements for change	Higher (2)	Higher (2)	Higher (2)	Intermediate (4.5)	Lower (7)	Intermediate (4.5)	Lower (7)	Lower (7)
Summary (seafarers)	Highest (1)	Low (5)	Higher (3)	Higher (3)	Lower (6.5)	Higher (3)	Low (6.5)	Lowest (8)
Overall rank (includes shipowners and seafarers)	Highest (1)	Lower (6.5)	Intermediate (4)	Higher (2)	Intermediate (4)	Intermediate (4)	Lower (6.5)	Lowest (8)

[a]Until 1980s.

Table 7-16. Overall Ranking, by Country, of Economic Favorability to Innovation.

Country	Overall Economic Conditions Favorable to Innovation	Shipowners' Economic Conditions Favorable to Innovation	Seafarers' Economic Conditions Favorable to Innovation
Norway	1.0	1.5	1.0
United Kingdom	2.0	3.0	3.0
Japan	4.0	5.0	3.0
Sweden	4.0	1.5	6.5
West Germany	4.0	5.0	3.0
Denmark	6.5	5.0	6.5
Holland	6.5	7.0	5.0
United States	8.0	8.0	8.0

its record of change (both innovative and noninnovative) was better by an even larger margin.

Sweden and West Germany. Sweden and West Germany were in a cluster with Japan for the fourth rank. A number of conditions favoring innovation were similar. Sweden's labor costs ranked third and West Germany's fourth. Sweden ranked fourth and West Germany sixth in national economic importance of shipping. Shipowners in both countries faced similarly high rates of decline in their tonnage capacity and engaged in relatively aggressive programs of new construction. These factors were all favorable for shipowners to act adaptively.

Shipowners' incentives in the two countries differed in one important respect. Sweden had relatively few ships reregistered under FOC's. In contrast, West Germany had a very large percentage of FOC ships, a condition that eased West German shipowners' incentives for staffing reforms. While the incentives for Sweden's shipowners were somewhat stronger than those for West Germany's, the incentives for Sweden's seafarers were weaker than those for West Germany's and therefore less aligned with those of the shipowners.

Holland and Denmark. The most strikingly similar pair was Holland and Denmark. They were tied for the sixth and seventh ranks in overall contexts favorable for change. In both countries lower labor costs and moderately generous government assistance acted to limit the incentive to change. Similarly, both had manifested less urgent conditions, considering that their fleet capacities actually grew from 1973 to 1983. This stability had the favorable effect of permitting longer-range planning. Two other factors were less favorable for Holland's shipowners than for Denmark's. Dutch shipping was less important to the national economy than Danish shipping, and Holland had a more modest rate of new building. While incentives for shipowners were weaker in Holland than Denmark, the reverse was true for seafarer incentives. The practices assuring employment for Holland's domestic seafarers were among the government-employer-union understandings that included acceptance of shipboard reform. Thus, Holland sharpened labor's incentives. Denmark followed the same employment practice, favoring domestic seafarers at the expense of foreigners, but did not make it part of a policy inducement, which blunted labor's incentives.

Taken as a whole their economic conditions were generally similar (and relatively unfavorable to innovation), but Dutch and Danish innovation records could not contrast more. Economic necessity suggests that Holland would be a low innovator, like Denmark, not dramatically more innovative, as was the case. Indeed, Holland's record of innovation was the least consistent with what one would have expected from the total set of economic factors considered.

Japan and the United States. Japan and the United States provide one of the most instructive comparisons and contrasts. I will analyze their economic contexts in more detail. Overall, Japan's context was intermediately favorable, comparable to those of Sweden and West Germany; the U.S. context was the least favorable, less favorable than the Danish or Dutch.

Japan and the United States had one particularly striking and important similarity—very high wage rates, yielding very high incentives for innovative change. The sizes of their flag fleets were relatively stable over the decade in question, helping to create relatively favorable conditions for planning. In fact, the U.S. case was the most favorable for planning among the eight countries— the United States increased its flag-fleet tonnage capacity by 57 percent and suffered a decrease of only 10 percent in the number of ships. This combination of stability and growth was, of course, not only a potential asset for planning and investing in change activities but also a potential liability, because it could mitigate the sense of urgency of shipowners and seafarers. Another factor, the high rates of flagging out, lessened the pressure to change. (America, with 60 percent of its managed fleet under FOC in 1981, ranked highest, and Japan, with 33 percent, ranked third.) Thus, in both cases flagging out was a relief valve, removing some of the pressure on shipowners for change.

The economic contexts just sketched were similar. Yet the totality of the American context was dramatically less favorable to innovation. What additional factors so radically altered the picture for these two countries? One striking difference was how the two governments defined the national importance of shipping. As expressed by Japanese government officials, shipowners, and labor-union officials alike, Japan's national economic interest required a strong merchant navy. Japan's dependence on raw-material imports and its economic policies of promoting exports made shipping strategic for the economy. The merchant navy was also a national priority for the United States, but for its role in national defense rather than for its importance to the national economy. In fact, the indexes in Table 7-5 confirm the difference between Japan and the United States in the economic significance of their flag fleets. In 1977, at the midpoint of the decade of labor cost pressure, shipping was more important for Japan than for any other country in our sample except Norway. It was least important economically for the United States, tied with Holland.

In view of differences in the national economic significance of shipping, it may not be surprising that policies differed so dramatically. Japan's government supported shipping in ways similar to many European countries and slightly more generously. U.S. policies, motivated in large part by defense concerns, gave large subsidies to shipping, larger than those in any other country. The subsidies were not contingent in any way on adapting to the competitive environment. Quite the opposite, they insulated the flag fleet from international market pressures, permitting it—noncompetitive internationally though it was—to grow in line with the growth of U.S. coastal trade and the expansion of the particular cargoes that had to be carried by U.S. vessels. Thus, there was little need for shipowners to reduce labor costs on their ships under the U.S. flag. If they lost a niche for vessels in the flag-fleet market, they could reregister them under an FOC and hire foreign labor at radically lower wages. Thus, U.S. subsidies completely offset other conditions favorable to innovation.

Closely related to the subsidized nature of the U.S. fleet was the slow rate of new construction. In 1983 the U.S. fleet averaged seventeen years; Japan's averaged seven years. Only 39 percent of the U.S.-fleet tonnage had been built in the past ten years; 60 percent of Japan's tonnage was less than ten years old. The slow rate of new construction in the U.S. fleet created a relative paucity of opportunities to tailor the design of vessels to a new organizational model and to use new ships as a lever in negotiating change with the union. The very limited but sharp reductions that did occur in the U.S.-flag vessels in the 1980s were negotiated for new construction.

Was there any need for U.S. maritime labor to change? As it happened, labor was almost as protected as the shipowners. Recall that U.S.-flag ships not only had to be built in America but also had to employ all-American crews, and that, in part because of protection policies, the number of ships declined by only 10 percent over the decade. Unions that managed the hiring halls spread the work around, and the total number of active seafarers remained relatively stable over the decade. The unfunded pension liability reinforced and exaggerated their interest in maintaining as many active seafarers as possible. Thus, seafarers in the United States would have had less incentive for change than their counterparts in any other country if shipowners had proposed work innovations during this period.

The economic contexts for labor in Japan and the United States also differed in an important way created by policy, not by inherent market forces. Japanese shipowners constructed some economic incentives as policy inducements for labor to accept change. The lifetime employment policies by shipowners, covering seafarers on oceangoing vessels, meant that the individual seafarer would not lose his job (the Japanese crews were all male) unless the company went bankrupt. Assurances that he would not lose his job deflected one potential source of opposition to change, and the need to avoid bankruptcy provided him with a positive incentive to support change. The lifetime employment policy elicited mutual commitment; a seafarer stayed with the same company over his career. The U.S. contrast with Japan in this policy is clear-cut: the U.S. seafarers who hired through the rotary hiring hall had no incentive to help any particular shipowner compete.

The Japanese seafarers' union secured policy commitments by shipowners that enabled it to participate in the modernization program, covering consultation, relocation, advancement opportunities, training, and pay. These inducements, which became integral aspects of the Japanese vision, were much more powerful in enlisting maritime labor support for innovative change than anything observed elsewhere.

This last contrast between Japan and the United States—centering on Japan's carefully constructed inducements for labor to join the modernization program—echoes a difference found in two other pairs. Norway was paired with the United Kingdom and Holland was paired with Denmark to reflect the general similarities in the economic contexts of the paired countries. Yet Norway and Holland differentiated themselves from the others in the same way that Japan differed from the United States. The shipping industries in Norway, Holland, and Japan devised policies that sharpened labor's incentives to change, whereas in the United Kingdom, Denmark, and the United States this did not happen. In fact, Danish and American practices blunted the incentives.

In reviewing the role of economic necessity, one fact is especially striking: there is absolutely no correlation between the level of labor costs and the amount of innovative change capable of reducing these costs. This does not deny that labor costs were important. However, other aspects of economic necessity were more important. The more general theme that emerges from the analysis is that policies were at least as important as raw market forces in providing economic incentives for shipowners and seafarers to innovate. Some of the policies were in fact shaped during the period in question to promote innovative change and thus reflect the exercise of metacompetence. The prime example involved employment policies in several shipping industries that elicited the support of labor. The policy aspects of economic necessity represent potential targets of strategic action and illustrate the role of metacompetence: the amount, character, and conditions for government support for the industry; barriers imposed by government and labor practices; and incentives affecting modernization of the fleet (discouraging it in the United States and encouraging it in other countries).

Combining Economic and Social Motivation Forces. The social and economic forces are combined and compared with innovation records in Table 7-17.

Considering both social and economic motivation, Japan, Norway, and Sweden had stronger overall motivation. Sweden therefore remains a mystery. Why, with relatively favorable economic and social contexts for change, did not more innovation occur?

Holland, which had intermediate social attitudes, had even weaker economic incentives (relative to other countries). Thus, Holland grows as an anomaly. With only intermediate social attitudes and relatively weak overall economic incentives, why was Holland able to be one of the more innovative countries? Of course, a clue is provided by one particular aspect of Holland's economic incentives, the policy inducements encouraging labor and companies to adopt the shipboard reforms. This foreshadows a relatively favorable institutional pattern in Holland.

Denmark's combined motivations are comparable to those of West Germany and Holland, yet these motivational forces failed to generate a corresponding amount of innovation.

The question taken into the next phase of analysis in Chapter Eight is whether differences in the institutional context will help resolve these anomalies.

**Table 7-17. Comparison, by Country, of Social and Economic Forces
to Innovation Records.**

Country	Innovation Record (Ranking)	Combined Social and Economic Motivation (Ranking)	Favorable Economic Conditions (Ranking)	Favorable Social Context (Ranking)
Norway	2.0	1.0	1.0	1.0
Holland	2.0	6.0	6.5	4.0
Japan	2.0	2.5	4.0	2.5
United Kingdom	5.0	4.0	2.0	7.5
Sweden	5.0	2.5	4.0	2.5
West Germany	5.0	6.0	4.0	7.5
Denmark	7.5	6.0	6.5	5.5
United States	7.5	8.0	8.0	5.5

Implications for Diagnosis and Action. A number of
questions about the conditions that combine to create economic
necessity and determine its role in innovative change were outlined
at the beginning of this chapter. They were advanced as being not
only relevant to theory but also as questions that should be
addressed in diagnosing the innovative capacity of a particular
industry or company. While they need not be repeated here, one
particular aspect of methodology used in analyzing economic
necessity deserves attention.

Figures 7-2 and 7-3 illustrate a technique as important to
diagnosis as to explanatory analyses. They show models constructed
to incorporate the many coping responses available to groups as
well as the several forces requiring some adaptive response. Thus,
they show how innovation is only one of the many possible
responses to pressures for change. They also clarify that innovative
change depends as much on the availability and attractiveness of the
options as on the attractiveness of the innovation itself.

The practical implication of the constructive role that may
be played by policy inducements for labor to support change is one
of the most important conclusions to be drawn from the economic
analysis in this chapter. It applies equally to innovative change in
U.S. manufacturing industries. Specifically, U.S. management and
labor, whether in autos, steel, aircraft manufacturing, or computers,

must find ways to provide the maximum feasible assurances regarding employment and retraining and to ensure an equitable sharing among stakeholders of the economic sacrifices and gains associated with performance in the marketplace. Only by devising policies covering this issue can the parties succeed to do what was done in Japan, Holland, and Norway in support of innovative shipboard change.

The national economic importance of an industry, say, machine tools and computers in America, also offers opportunities for policymakers to promote innovative change. However, even when the importance is high and readily apparent (as in shipping in Norway, Japan, and the United Kingdom), this fact by itself does not galvanize the support of the stakeholders. The fact of high objective importance must be carefully nurtured and its implications carefully spelled out by all groups, as it was for Norwegian and Japanese but not British shipping. (In the U.S. case the fact that exports had doubled as a percentage of manufacturing, from about 10 percent to 20 percent, during the period studied was not exploited for the increased importance that accrued to the shipping sector, but it could have been.)[9]

An industry can be important to the national economy in ways not captured by the indicators used in this chapter. For example, the U.S. steel and automobile industries are important to other industries in the economy because they provide markets for the emerging high-tech and service industries often viewed as replacing them. By clarifying the importance of an industry to other industries and the national economy, policymakers may sometimes increase the strength of the forces for change.

The idea reinforced in this chapter, that pressures can be so weak that they do not provide adequate impetus for change of any kind and so strong that they discourage innovative forms of change, suggests that ideally policymakers would formulate policies that amplify, accentuate, or supplement market pressures under some conditions, and that reduce the severity of market pressures at other times.

The effect of new-ship construction improving the ratio of costs and benefits of innovative change initiatives has practical implications often not fully appreciated. My observations of U.S.

manufacturing industries found that in these settings, just as in the shipping countries studied, newly constructed facilities improve the net incentives to innovate for both unions and employees. Thus, the policies of government, employers, and labor unions that encourage modernization of plants and equipment also encourage social innovations that enhance competitiveness.

Chapter 8

Institutions That Facilitate Innovation

Chapters Five through Seven have covered the what and the why of innovative change but not the how. Thus, this chapter, on institutional context, and the next one, on the choices individuals make, move us from the models that guide innovation and the underlying economic and social motives that drive (or block) innovation to factors that facilitate (or constrain) the innovation process.

Proposition Four asserts that the capacity for innovative change is affected by institutional arrangements, principally those involving labor, employers, and government. The institutional properties that facilitate the innovation process include the internal unity of the groups, the existence of problem-solving mechanisms that link them together, and a cooperative orientation toward each other. Another property is the requirement for approval at various steps in the process.

These properties can affect each of the functions essential to an effective process. Institutions can affect sponsorship—whether an innovation is championed and a dedicated constituency built. Institutions can affect consensus—whether those who need to agree

186

Figure 8-1. Role of Institutional Forms in Innovative Change.

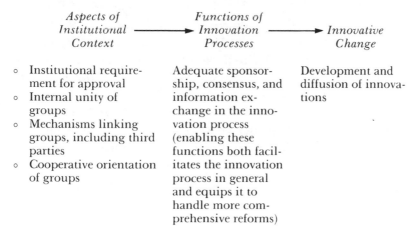

Aspects of Institutional Context	*Functions of Innovation Processes*	*Innovative Change*
○ Institutional requirement for approval ○ Internal unity of groups ○ Mechanisms linking groups, including third parties ○ Cooperative orientation of groups	Adequate sponsorship, consensus, and information exchange in the innovation process (enabling these functions both facilitates the innovation process in general and equips it to handle more comprehensive reforms)	Development and diffusion of innovations

do agree. Institutions can affect the transfer of information and social technology—whether usable knowledge about innovative concepts and experimental results is generated and disseminated.

The role of institutional forms in innovative change is summarized in Figure 8-1. Thus, the task of this chapter is to explore whether these ideas help explain the innovation in shipping.

Two Examples of the Innovation Process

The importance of the process functions—sponsorships, consensus, and information—can be shown by reviewing the experiences of Norway and the United Kingdom. In each the innovation process has been well documented. Neither experience is offered as typical of any others, but they illustrate the process issues that must be managed in all eight countries. The examples contain successes and failures and thereby set the stage for a discussion of the roles of institutions and competence.

Innovation Processes in Norway. In Norway pilot studies of interdepartmental flexibility were conducted between 1966 and 1968, project ships were organized between 1969 and 1974, and spread of the innovations started in the earlier periods continued through 1983.[1]

In Chapter Four we described some of the activities in the leading company, Leif Hoegh. Here we add to that description by examining industry-level activity and how it related to progress at the company level. At the suggestion of the Oslo Work Research Institute (WRI), a new industry mechanism was formed to consider changes in staffing concepts. This occurred in 1969, when new legislation permitted smaller crews and general-purpose ratings. The mechanism, called the *contact group,* comprised representatives from four unions, the shipowners' association, and three government directorates. Although individual membership varied over time, WRI researchers were active in all of the group's meetings. Over the first six years some twenty-five key people in Norwegian shipping were involved in thirty half-day or full-day meetings, discussing in detail plans, results, and their policy implications. Participants were careful to remind each other that they were not authorized to endorse new principles on behalf of the institutions they represented. The contact group was thus an open forum for exploring options, confronting differences, and clarifying—if not endorsing—organizational principles. Policy discussions that occurred within unions, companies, employers' associations, and government bodies and between these in other settings were informed—if not instructed—by the discussions within the contact group. One important principle emerged during the early phases of the projects and was accepted in practice. This principle was to create freedom for local experimentation and to protect the developments until some concrete experience could be evaluated. Einar Thorsrud, the leading researcher involved in the process, observed, "Perhaps without being aware of it, people in policy-making positions started to accept the need for a continuing learning process, which seemed necessary for any basic change in policy to become effective in day-to-day working life and in the institutions of shipping and seafaring."[2]

Hoegh, the shipping company chosen to conduct the first field trials, formed a project group of managers and seafarers. The seafarers selected were designated as future crew members for the project ship. The project group visited the sites of work experiments in industry to learn from workers, managers, and union officials about the issues they faced. Committees composed of top and middle managers also met, sometimes with the researchers, to hammer out the objectives of the project and identify constraints. They decided that the objectives were to better develop and utilize seafarers' capabilities; improve the work culture; and adapt to technological, economic, and social changes. The project participants themselves saw the objective as "reversing bureaucratic tendencies." Both groups identified constraints on the organizational options that could be considered. These were safety rules, regulations, labor contracts, and certain operational requirements. Only a broad outline of alternatives was developed before the project group began planning changes.

The first Hoegh project ship, *Mistral*, which started in 1970, was discussed in Chapter Four. *Mistral* confirmed the feasibility of the new shipboard organization. After one year this project was evaluated at the ship, firm, and sector levels. The crew members themselves decided they wanted to continue with the new way of working. The company also confirmed its satisfaction with the results by proposing a second and more advanced project. The contact-group members expressed their satisfaction with *Mistral* and approved the second Hoegh project ship, *Multina*, on the basis of quarterly progress reports they received on the *Mistral*, meetings they had with three observers who sailed with the ship, and personal visits they made to the ship in Rotterdam. Their evaluation took the form of a conclusion that they had "no objection to continued try-out."

Gradually, informally, and implicitly, the contact group began playing a more direct role in the policymaking process. Its activities sometimes became contentious. One confrontation occurred about crew members alternating between deck and engine work on the *Mistral*. Another focused on the introduction of a common mess room and dayroom for the whole crew. The confrontations produced a compromise to allow the trial of these ideas on the ships without attempting to agree on their merits. A serious dispute occurred when one crew proposed to the contact group that it be allowed to vary the size of the shipboard crew during the year according to work load. This proposed arrangement was intended to take into account, for example, the fact that during the winter the weather in the Atlantic Ocean limits the outside maintenance that can be performed. The two crew members who pleaded their case before the contact group had to return to the ship and report that the shore organizations were not yet ready for this reform.

One important development in the spread of the new practices started in 1975, more than three years after the first ship had been evaluated. The crew on *Balao,* of the Klaveness Company, requested an opportunity to compare experiences with the crews of other project ships in the industry, including the two Hoegh ships. Seafarers from a number of the ships planned a conference in which direct participants from six ships in the Norwegian fleet met to exchange what they were learning. Researchers, company representatives, trade-union officials, and government officials were invited as observers. The agenda for these Ship-Meets-Ship workshops, as they were called, included issues related to participation, integration between deck and engine, and new policies on layout of cabins and common rooms. The agenda also covered labor contract changes and new forms of education that were required to support shipboard reforms. Reports of the discussions were sent to the crews, the contact group, and the companies involved in the change projects.[3]

Diffusion of the new concepts was promoted by other developments reported in Chapter Four, including the 1979 Frame Agreement, which specified the benefits seafarers would receive in exchange for increased role flexibility and decreased staffing levels, and the 1983 legislation, which lowered minimum staffing scales.

The trend toward adoption of the models pioneered in *Mistral, Multina,* and *Balao* was clearly established by company-level and industry-level developments over the 1970s. The slow nature of the evolutionary change in Norwegian shipping was also clearly confirmed. First, individual project ships required a year to plan and arrange and at least a year or two of implementation before they could be evaluated. Several experiments, each based on the last, required no less than four years. Second, policy discussions involved the assimilation of new data; consideration of ideas that challenged current beliefs; careful assessment of groups' self-interest; exploration of alternatives, each with different meanings for different groups; and hammering out a consensus to allow a change in policy. Such discussions had to be conducted at both the industry and company levels (at least in Hoegh). Third, company training of crew members involved in the new work forms had to be arranged on top of normal schedules. This limited the rate at which ships could be converted to the new design. Fourth, changes in the maritime education required still another set of deliberations. It took many years to develop new policies, translate them into curriculum and certification requirements, and make the changes.

Innovation Processes in the United Kingdom. In the United Kingdom pilot studies of flexibility occurred in a tanker fleet in 1967. An industry effort to promote change, the Sealife Programme, lasted from March 1975 to December 1979. An informal group of companies, called the Eighties Group, carried on discussions of their change programs after Sealife was shut down and was continuing to meet in 1983. Like the Norwegians' activities, the British experience involved efforts at the sector and company levels. The efforts in the two countries, however, had contrasting dynamics and results that were due primarily to differing institutions examined in this chapter and secondarily to behavioral choices treated in the next chapter.

ESSO Ltd. and the ratings' union agreed in July 1967 to a new *integrated crew concept,* featuring interdepartmental flexibility, watch duties for all crew members, permanent employment, ship assignment continuity, a management team, and reduced crews.[4] Tavistock Institute of Human Relations, contracted by the company to study the new practices, found varying attitudes toward them. The senior officers, who had volunteered for these pioneering ships, were positive; the junior officers were negative; and the ratings had mixed feelings. The Tavistock researchers concluded that the concept was not yet appropriate to the general population of U.K. seafarers. However, they urged that the ideas be pursued with subgroups of seafarers whose values and attitudes were more compatible with the concepts of an integrated crew. They proposed that these subgroups could be identified with selection techniques.

ESSO allowed this effort to lapse for many years but in the middle of 1974 began a related program. In the meantime, the experience of ESSO in the United Kingdom was utilized in other countries in the early 1970s. The Tavistock researcher became professionally committed to work in the shipping industry and organized an international conference on the subject in Holland in May 1969. Research institutes and shipping companies from seven countries took part.

This early experiment in 1967 in a major U.K. company fully anticipated the paradigm that would later emerge in the northwestern European shipping industry, and it was documented by the most prestigious behavioral science institute in Europe. Yet no parallel innovations were to occur in the United Kingdom for another decade. When innovations similar to ESSO's did occur, they grew more directly out of a new research program, Sealife, and were based more on the Norwegian example than on the ESSO experience.

The Sealife Programme was started in 1975 as a joint venture among owners, unions, and the Department of Trade to examine ways of improving life at sea.[5] This interest reflected the severe problems that U.K. shipowners had recently experienced in meeting their labor requirements. The program was funded entirely by shipowners and was guided by a steering group, composed of two shipping-company executives, one of whom served as chairman; representatives from each of the five maritime unions; officials from the Department of Transportation; and representatives of the British shipowners' association, which administered the central labor-supply system.

The first study undertaken by the program staff was based on a system for shipboard work analysis done several years earlier at Flensburg College in Germany. The Flensburg study, in the tradition of industrial engineering, developed tools to measure time and skills requirements for each task aboard a specific class of ships over a specified voyage under varying assumptions about weather, port facilities, crew sickness, and equipment failure. The study had demonstrated analytically the great advantage of flexibility in manpower deployment in meeting the work-load peaks and valleys of various shipboard activities. Sample voyages on comparable U.K.

vessels were used to collect data, which were fed into the Flensburg programs. The results on British ships were similar. They clearly implied the technical feasibility of alternative work organizations and reduced crew, provided jobs could be redesigned, training reorganized, and departments eliminated. However, the results were resisted or rejected by several groups in the industry.

The nature of the resistance to this study was instructive because, as Peter Sharpe, the chairman of Sealife, wrote later, this first output from the program met with the types of reactions that were to become themes of Sealife's difficulties. First, the technical complexity of the report made it inaccessible to the average shipping executive. Second, the unions were very concerned about the staffing and organizational implications of the study. Third, the section within the shipowners' association that administered the central labor pool disagreed with the thrust of the study: that companies should do more of their own recruiting, training, and assigning of seafarers.

Why did this study, which even in retrospect the program's chairman regarded as "potentially one of Sealife's most important," produce, in his words, nothing more than a "dull thud"? To anticipate the primary questions addressed by this chapter and the next, was it due to institutional constraints or to poor judgment? Both, but mostly institutional constraints, according to the Sealife executive.

> Ironically, in view of its painful relevance in 1980, it [the analysis of shipboard activities] was commissioned too early in our understanding of the problems of industry-level change to have a reasonable chance of paying off . . . with hindsight it could be argued we did not market it hard enough for its true potential to be appreciated. Whilst this is probably true the dominant factor at the time was the fragile nature of the Sealife coalition. . . . As happened on later occasions a divided Steering Group produced no hard follow-up or dissemination.[6]

A second area of study, treating organizational issues on board and ashore, lasted over the five-year program. Preliminary studies with a large tanker company and a small tramp company showed the damaging effects of casualism and lack of continuity on board. However, when the Sealife staff tried to recruit companies to serve as "willing testing grounds" for the development of new forms of organization, they experienced great difficulty. This difficulty, combined with the earlier response to the replication of the Flensburg study, created anxiety within the Sealife staff and raised questions among company sponsors of the program.

In July 1976 the staff planned to initiate change processes in thirty to forty companies by the end of 1979. By December 1976 the staff had visited directors of the forty leading shipping companies. Six firms accepted help from the Sealife staff, but most of the work dealt with officers and shore staff in the spirit of conventional management consulting. Only two of the participating firms, discussed below, engaged in the change activities of interest here. Among many reasons identified by Sealife staff for the "consumer resistance" were "fear of involving a tripartite organization in private company problems" and disagreement with the consultants' "experimental approach" to solving the industry's problems.

In view of the limited opportunity for Sealife staff to sponsor change projects in company settings, they devoted considerable effort to arranging "clubs," meetings of potentially interested companies. The clubs disseminated findings of Sealife's studies and facilitated the exchange of experience among companies. Many companies attended these meetings with the understanding that representatives from unions and government agencies would not be involved. Sealife staff were ambivalent about the clubs under these circumstances, because while they promoted shipowners' thinking, they also denied the soundness of the basic tripartite idea on which Sealife was founded.

In due course, Sealife secured the cooperation of two companies, Denholm and Bibby Brothers, each of which supplied a project ship. These experiments were patterned after Hoegh's trials in Norway. The innovations were implemented successfully in one of the project ships but encountered severe problems in the second. These experiments reinforced the conclusion that limited innovation models would not work, and that the new organization must reflect comprehensive change, including especially continuity of assignment and delegation of authority to ships' officers. Some of the difficulty in these trials related to the role of Sealife as the sponsor, a point I will explore later. Subsequent change programs by other companies, including P.A.L. and Jebsens-U.K., built on and extended these Sealife projects, but, as stated repeatedly, they did not constitute an industrywide trend.

A third area of work, employment issues, had still a different history. It was understood to be controversial from the outset. On the one hand, in announcing the launch of Sealife, the director of the employers' association had emphasized that the program "should not embrace matters such as terms and conditions of work, which are properly the subject for negotiation."[7] On the other hand, the unions regarded the industry's employment package as clearly related to its ability to recruit satisfactory manpower; they wanted the employment package to receive a fair share of research.

When terms for a feasibility study of employment issues were set, the problem became one of staffing it with researchers whose independence would be accepted by all groups. When such a team was identified, the problem became one of dealing with all the proposals the team produced, nine in number. The problem stemmed from the fact that the studies could raise questions about the effectiveness of the two institutions administering the central supply of labor and conducting central industry bargaining. It was finally decided in April 1977 to put to the industry at large the recommendation to study the hiring-pool system. Sealife staff solicited individual reactions from thirty-six key figures in the industry and on the basis of favorable replies commenced the study. Two years elapsed between the feasibility study and the issuing of a preliminary report for one of the nine studies it had proposed. As expected, the completed study of the central labor supply reinforced the pressures for labor policy reform and for companies to rely less on casualism.

Another development in the U.K. shipping industry was a by-product of Sealife. The ratings' union undertook a major organizational development program with the assistance of Tavistock, resulting in reforms that decentralized its structure to permit more company-level bargaining, ship-level problem solving, and direct participation of seafarers in union activities.

In his final report on Sealife the program's chairman observed, "Sealife's machinery began to reveal its frailty as soon as it became clear in 1978 that fundamentally important questions about job territory and the traditional occupational structure were not permissible areas of inquiry or experiment."[8] He also spoke directly to the difficulties created by the institutions with a stake in Sealife and the need for employers to mount an effort for reform.

> The tripartite process has been helpful in exposing and examining some of the main sources of rigidity. Similar tripartite processes may not be effective in producing corrective changes in institutional policies. While consultation will continue to be vital to effective change, what seems now most needed . . . is for one of the power groups to muster sufficient unanimity among its representatives to mount a determined attack on current employment conventions and the policymaking machinery that underpins them . . . such unanimity is going to be difficult to build on the employers' side. Nevertheless, this may be easier than finding a formula for the integration of the five unions and their widely different policy programs and structures.[9]

While Sealife frustrated its dedicated leaders and staff, its continued functioning in the midst of criticism and opposition was a remarkable achievement. While its chairman expressed deep disappointment that there were no changes in industry-level institutions and that only between five and ten companies were significantly affected by Sealife, his expectations may have been unrealistic, and the changes that did occur represented a measure of success. In any event, the Sealife case permits us to ask both why it did achieve some positive results and why it fell so far short of expectations.

Why Institutions Can Influence the Innovation Process

The experiences of Norway and the United Kingdom provide anecdotal evidence that institutions can help and hinder innovation. Before examining more systematically how institutions exercise their influence, addressing in turn their effect on consensus, sponsorship, and technology-transfer processes, I will review why they can exercise influence.

As noted in Chapter Three, the shipboard organization, roles, duties, working conditions, and staffing requirements were not only covered by union-management agreements but were also subject to detailed government rules and regulations. The government's attention to such details derived from their concerns about safety of ships and the welfare of seafarers. Regulations were especially important with a casual employment system because they coordinated the seafarers' expectations about working conditions and the shipowners' expectations about seafarers' qualifications. As often happens, these rules took on a life of their own, often outliving the conditions that made them appropriate in the first place.

Shipping institutions were relatively closed to new insights and knowledge. Roggema and Smith attributed this closedness to the fact that "the shore-based institutions have developed to a large degree as a reflection of the structural characteristics of the shipbord organization."[10] They pointed out that demarcation lines on board ship are reflected in the structures of unions, academies, management organizations, and government departments, and that in each of these shore institutions most of the officials were ex-seafarers from corresponding ranks and departments. These factors promoted conservatism in shipping.[11] Thus, it was especially remarkable whenever groups in this industry were able to grasp the need to move to radically different organizational forms and were able to implement the changes.

These characteristics had unique implications for each type of innovation, primarily because the innovations were initiated in different ways and had different approval requirements.

Institutional factors were the least important for the trend toward greater participation and officer delegation. In no case did

I find participation subject to explicit institutional agreement. Similarly, top management could delegate more responsibility to their officers without union or government approval. Ideally, shipowners would be able to persuade the maritime academies, the only relevant industry institution, to add more managerial courses, but that would be only helpful, not essential.

Changes that affected social integration were subject to more institutional processes. These changes were proposed at different times and places by different groups. Ratings' unions took the initiative in negotiating better perks. Officers had concerns about the narrowing of perks between ratings and themselves, but their agreement was not formally required. Shipowners usually initiated common shipboard facilities for ratings and officers. The unions had to approve many of these changes in facilities because their agreements specified minimum mess facilities and other accommodations.

Institutions were still more important for employment continuity. The initiative and approval requirements for this change were the most varied. Labor in Sweden, Holland, and West Germany had promoted the laws that required regular employment for seafarers. Similarly, labor in Norway negotiated certain provisions for permanent employment. Some companies in Norway and other countries where it was not law often offered regular employment for their own reasons. Unions in Denmark and the United States often prevented their members from accepting the companies' offers. Finally, seamen often declined the offers.

Role flexibility required the most institutional approvals. The point can be illustrated by analyzing what forms of consensus were required for the introduction of officer role flexibility in Norway. A company could propose this practice. (Hoegh of Norway did so after its successful *Multina* experiment.) Agreements by the two officers' unions were required. (These were not forthcoming, primarily because the deck-officers' union was especially threatened by the idea of integrated-officers' positions, which deck officers feared would be filled mostly by engineers.) The Norwegian government's approval was also required. (After a long and trying process, the law was changed in 1978 to permit the innovation.) Then maritime educational institutions had to be persuaded to change their curricula. (Eventually they were.) Finally, individuals would need to agree to accept assignments involving the new role. En route to government approval the initiating company needed the support of the Norwegian shipowners' association. These stiff requirements derived from institutional arrangements, many of which were typical of the countries studied. Some, however, were peculiar to Norway, such as the separate unions for deck officers and engineering officers. Multiple unions with a direct stake and a veto raise the consensus requirement, a point formalized below.

Invariably proposals for role flexibility came from ship-owners. Labor unions became active in setting the conditions for the trials of this practice and still more active in evaluating their results. When role flexibility came up for policy approval, the owners became prime movers once again, although by now often joined by other individuals in labor or government. In the diffusion stage, when role flexibility was an approved option for the industry, individual shipowners usually made the critical decisions. Their choices became increasingly constrained as the pool of traditionally trained seafarers dried up, and only GP ratings or integrated officers would be entering the industry. At this stage, depending on the total package of changes, including compensatory adjustments in benefits, the union sometimes became an advocate of the practice.

Thus, consensus requirements were usually raised and lowered through the innovation life cycle. Obtaining government dispensation for a trial implementation of role flexibility was usually easier than gaining permanent policy approval, for instance. When the policy change was approved, it became much easier once again for a given company to implement.

The discussion of the need for consensus has emphasized the role of formal requirements, but there were other reasons why a party chose to seek consensus before acting. Even when the law did not require it, regulators often sought agreement between labor and management before they would approve a shipowner's request. They did this for both political and practical reasons. Similarly, even when managements were not contractually obligated to get union approval of a proposal, they often wanted the concurrence of their unions in order to elicit their cooperation on other matters. Thus, in reality, parties often had a say in the process, even when they had no formal right to approve or disapprove a proposed action.

The seafaring unions in all eight countries were sufficiently powerful that management needed to take their interests seriously. For example, they all could block proposals for role flexibility that affected their members if they concluded it was in their interest to do so.

Influence of Institutions on Consensus

Of the three ingredients for effective innovation—sponsorship, consensus, and information transfer—achieving the necessary consensus was affected most by institutional systems. Institutional arrangements varied in two ways. They varied in the amount of consensus normally required, based on law, prior agreement, past practice, or the policy of the initiating party. They varied in the degree of difficulty they normally created for the consensus process.

Consensus requirements and consensus difficulty enter into a number of specific propositions, all extensions of Proposition Four, about institutions, set forth in Chapter Two. The two attributes combine to determine the overall consensus capability of the institutional system. The first proposition specifies the hindering effect of a requirement for centralized approval, that is, approval by industrywide institutions in addition to company-level institutions.

The more numerous the requirements for an initiating party to obtain approval from sector institutions (government agencies, shipowners' association, national unions), the more difficult it is to innovate, and the longer it takes to move an innovation from conception to established practice.

This proposition by itself would predict that Norway would have been less able to innovate than the United Kingdom. Taking other factors and their effect on the ease or difficulty of achieving consensus into account will modify this picture, however.

The most obvious attribute affecting the difficulty of achieving consensus is the orientation of the institutions in their relationships with the other institutions and the availability of forums at the level where consensus is required. Relations can range from adversarial in orientation to ones of mutuality or mutual reliance. The second proposition treats the hindering effects of adversarial relations.

When approval by sector institutions is required, the absence of tripartite forums, third-party facilitators, and a lack of spirit of mutuality in relations at the sector level will discourage innovation and will bias the innovation toward simpler forms. The absence of union-management problem-solving forums and adversarialism at the company level has a similar and additional effect on innovation.

Note the qualifying phrase, specifying that consensus must be required in the first place if adversarial relations are to have a direct effect on innovation.

Disunity in stakeholder groups complicates intergroup negotiations or problem solving. Hence, the next three propositions, about the effects of the fragmentation of labor, fragmentation of government, and dissension among shipowners.

When union approval is required at any level, the multiplicity of unions and rivalry among them decreases the capacity of the institutional system to innovate.

Whenever government approval is required, the more numerous the separate agencies that have a stake in the innovation the less capacity the institutional system has to innovate.

Whenever union or governmental approval is required by industrywide institutions, and therefore shipowners need to act as a group, the diversity of shipowner interests and the weakness of the shipowners' association will decrease the capacity to innovate.

These three types of fragmentation plus the adversarial relations among institutions all act to increase the difficulty of reaching consensus.

The final proposition refers again to a factor that heightens the need for consensus. It treats uniformity policy. Industry-level decision making tends to produce decisions that apply uniformly to all companies and all ships in the industry. But this is not logically required, nor was it always the case. While the countries studied retained centralized decision making, over the period covered by the study decisions about staffing and other practices were increasingly made on a ship-by-ship basis, taking into account the technology, trade routes, and qualifications of the crew. A related trend was illustrated by frame agreements specifying the quid pro quos that individual shipowners and their unions could buy or not buy into on a company-by-company basis. The 1979 Norwegian Frame Agreement and Japan's special treatment of ships in its modernization program were examples of this trend. Thus, the uniformity proposition:

The less actual diversity (from company to company or ship to ship) permitted by shipowners, government, and unions, the more difficult it will be to innovate.[12]

The first factor (numerous consensus requirements) and the last (uniformity of practices) raise the demands for consensus. The others, dealing with adversarialism among and fragmentation within groups, make consensus more difficult. I refer here to the effects of institutions. Skilled individuals can sometimes personally overcome the hindering effects of institutions, a point developed in Chapter Nine. Also, while I have chosen to phrase all the propositions as hindering innovation, this was arbitrary. It would be equally appropriate to state how these factors can help the innovation process.

Considering ranges from high to low requirement for consensus and from high to low difficulty to reach consensus reveals a number of interesting possibilities. The most favorable condition is when there are few needs for consensus and little difficulty in achieving it. This yields a high net consensus capability. The least favorable possibility is when the requirements for consensus are high (due to centralized decisions about uniform practices), and it is also very difficult to engineer consensus (due to adversarialism and internally fragmented groups). This condition creates a low net capability for consensus.

In terms of net capability for institutional consensus, I find the following clustering: (1) Holland and Japan, (2) Norway, (3) Sweden and West Germany, (4) Denmark and the United Kingdom, and (5) the United States.

Japan, Holland, and Norway had more favorable consensus positions, but each got there by a different route. For example, Holland's institutions enabled innovation more than Norway's, not because they made it easier to achieve industry consensus, but because they required less of it. Compared to those of Holland, Japan's institutions had imposed higher consensus demand, but they also made consensus an achievable objective. Norway had relatively favorable conditions compared to the other five countries. Its requirements were almost as high as those of Sweden and West Germany, but its consensus capacity was even higher.

Institutions in the other five countries, for varying reasons, had more frustrating circumstances affecting consensus processes. Institutions in West Germany and Sweden imposed high requirements for consensus but were characterized by conditions that made it moderately difficult to achieve. Denmark, the United Kingdom, and the United States suffered a worse fate. They had intermediate requirements for consensus accompanied by conditions that made it exceedingly difficult to achieve.

Now I will review the arrangements that determined the requirements and difficulties related to consensus in each country.

Holland, Norway, and Japan. Holland and Norway are discussed together first, even though Holland's institutions scored higher, on a par with those of Japan. Chapter Four showed their innovation and diffusion records to be remarkably similar. Here they present an interesting set of contrasts and similarities in the institutional systems within which these innovations occurred and were managed. Both systems were favorable but different.

The greatest difference between them—especially in the 1970s—was the number of approvals that a shipowner had to obtain before proceeding with innovation. Hoegh, whose experiments began in the early 1970s, only went forward after approval was given by the tripartite forum, the contact group. In Holland, Shell, whose pioneering role was similar to Hoegh's, was outside the industrywide bargaining structure and did not need to secure union, government, or shipowners' association approvals at the sector level. In beginning its complex innovations, Shell consulted the ratings' union at the company level. A similar pattern was reported in the case of officers later in the 1970s. In both innovations, the ground was first broken by Shell, the innovations proved effective, and a lag of several years occurred; then Nedlloyd and the rest of the industry followed, with the interest and support of the Dutch government. Once other Dutch firms began to consider new staffing policies, the process was similar to that in Norway. A tripartite committee decided the conditions for experiments, monitored them, and helped derive the industry policy implications from them.

A number of factors in addition to the tripartite forums made it feasible for the Norwegian and Dutch institutions to reach consensus. In both countries the employers' associations were active and cohesive; in Norway it was especially strong, deriving in part from the strong traditions of the country's shipping industry. Shell B.V. Tankers, Holland's prime innovator, frequently provided the shipowners' association with key personnel who served as vehicles for diffusion of innovation. In both cases the government agencies dealing with the shipping industry were well coordinated. In Holland in particular the government officials involved in planning in the shipping sector endorsed workplace consultation and social integration as keys to the industry's future. An absence of adversarialism marked the shipping industries in Holland and Norway (until the early 1980s). A major factor favoring Holland was its simpler union structure—there was only one union for officers and one for ratings, and these cooperated closely. Norway had four unions, three for officers and one for ratings.

During the 1970s the rules of the game changed in Norway. The parties lowered their insistence on uniform practices and their reliance on industry-level decisions, lowering the amount of consensus required. For example, the optional set of quid pro quos set forth by the 1979 Frame Agreement created more local choice and resulted in more diversity of practice.

Finally, in 1983 the Norwegian government changed the game itself, no longer acting as a participant in the consensus processes. By legislating permission for shipowners to adopt practices that previously they could only adopt with the unions' approval, the government affected the industries' capacity for achieving consensus in a number of ways. The prospect that the government might remove other issues from the consensus process in the future might cause the parties to strike a deal with each other, but it also might raise the aspirations of one or both of the parties, making it even more difficult for them to come to terms.

In any event, the legislation antagonized the union leaders, who resented the unilaterally imposed terms and claimed they had not been adequately consulted. The unions' relations with the government and management became more adversarial. In the longer term the probable effect of the legislative intervention was to weaken the consensus processes. If the processes lost credibility in the eyes of union officials and shipowners, neither would invest the effort to rebuild their effectiveness.

Meanwhile, in Holland in 1983 the unions tried to solidify their presence in the tripartite process. While satisfied with their role in industry planning for shipboard changes, they wanted it to become a right rather than a privilege extended out of the generosity of the government and the shipowners.

Japan's institutions and their implications for consensus were similar in some ways to those of Norway. In both countries a mechanism involving four parties was established at the industry level to deal with innovative changes, progressive companies were recruited to actually implement trials, and the shipowners' associations were strong and internally unified. In both cases, laws and policies required some form of consensus. The power of Japanese and Norwegian unions created an imperative for still more consensus. In the two nations, the parties negotiated a framework allowing some options for individual shipowners and their union counterparts at the company level. Japan's parallel to the Norwegian Frame Agreement was the terms of the modernization program, which allowed companies to participate or stay out (for the short term, at least).

The number of unions was the most striking difference between the two countries—and it was major one. A single union represented all Japanese seafarers compared with Norway's four. The All-Japan Seaman's Union (AJSU) and its members were initially opposed to many of the proposed changes. The union was persuaded to support the modernization program by many factors, including its own desire to strengthen the flag fleet and preserve jobs and its satisfaction with policy commitments conceded by management. In any event, as an AJSU spokesman himself reported, the unified structure made it much easier politically for the union to support the changes. Because they represented all groups of employees affected in all departments and at all levels, they were in a position to ensure that the changes and the provisions for new training opportunities—the costs and benefits—were as evenly distributed across all groups as possible.

Sweden and West Germany. The approval requirements in Sweden and West Germany were similar. In effect, both governments had placed an increasing emphasis on labor and management reaching agreement, standing ready to approve their agreements. In both cases a trend toward ship-by-ship approval reduced the demands for consensus. Nevertheless, my conclusion is that both Sweden and West Germany retained relatively centralized decision making and required fairly uniform practices throughout their industries. These requirements equaled or somewhat exceeded those of Norway and Japan.

Sweden's institutions created intermediate difficulty in reaching consensus. It had a unified employers' association and three unions, compared with Japan's one, Holland's two, and Norway's four. With the return to a Social Democratic government in 1982, the shipping industry was administered by only one agency. The institutional climate could generally be described as constructive.

Conditions in West German shipping were slightly more favorable for reaching consensus than those in Sweden, although not as favorable as one would expect, given West Germany's larger institutional framework and culture, which usually encourages coherence among the major actors in a particular industry. West Germany's shipowners' association was hampered by the disagreement between the two largest firms, Hapag Lloyd and Hamburg Sud, about what staffing practices should become the industry norm. Although association officials appeared to align themselves with Hapag Lloyd's position, the division between these two firms weakened their ability to pursue change. West German industry was able to set up an informal tripartite institution in the early 1970s to deal with GP crew issues and another in the later 1970s to oversee Hapag Lloyd experiments. However, a conflict between the two seafaring unions—again an anomaly in West Germany, given its usual one industry–one union structure—undermined the cooperation necessary to diffuse the Hapag Lloyd model further. A major problem was that one union represented mainly ratings and some officers, while the other represented only officers.

The United Kingdom and Denmark. A would-be innovative shipowner in the United Kingdom faced modest consensus requirements. The government did not insist that the unions and shipowners agree on a matter before it would allow trials. Moreover, company-by-company bargaining had become increasingly common, a trend favored by the seamen's union in the early 1980s. The union had actually revised its own internal structure to reflect and promote this trend. This enabled experimentation first within and then subsequent to the Sealife Programme. As an additional clue that government approval was not the bottleneck factor, shipowners generally maintained several billets more than the government's scale required.

British institutions created barriers that frustrated even the modest amount of consensus they required. The United Kingdom could stimulate very innovative work in the Sealife Programme, yet it could produce almost no industrywide trends. The employers' association was dominated by many small firms with diverse commercial interests and, as a result, was unable to agree about policy changes. The five unions were adversarial; they had a rigid, craft-based, and profession-based structure; and they could not coordinate union policies at the industry level. The antagonism between the deck-officers' and ratings' unions deepened during the 1970s, in part due to their disagreements over proposed innovations. Finally, the Thatcher government's emphasis on free-market forces had eliminated the government as a potential force for adapting shipping institutions. Yet the government still had multiple ministries influencing policy for the maritime trades.

The Danish case was similar, although slightly more consensus was required than in the United Kingdom. Denmark's capacity was handicapped in some of the same ways as the United Kingdom's, by a weak employers' association and a rigid, adversarial, craft-based union structure.[13] The Danish employer community had the advantage of being much smaller and less diverse than the United Kingdom's, but its union structure, with seven unions, was even more fragmented than that of the United Kingdom. Denmark was the only northwestern European country in which the engine-room and deck ratings were represented by separate unions. Fragmentation, coupled with the radical ideology espoused by the leadership of the deck-ratings' union, prevented GP's from being introduced into Danish shipping.

The United States. A review of the U.S. shipping industry leads inescapably to the conclusion that it had the most fragmented and least collaborative institutions of any country studied. It is worth examining the U.S. situation in detail because it best clarifies the disabling effects of certain institutional patterns. The number of seafarers' unions in other countries ranged from one in Japan to seven in Denmark; no less than eleven national unions in the United States represented about 90 percent of the unionized seafarers. The union structure not only reflected eight different trades, but, because many unions represented two or three trades, it also ensured that there were at least two unions representing each trade. The fragmentation of the structure generated rivalry at the boundaries of related trades, and its overlapping missions created direct competition among unions to represent each trade.[14] As in other countries, fragmentation by craft complicated the task of achieving role flexibility. In addition, rival unions for the same craft intensified the cautiousness of union leaders in accepting any changes that might be unpopular with their members. A small "update" item in an industry periodical signals the sour climate fostered by and reinforcing the structure.

> *On the maritime union front,* attention is being paid to the sharply increased sniping between Jesse Calhoon of the National Marine Engineers Beneficial

Association (MEBA 1) and Frank Drozak, president of
the Seafarers International Union (SIU). "If manning
standards are tightened," said a neutral source,
"Drozak wants the jobs that Calhoon would lose.
There are SIU 'Qualified Men in the Engine Department' (QMED) just waiting to fill Third Assistant
Engineer slots on ships where Thirds are redundant,
or not needed at all." "I don't believe that 1984 is
going to be a tranquil year," said a MEBA source.[15]

Ironically, the competition among unions for members and
jobs had on some occasions promoted rather than inhibited
concessions on wages and staffing. Coalitions of unions offered
shipowners concessions for newly constructed ships, provided their
coalition could represent the ship "from top to bottom," that is, the
entire crew. Thus, a form of free enterprise developed among some
unions intent on preserving their own union as an entity. The
impact of this practice on average crew sizes in the industry was
limited because the unions said they could not justify to their
membership similar changes on the ships they already represented
and because the rate of new construction in the United States had
been so low.

Efforts had been made to merge some of the unions and unify
the structure. Harvard labor economist John Dunlop, who had
personally helped limit destructive jurisdictional rivalry among the
crafts in the construction industry, headed an effort to achieve
similar results in the maritime industry but was without success.

The U.S. shipowners' community was also more divided
than that in any other country. In the other seven countries,
shipowners' associations varied in internal cohesion and influence,
but in all cases a single national association represented owners of
oceangoing vessels. In the United States there were several national
associations, all relatively limited in scope and influence over their
members. United States antitrust laws, domestic competition, and
an American ethos of individualism inhibited collaborative
undertakings by these associations.

This industry fragmentation was pervasive in its form and
effects. A committee sponsored by the National Academy of

Engineering reviewed the status of ship-operations research and development in the United States and drew conclusions that support this generalization.[16] The committee found less support for ship-operations research and development in the top management of U.S. shipping committees compared with those of other countries and less general acceptance of the results by shipowners. They attributed the findings in part to the fragmentation of the industry and to the lack of active participation by shipping-company managers in the research and development sponsored by the Maritime Administration (MarAd) and industry associations.

Two governmental agencies dealt with the shipping industry in the United States. The Coast Guard was concerned with safety and related matters, and MarAd was charged with promoting the industry and administering various subsidies. Both agencies could be involved in the approval of staffing. The Coast Guard issued certificates of inspection that specified a minimum staffing scale to ensure that vessels conformed to prescribed rules and took into account general safety considerations. MarAd approved crew complements for vessels operated under subsidy.

Although some innovations were categorically constrained by certain U.S. laws and rules, minimum staffing scales were not. They were determined administratively by the Coast Guard, which provided its field organization with policy guidelines for the issuing of certificates of inspection.

While the Coast Guard had approved staffing reductions proposed by ship operators, it had done so conservatively.[17] For example, it had been conservative by requiring personnel to attend to automation that was designed to be left unattended and was unattended in other countries. However, in 1983 a Coast Guard representative claimed the service was receptive to more frequent proposals for lower and more innovative staffing plans than it had received from shipowners in the past, implying that obstacles to change lay more in the policies of shipowners and unions and in their relationship to each other than in the Coast Guard's decision making.

To understand more fully the role of U.S. government bodies in providing either coherence or confusion in the shipping industry, we need to examine the political context. Because of the

importance of subsidies to the industry, every interested group—
including unions, ship operators, and shipbuilders—actively
lobbied merchant-marine committees in the Senate and House of
Representatives. An index of the seriousness of this activity is the
fact that the median amount of money given by political action
groups to members of merchant-marine committees during the first
six months of 1983 was greater than that given to any other
legislative committee.[18] During the 1983–84 election season, the
political-action committee of one union, the Seafarers, gave $1.3
million to congressional campaigns, more than all but five other
groups—National Association of Realtors, American Medical
Association, National Association of Home Builders, United
Automobile Workers, and National Education Association. The
Seafarers, whose membership totaled less than one hundred
thousand, contributed to the campaigns of thirty-six of the forty
incumbent members of the House Merchant-Marine and Fisheries
Committee, with half of the thirty-six getting at least $5,000
apiece.[19]

In some earlier eras the political agendas of shipowners,
builders, and unions were better aligned. In 1983, as subsidies for
shipbuilding were reduced, and the government was attempting in
other ways to induce the industry to become more efficient, each
group found its own legislative interests differing from those of the
others. This added to the tension within the industry and the widely
felt resentment of labor and management toward the government.

Modifying the Institutional Capabilities for Consensus. The
shipping institutions in most countries adapted during the decade
of severe and sustained competition by either lowering the
consensus requirements or decreasing the difficulty of achieving it.
In the language of this book, they managed the institutional context
to increase the capacity for innovative change; they exercised
metacompetence.

In many cases they had devolved authority for decision
making from the industry to the company level; in other cases (for
example, Sweden, the United Kingdom, Japan, and Norway) they
increasingly made decisions that were ship specific, albeit via
industry decision mechanisms. Also, in some countries the

government singled out safety as the only criterion that industry-level processes would take into account, in effect lowering the requirement for consensus. Decisions that took other considerations into account were made by more decentralized mechanisms, primarily union-management negotiations.

To ease the task of reaching consensus, the parties often created new forums to facilitate consensus. This happened in Japan, Norway, and Holland. Unfortunately, the union structures did not change except in the United Kingdom, where in the early 1980s the masters' union joined forces with the deck-officers' union. If anything, the relations among fragmented unions had grown more strained over the decade.

Another aspect of the institutional framework that changed as a result of the initiatives of one or more of the parties was the orientation of the shipowners and seafaring unions to their relationship. Earlier I noted that relationship orientations, including those of labor to management and vice versa, can range from adversarial to mutual reliance, and they did. The power of labor vis-à-vis management also can range from high to low, although in the sample of countries all the unions were strong; the differences in the sample were not significant.

A matrix of the two power and two orientation possibilities will help portray a few of the institutional changes that occurred during the period studied or were possibly emerging at the end of the period (see Figure 8-2). In 1983 the positions of labor relations in the United States, the United Kingdom, and Denmark were high power and adversarial, a pattern distinctly unfavorable to innovative change; the others were high power and cooperative (or mutually reliant), a pattern that permitted but did not ensure innovative change. The shipping industries in the two southeastern Asian countries—Taiwan and South Korea—are included in the matrix to illustrate a labor-relations pattern not represented in the sample, one typical of the countries that were offering increasingly stiff competition to the traditional maritime countries studied.

The most important shift engineered in the labor-management relationship occurred in Japan, after the bitter industrywide strike in 1972 enabled seafaring labor to consolidate its power, and marked the zenith of adversarial relations in Japanese

**Figure 8-2. Power and Orientation in Seafaring Labor Relations
in 1983.**

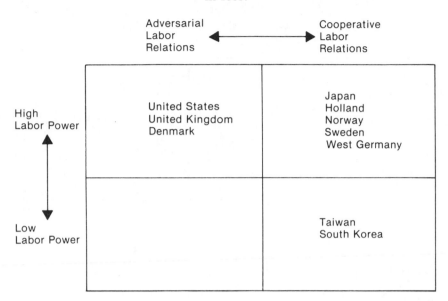

shipping. Beginning in the mid 1970s shipowners initiated a successful movement toward cooperation and mutual reliance while respecting labor's strong power base (see Figure 8-3). The product of this movement and its vehicle was the modernization program.

A second illustration of a change with the potential in 1983 of becoming more significant were the developments in Norway in the early 1980s. Against a history of reinforcing the moderately cooperative relations between labor and management during the 1970s, the conservative government's unilateral changes favorable to shipowners tended to diminish labor's power and fostered more adversarialism. The government was attempting to promote innovative changes by giving shipowners more latitude to implement changes without the approval of labor. It is uncertain whether the decrease in labor-management consensus requirements would be more than offset by the decreased capacity for labor and management to agree in areas where they still needed to do so.

Other institutional innovations and adaptations occurred,

Figure 8-3. Shifts in Seafaring Labor Relations in Japan and Norway.

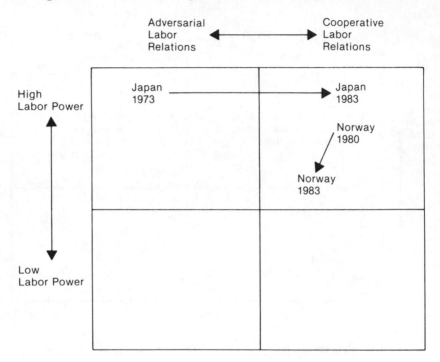

but they related to sponsorship and other aspects of managing the innovative process. These are discussed in the next section.

Influence of Institutions on Sponsorship and Technology Transfer

Institutions assist directly and indirectly in the information, education, and advocacy essential to innovation. The direct mechanisms include such industry research organizations as the Oslo Work Research Institute program in shipping beginning in the 1960s, the West German Flensberg College research into work loads and staffing in early 1970s, the West German Ship of the Future program launched in 1977, the U.K. Sealife Programme from 1975 to 1979, and the Japanese modernization program begun in 1977. The programs were usually funded by industry and government and often included union representatives in their oversight committees. Japan, Norway, West Germany, and the United Kingdom were more active than the other four countries in using formal research in the work-innovation process.

Conferences were organized by academia, industry, government, and unions and attended by company- and industry-level representatives. These mechanisms often exposed shipowners to ideas they later sponsored in experiments. Position papers were issued by government agencies and industry associations to generate awareness and interest in innovations and to hasten their adoption throughout the industry.

Semiformal institutions were established to facilitate ongoing exchanges between participants involved in leading-edge projects. Examples of these semiformal networks included the Eighties Group in the United Kingdom and the Ship-Meets-Ship conferences in Norway. The latter illustrated the value of such networks. They reinforced the interest of participants, clarified that the innovations were becoming increasingly an industrywide movement, encouraged the transfer of information about techniques, and built a network of acquaintances that could lead to further correspondence and visits. These networks helped promote industrywide change in Norway.

The indirect effects of institutions on sponsorship and technology transfer were as important as the direct ones. We refer to the secondary consequences of the institutional factors analyzed earlier for their primary relevance to the consensus process. Industry approval requirements and an industry policy of maintaining uniform practices provided occasions during which leaders of different unions had to deal with each other. Shipowners likewise had to deal with their peers. These contacts spread information about innovative developments in the industry and ensured that government officials were aware of developments. The more internally unified the labor movement and the shipowners' association were, the more likely productive exchanges were to occur between them.

Let us explore these dynamics by revisiting the Hoegh-Shell comparison discussed earlier. Recall that Shell's first use of GP ratings required only minimal union involvement and did not require agreement at the industry level. Although the practice of

using GP ratings diffused rapidly throughout Shell's fleet, it did not
go beyond Shell until many years later. The rest of the industry then
chose to conduct new project ships rather than base policy on
Shell's decade of experience.

Recall also that in Norway the Hoegh experiments with GP
ratings and other innovations from 1970 to 1975 were discussed,
debated, approved, and monitored by the contact group composed
of all interested parties. As a result, the Hoegh experiments
produced industry-level learning. Other key industry officials, in
addition to Hoegh managers and their direct union counterparts,
developed an informed commitment to a new shipboard model.
Soon after, two other Norwegian firms initiated changes.

The different decision processes in the Hoegh and Shell cases
had very different implications for sponsorship and transferring
knowledge. The fact that Hoegh's experiments were partly industry
property, approved and monitored by an industry group, resulted
in slower diffusion of the new model within Hoegh, but it also
helped explain why Hoegh's influence on the Norwegian industry
came sooner and was more direct than Shell's influence on the
Dutch industry.

The types of institutional process by which proposed new
approaches were developed, approved, and monitored also
influenced the type of changes that were copied. Sometimes
followers oversimplified an innovation, copying, for instance, only
the most readily understood aspect of a complex new approach.
Some institutional mechanisms promoted the tendency to oversim-
plify; others helped avoid that tendency.

The problem of oversimplifying can be appreciated by
reviewing the Brostrom case. The model proved to be safe, cost-
effective, and satisfactory to crew members. It had the following
well-publicized aspects: (1) a sixteen-person crew, (2) six GP crew
members, and (3) an operational strategy that transferred all main-
engine maintenance to shore-based facilities. These three aspects
were what other Swedish managers and government and union
officials referred to when they spoke of the "Brostrom approach."
When they considered the general applicability of the approach,
they especially focused on whether it was practical for other
shipping companies to transfer maintenance functions to shore-

based crews. These individuals were missing important lessons. When one examined less publicized aspects of the Brostrom model and listened closely to what Brostrom's management considered to be the basis for the model's success, one could sketch a more complex picture.

The crew concept was negotiated with the unions, which became partners in monitoring the ships. Crew members, who were required to be experienced, were volunteers. Management gave more voice to crew members and was responsive to their stated needs. Role flexibility was accompanied by involvement in work planning. The manager with line responsibility for these ships emphasized that all of these practices were effective only if they resulted in a "motivated, spirited crew." What this manager understood so clearly was not even vaguely appreciated by observers in the Swedish shipping industry.

Thus, what did not exist in Sweden in the later 1970s and early 1980s, and what had existed in Norway as early as the period from 1970 to 1975, was an industry-level process by which institutional representatives could more fully appreciate the comprehensive nature of the new staffing models used by pioneering companies.

The contact group, the tripartite committee, and the modernization committee help explain why Norway, Holland, and Japan were more effective in diffusing complex innovations. Sweden, Denmark, and the United States had no comparable mechanisms capable of creating industry-level ownership of experiments and learning from them. The United Kingdom tried but partly failed in its efforts to develop such a mechanism. In West Germany an industry committee dealing with general-purpose crew issues had been established in the early 1970s. It played a role in the Hapag Lloyd experiments in the late 1970s, but it was somewhat less effective than the Norwegian, Dutch, and Japanese mechanisms.

As we saw in Chapter Seven, a new model favored by sponsoring groups at the industry level was often made more attractive by policies that encouraged individual companies and their unions to adopt the model. The analysis of their institutional capabilities in this chapter clarifies why Holland, Norway, and Japan were better able to develop such economic policies and rules.

Implicit throughout this chapter is the idea that the structural features of institutions influenced the quality of relationships among labor unions, shipowners, and government, and that the quality of relationships influenced how much innovation occurred in a national industry. Frequent discussion, mutual respect, and trust among these institutions enabled consensus and also enabled learning at the national, industry, and firm levels.

Summary and Conclusions

Explaining Innovation Records by Institutional Forms. According to the theory outlined in Chapter Two, institutions effect innovations by two routes: first, by quickening or slowing the rate of innovation activity; second, by biasing the content of the model that emerges to guide the industry. Institutions influence the ability to achieve the required consensus, shape sponsorship at the industry and company levels, and facilitate learning and communication. Considering these different routes and types of influence, in Table 8-1 I rank the countries in the right-hand column arrayed next to the three-way clustering of innovation performances. The two rankings are highly consistent. The institutional proposition has high explanatory power. It merely suggests that additional country differences would be found within each of the three clusters.

To review how the several separate analyses produced the ranking shown in Table 8-1, we can start with the institutional effect on consensus summarized in an earlier section: Japan and Holland were most favorably endowed; followed by Norway; West Germany and Sweden; Denmark and the United Kingdom; and finally the United States. Consideration of sponsorship and technology transfer strengthen all three in the top cluster—Japan, Holland, and Norway—but Holland less than the other two. All three countries had active research, information, and education programs, and officials in their shipowners' associations and government agencies strongly advocated work innovations. Their consensus activities also contributed to diffusion. West Germany is

**Table 8-1. Ranking of Countries' Innovation Records Compared
to Institutional Contexts.**

Country	Innovation Records	Institutional Contexts Favorable to Innovation
Norway	2.0	2.5
Holland	2.0	2.5
Japan	2.0	1.0
United Kingdom	5.0	6.0
Sweden	5.0	5.0
West Germany	5.0	4.0
Denmark	7.5	7.0
United States	7.5	8.0

strengthened relative to Sweden because of industry research
(Flensburg and Ship of the Future) and industry-level monitoring
(the Hapag Lloyd experiments). The United Kingdom is strengthened relative to Denmark and the United States by virtue of its
ambitious if very frustrating Sealife effort and the Eighties Group
that grew out of it.

What effect, if any, did the institutional factors explored here
have on the nature of the models that guided the different shipping
industries? Chapter Five concluded that the comprehensive model
was more robust and more likely to be successfully diffused,
assuming that it could be agreed to and implemented. These
assumptions were more than pro forma. Now we can appreciate
why in more specific terms. The comprehensive innovations are the
most ambitious, in terms of attempting to satisfy safety, costs, and
social-effectiveness criteria. They also are the most demanding, in
terms of each of the three ingredients of the innovation process. By
deductive logic, I proposed that institutional systems that had
limited capacities to achieve consensus, provide sponsorship, and
transfer technologies would prefer innovations that did not require
any institutional approval, such as delegation to officers. These
same institutional systems would prefer the simple versions of
innovations that did require approval, such as the limited role-
flexibility model. Thus, in this case the two effects of institutions
are parallel. The institutional factor becomes the most plausible

explanation for the differences in the models that evolved to guide innovation activities in the eight countries.

There is still one more consequence of institutions to be noted. They influence economic necessity. Chapter Seven showed that some aspects of economic necessity related to raw market pressures and were entirely independent of institutional patterns. However, it also showed that the overall strength of economic necessity for shipowners included the amount and nature of government assistance. The careful tailoring of government assistance to protect and support the industry but also help it adapt was made possible by the types of institutions found in Holland, Norway, and Japan. Similarly, continuation of the type of industry subsidies that killed the incentive for shipowners to innovate was partly a consequence of the type of institutions observed in the United States. The overall strength of the incentives for labor to change was also influenced by industry labor policies and relative employment pressures. Again, in the cases of Japan, Holland, and Norway these policies provided inducements for labor to change. These substantive labor policies were partly a product of institutions in these three countries and instances of the exercise of metacompetence.

The analysis of institutions helps resolve most of the anomalies identified at the conclusion of the treatment of motivational forces. What Holland lacked in strong social and economic forces for innovation, it partly (but not completely) made up for by more enabling institutions.

The United Kingdom's relatively poor performance compared with the motivational forces for change (it had the second-highest economic necessity) is more than fully explained by its fragmented institutions and adversarial relations. Denmark follows a similar pattern.

Sweden remains more of a question mark. Its institutional framework was in line with its moderate record of innovation, but that leaves unexplained why it did not act on the relatively strong economic incentives and favorable social attitudes.

Implications for Diagnosis and Action. The role of institutional forms analyzed in this chapter illustrates why it is important to analyze the institutional context as part of the process of developing policy. Any attempt to formulate industrial policy for U.S. industries should give as much attention to institutional reform as to changing economic policies. Indeed, because approval of policies that promote adaptation may depend partly on the quality of the working relationships among labor, business, and the relevant government agencies, institutional change and innovation may be the more urgent task.

The importance of institutions will vary from setting to setting, and therefore a preliminary step in the policy process is to make an assessment of the general relevance of institutional features. A threshold question is whether interinstitutional approval of an innovation is required before it can be implemented. A contrast was drawn in shipping between role flexibility, which required complex approval steps, and forms of participation, which usually could be implemented by an employer without union or government approval. Interestingly, in most American industries participative mechanisms similar to those introduced in shipping require the support or tacit acceptance of unions (where unions are present); otherwise they are not effective.

The centrality of institutions, including government agencies, derives from the extent to which organizational practices are either prescribed by law and regulations or by detailed labor-management contracts. Few, if any, other U.S. industries have as detailed government regulations covering workplace behavior as I found in shipping, although coal mining has many. However, the provisions and controlling precedents under labor agreements in many U.S. industries, for example, basic steel, are almost as detailed in prescribing and proscribing work practice as the agreements and regulations in seafaring combined.

If institutions are found to be important, the diagnosis turns to an assessment of the requirements for consensus, comparing them with the difficulty of achieving consensus. Reform can be designed to lower the former or decrease the latter.

Institutional reform increases the likelihood of consensus by lowering the consensus requirements, for example, devolving bargaining activity from the industry level to the company level (as in the American steel industry) or from the company level to the

plant level (as in American autos and other industries). Decentralization of decision making requires another change as well. When
individual parts of an industry (and a company) have the autonomy
to innovate, it becomes more important to create other mechanisms
to ensure diffusion from part to part. Hence, the need for
industrywide (and companywide) mechanisms for monitoring, if
not approving, local trials.

Reform can also attempt to decrease the difficulty of reaching
consensus, for example, if the leadership of labor and management
reciprocate cooperative initiatives to move their relationship from
adversarialism toward mutuality and create labor-management
forums at various levels of their hierarchies to promote joint
problem solving and planning. Government entities can take the
initiative to create tripartite forums, which has occurred on only a
few isolated occasions in the United States in the past.

The most striking finding about the role of institutions in
shipping is the importance of internal coherence or unity of
stakeholder groups and especially within the seafaring labor
movement in a particular country. Disagreements within groups
makes it extremely difficult to reach consensus between groups. I
expect this internal condition of stakeholder groups to be important
in other settings, including airlines and construction, two U.S.
industries where multiple craft unions inhibit work innovations.
Where fragmentation exists, it often should be considered a special
target of institutional innovation and reform.

Chapter 9

Individual Competence for Managing the Process

Effective innovation depends not only on a favorable institutional context but also on the competence of the individuals who manage it. Competence involves skills, knowledge, and mind sets at a point in time and the ability to learn from others. Whereas institutional arrangements make it possible to get participation, competence involves the judgment about whether, when, and how to use participation. Whereas institutions make achieving consensus more or less difficult, competence includes the skills and attitudes helpful to orchestrating the consensus process. And whereas institutions make intercompany learning more or less difficult, competence can facilitate that type of learning.

The role of competence to manage the innovation process within a given institutional context (Proposition Five) is summarized in Figure 9-1.

This chapter will illustrate how competence in the innovation process made a difference in specific change programs and will clarify why it belongs in a theory of the determinants of innovative performance. The competence proposition will not be tested with comparative data in the same way that the other four propositions

Figure 9-1. Role of Competence in Managing the Innovation Process.

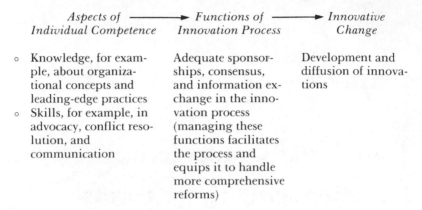

Aspects of ──────▶	*Functions of* ──────▶	*Innovative*
Individual Competence	*Innovation Process*	*Change*
○ Knowledge, for example, about organizational concepts and leading-edge practices ○ Skills, for example, in advocacy, conflict resolution, and communication	Adequate sponsorships, consensus, and information exchange in the innovation process (managing these functions facilitates the process and equips it to handle more comprehensive reforms)	Development and diffusion of innovations

were treated in the preceding chapters. The data on this important but somewhat elusive factor were too uneven to permit such an analysis.

Competence Illustrated

The idea of knowledge, skill, and mind sets accumulated by an industry is aptly illustrated by the discussion in Chapter Eight of the Norwegian contact group. The Norwegians believed they had built a capability that was an even more important asset than their current practices. To paraphrase one Norwegian, "We have built a network of people and companies who have expertise and who know how to exchange it, and more importantly we have created a tradition of experimentation." The capability of the Norwegian industry was an aggregation of the competencies possessed by seafarers, managers, union leaders, government officials, shipowners' representatives, social science researchers, and maritime educators.

The development of competence can also be illustrated by describing the lessons learned by individuals associated with Bibby Brothers, one of the British companies that Sealife's staff recruited for its field experiments. Bibby Brothers learned much from the experience of its first project, a containership in which policy changes affecting ratings were initiated by Sealife staff. In subsequent projects change was initiated by management (not researchers), targeted at officers (not ratings), and involved field trials on three liquified petroleum gas (LPG) carriers (not one containership). Five lessons prompted these shifts in the strategy of innovation.

Lesson 1: Bibby managers discovered how changes in role relationships between ships' officers and the shore departments were needed to pave the way for implementing changes in the way officers managed other crew members. An account by a researcher involved in the Bibby work captures the dynamics of the learning process as well as the nuances of this particular lesson.

> The concept of shipboard management was related to other change programmes but was also a result of experiences on the container ship project. In that project the attempt had been made to create a greater involvement and enriched job content for ratings. In order to achieve this we established continuity of senior officers on board the ship . . . took advantage of a fairly stable group of ratings who seemed to return to the ship again and again. Although continuity of senior officers helped to promote a greater sense of accountability and directly improved performance, it was extremely difficult to achieve effective work planning and delegation on board the ship. Although there was a greater . . . accountability, it was still defined in a traditional way. It was clear that if we could redefine the accountability and reporting relationships of the senior officers we could achieve more effective teamwork on board the ship.[1]

Lesson 2: Bibby Brothers' managers and the researchers concluded that, to be taken seriously, trials must have credible sponsorship. Outside researchers had not been credible sponsors of the first project; therefore, management would need to show its own commitment for future projects. Again, in the words of the researcher involved,

The difficulty (in the earlier project) stemmed from several factors, most importantly Sealife was an external change agent, initiating change. The projects were experiments and the crucial questions were: Were they for real? Was management really committed to the changes? What were management's objectives?[2]

Lesson 3: Bibby managers found that an isolated project ship tended to be discounted and resented by others in the organization, a tendency that made it difficult to spread successful innovations throughout the fleet. Thus, they involved three ships in the second program.

Lesson 4: Bibby managers learned to select pilot sites that would be credible in subsequent diffusion efforts. Compared with the containership used in the first experiment, the three LPG carriers in the subsequent trials were "a section of the fleet of much greater visibility and importance in the eyes of the sea staff and shore management both in terms of prestige and commercial objectives."[3]

Lesson 5: Finally, Bibby management deepened its appreciation of a principle it had already applied in the first project: the need for extensive consultation involving the "targets of change." In the follow-up project management asked union officials to participate in a monitoring group, which met every six months. The group helped allay suspicion and gain acceptance of change.

Like the Norwegians, who claimed a storehouse of useful knowledge and skill, the Bibby Brothers' managers, union officials, and researchers could claim they had gained both competence and confidence in managing the innovation process. We turn now to a more extensive review of the types of skills, knowledge, and other personal attributes helpful to the management of the innovation process. Table 9-1 organizes the choices and activities involved in this process by whether they occur in the early, middle, or later phases of the process and whether they relate to sponsorship, consensus, or the transfer of information and social technology. All three ingredients play a role in each phase. Each phase requires sponsorship, albeit different kinds. Each phase has its own requirements for consensus, but they vary in terms of the amount

Table 9-1. Aspects of the Innovation Process That Require Competent Management.

	Early Phases: New Approaches	Middle Phases: Trials	Later Phases: Diffusion
Sponsorship	Raising consciousness about problem Championing a concept or approach to the problem Involving third party who advocates a new concept or approach	Selecting most credible pioneers and sites for trials Invoking the power and prestige of legitimate authorities to add credibility to trials and change	Advocating widespread adoption
Consensus	Agreeing to address problems Agreeing to objectives of change programs Agreeing to promising solutions Using third-party facilitators	Agreeing to try new techniques Agreeing to terms of trial and how to assess Gaining commitment by participants to trials by selecting, informing, and involving them Agreeing on results of trials Using third-party facilitators	Agreeing to policy and providing inducements for widespread change Agreeing to corollary changes, for example, in educational and certification programs Using third-party catalysts
Transfer of Information and Social Technology	Analyzing the problem Forming concepts and translating into techniques and structures Learning from research and the experience of others Tapping special expertise	Monitoring and learning from trials about efficacy of new concepts and implementation Training in new techniques Using objective third parties for documentation research	Disseminating findings by research publications, education, conferences, and visits to early adopters Recruiting third-party educators to help in dissemination

of consensus required and whose concurrence is particularly critical. And in each phase certain types of information and knowledge must be transferred into the process, gleaned from the process, or made available to other parts of the larger social system potentially affected by the innovation.

Sponsorship

Sponsorship is used broadly, referring to the championing of innovative ideas as well as the provision of critical support for innovation activities.[4]

In order to ensure that a new concept was translated into an operational technique and seriously considered by the various groups concerned, someone had to have the imagination, courage, and persistence to champion it.[5] A champion usually also worked to raise the consciousness about the problem for which the new concept was a solution.[6] Behind the path-breaking efforts of the Hoegh Company was a member of the Hoegh family committed to progressive management approaches as part of the firm's competitive edge. In Denmark the DFDS shipboard management concept was introduced and championed by a new company chairman fresh from Norway.

Although it was not typical for such sponsorship to come from outside the principal stakeholder groups, the Oslo Work Research Institute (WRI) in Norway played an effective advocate role. The Oslo researchers had strong beliefs about the content of the change and the change process. As I noted in the opening paragraph of Chapter Five, they insisted that the organization be viewed as a "sociotechnical system" and the ship be treated as a "twenty-four-hour society and not only as a workplace."[7] They had a third condition, that "no public authority should be allowed to direct or sanction the research or the utilization of results." They envisioned the type of forum that was created later to represent all the major interest groups. Thus, the researchers championed certain concepts, concepts that were in retrospect extremely important. In the language of this book, the first and second conditions constituted a vision of comprehensive change, and the third dealt with the need for multiple groups in sponsoring and sanctioning the changes.

Effective sponsorship involved making good choices about what to advocate. Was it a specific solution or the commitment to attack a certain problem? Was it a specific innovation or the spirit of innovation? Was it a new policy or a process for formulating new policies? The more successful efforts involved initially sponsoring a spirit of innovation, a learning process for developing new policies, and a commitment to attack certain problems. For example, in the case of the Hoegh Company in Norway, the early participants in the process could not settle on specific changes, but they could agree on a problem to be attacked, bureaucratic rigidities. Later, still unable to agree on what specific policies to support, the sanctioning group could argue for an experimental strategy of learning and policymaking. Eventually, of course, the company did sponsor a set of specific innovative policies and a philosophical framework for them. The experience of Hoegh and other companies was that attempts to develop strategic commitments to change at the top were more effective when they were based on a foundation of relevant experiences in some part of the organization, often locally initiated. The specific experiences serve both to operationalize the more abstract concepts contained in the strategic commitment and to build confidence in them.

Innovation activities were more effective when sponsors clarified their underlying purposes and philosophies. The Sealife Programme as a whole and several of its specific projects were hampered by a lack of clearly stated objectives. It was particularly important to clarify whether the objectives were commercial, humane, or some combination of the two. Although there was an advantage to being explicit, sometimes the duality of the objectives was implicit in the situation. In the proposal stages, Germany's Hapag Lloyd and Sweden's Brostrom emphasized commercial objectives and only referred incidentally to human advantages, although Brostrom's gave more attention to the social benefits when the seafarers and their unions reacted positively. It is significant that these companies initiated changes in the late 1970s, when survival issues made it obvious to all concerned that commercial success of flag vessels translated directly into employment security. At the other end of the spectrum, Hoegh's changes emphasized the quality of work life, but at a time when a manpower shortage made it obvious to all that attracting better talent translated directly into commercial success. Finally, P.A.L. set forth one of the most balanced set of objectives in its effort to enlist the unions in sponsoring the change. P.A.L.'s top management had learned through Sealife the difficulties of not following this route. Their strategy, unusual in the United Kingdom, was the normal approach of the Japanese.

To be effective, stated objectives and the policies they supported needed to be credible. New policies were more credible when they were seen as responsive to competitive pressures and reflective of an explicit management philosophy. The innovations of Shell B.V. Tankers in Holland were stimulated by the threat of corporate headquarters to transfer part of the fleet to Shell's tanker subsidiary in the United Kingdom. This external pressure, combined with the concern that Shell had shown for human aspects of their business in the past, enhanced the credibility of management's commitment.

Management's credibility was also enhanced in Shell B.V. Tankers and other companies when their top executives put the power and prestige of their positions on the line. Strong top management commitment was cited as an important ingredient in the success of the projects initiated by Hoegh (Norway), DFDS (Denmark), Hapag Lloyd (West Germany), Shell B.V. Tankers (Holland), Brostrom (Sweden), and P.A.L. (the United Kingdom), all pioneering companies discussed in Chapter Four. This factor was missing in some other cases, where projects were directed principally by the researchers, and management's interest and commitment were either unclear or explicitly hedged by a wait-and-see stance.

At some point in the innovation process, the sponsorship of ideas gave way to the sponsorship of trials. Especially in the earlier stage of an industry's transition to a new model, one or a few companies became the vehicle for "experiments," "projects," or "trials."

The selection, including self-selection, of the company to sponsor field trials was important because the characteristics of the company influenced the credibility of results.[8] Firms that were seen as leaders within the industry and as typical in their operations were more effective in pioneering change. The Japanese were very careful in selecting the initial companies to participate in the modernization program. Hoegh and Hapag Lloyd also appear to score high on the criteria cited above and were more effective pioneers as a result. Brostrom, because of its unusually effective shore-based experience and facilities, was less effective as a general model. Shell was discounted somewhat by other shipping companies because of perceived differences between a division of a large oil company and independent ship operators; on the other hand, its size and positive reputation in Holland's shipping sector gave it considerable influence. DFDS was a small, peripheral company in Denmark's shipping, which may help explain why its internally effective shipboard management innovations did not diffuse throughout the country's fleet. P.A.L. had the same limitation in U.K. industry.

Companies launching change programs employed two somewhat contrasting strategies to set the stage for companywide change. One involved the "sheltered experiment"; the other was based on "workshop" techniques. Planners needed to know the strengths and weaknesses of each so that they could make an informed choice between them.

The sheltered experiment was an approach commonly utilized in this type of social change.[9] It relied heavily on the experiment to demonstrate the efficacy of the proposed policies and to fuel the diffusion process. It involved three parties: (1) the managers and union officials who authorized a project; (2) the outside consultant or researcher who helped the authorizing group determine what to change and how to change it; and (3) the target group, that is, members of the organizational unit that will undertake the change. The experiment was sheltered in the sense that normal organizational rules were suspended to permit the trial conditions. Applications of this technique in Norway and the United Kingdom revealed difficulties, one of which was the tendency for sharp demarcations to exist among the roles of the three groups and between these three acting groups and the rest of the organization. The authorizing group often allowed too much sponsorship to remain with the consulting group, thus undermining the seriousness with which the experiment was viewed by the target group and the rest of the organization. The authorizing group for a sheltered project seldom included all the constituencies whose power and authority affected the success of the trial, and the target group never included all of those who had a strong interest in the innovation. As indicated earlier, those sharply excluded from the project tended to dissociate themselves from the ideas it represented.

The experiences of Shell illustrated the competent use of the workshop technique.[10] By the early 1970s Shell top managers had concluded that fundamental organizational change would be necessary. They were aware of a tendency for single sheltered experiments to become isolated and discounted as a basis for further diffusion. Therefore, they embarked on a process of involving the whole company, an approach in which all levels and all departments of the company became active in analyzing the problems and defining solutions. They began with three workshops, each attended by a cross section of managers and employees.[11] Each workshop considered what organization would be needed in the future to improve operational performance and to provide satisfactory careers in view of projected technological and social developments. To the surprise of senior management and workshop participants, ship and shore staff were in wide agreement on the direction of change. The workshops also considered what steps could be taken to implement the change. Management set up a senior management steering group and a separate working group to coordinate the development work. Thus, the workshops confirmed a direction for change and also created a wide base of commitment for this change.

Another choice in the trial phase of the innovation process is the number of trials to be sponsored concurrently. Hoegh began the *Mistral* project in 1970 and *Multina* a year later. This stepwise involvement of two ships from the same firm had been advocated by the WRI researchers. They had learned from other settings that several projects eased the pressure on any one of them, and that the contrasts and similarities in their experiences created additional possibilities for learning. Shell began four project ships within a few years, based on the same reasoning and Hoegh's experience.

Japan, whose effort benefited from Norwegian and Dutch experiences, started an even larger number of pilot ships in the same time period. In contrast, the single Bibby Brothers and Denholms project ships encountered difficulties in their implementation. Since each company had only a single data point of its own, managers and seafarers in each of these companies tended to attribute the whole of the specific experiences they were having to the concept itself. Multiple trials would have allowed them to sort out what was common and therefore probably inherent in the concept, and what was unique to each case and therefore caused by other conditions.

A final issue of sponsorship is the period during which it must be sustained. A major lesson reinforced by every change effort was the long time required to effect change throughout a company's fleet and throughout a country. The discussion of the Norwegian experience in Chapter Eight identified the factors that combine to make the process a slow one. Suffice it to note here that this slow process required sustained sponsorship, a fact acknowledged in the name of Shell's change program launched in 1975, "Project met de Lange Adem," meaning a project with a long breath. The Japanese industry representatives emphasized repeatedly that the industry was embarked on a gradual implementation program.

Consensus

The important economic, social, and institutional stakes associated with the shipboard innovations made conflict an inevitable aspect of the innovation process and therefore made the ability to manage differences constructively an important aspect of competence. For example, the differences that cropped up in the Norwegian contact group centered on proposals for a single mess, for officers to work in both departments, and for crews to change the size of their onboard complement throughout the year. These differences occurred between owners and unions, researchers and owners, and unions and researchers. The Sealife Programme encountered even more damaging conflicts between owners who supported Sealife and owners who opposed it; between the seamen's union, which wanted to equalize status and perks, and officers' unions, which did not; between Sealife staff, who wanted to eliminate casualism, and the employers' association department, which had responsibility for the hiring-hall mechanism; between the Sealife staff and the unions, over the replication of the Flensburg engineering study of shipboard work loads; and between employers and unions, about whether pay, role flexibility, and other terms of employment should be studied by Sealife.

The effectiveness of the process in all countries depended on how skillfully the parties engaged in dialogue and managed conflict. The more consensus they developed early in the process, the more coherent their efforts. It was important for sponsors of a change that required the cooperation of other groups to produce a common resolve to address a set of problems, build consensus about the objectives of change, and reach tentative agreement about directions of change.

Initiators had to give careful consideration to what type of consensus was institutionally required at each stage, how much additional consensus seemed advisable, and how to generate it. In view of the uncertain and creative nature of the innovation process, it was possible to err on the side of neglecting the input of the union and other groups or on the side of seeking too much consensus too early about the merits of the innovation. Neglecting input ran the risk that those excluded from the process would resist the trial implementation and disapprove the subsequent results. Another risk was that the innovation would be less balanced in addressing the interests of all the groups. Seeking wide consensus about the concepts at the early stages ran the risk of premature evaluation. After a trial the parties would have more informed bases for evaluating the innovative concepts.

Circumstances influenced judgments about how much consensus was sought at each stage of the process. Shell B.V. Tankers only discussed the rating role-flexibility concepts with the union before moving from the proposal stage to the trial stage. In contrast, an early aspect of Japan's modernization committee's effort was to work out many of the policies that were preconditions for the union's support for the radical change progress. Similarly, Brostrom's decision to order the construction of six vessels from a Japanese shipyard was made contingent on the unions' agreements covering the proposed work organization. (In this case the parties intended to go directly from planning the new model to institution-alizing it, without an intermediate trial stage.) In West Germany, the parties agreed contractually to a detailed plan specifying not only the innovations to be tried, that is, reduced crews, role flexibility, and vessel continuity for crew members, but also other conditions, including the number of ships, the trial periods, and the methods for gathering evaluation data. The unions insisted on such an agreement, and when a specific condition was not met, the officers' union used that as a reason for withdrawing support for the experiment. In point of fact, by withdrawing this union was also registering opposition to the innovation itself.

Third parties played constructive roles in assisting the development of consensus. I have the most evidence about the roles of Norwegian WRI researchers, the most active third party in any country's shipping industry. The Norwegian contact group was established apart from existing tripartite committees in order to deal with the general problem of shipboard change. It was vested with limited formal power. It became a forum for exploring ideas, providing the parties engaged each other. The researchers facilitated this engagement and helped shape group norms. One norm was to preserve a certain productive ambiguity; in particular, while the contact group was formally not a policy group, it nevertheless played an integral, if informal, role in developing policy. A second norm enabled parties to confront each other and to modify views on the basis of dialogue and new information. Another norm permitted a trial to go forward for learning purposes rather than attempt to reach a consensus in advance on the probable merits of the proposed innovation.

Consensus activities were focused not only on reaching agreement among institutions but also on promoting consensus among direct participants in the innovations. Both types of consensus were important. While consensus among institutions was necessary in order to go forward with change, consensus among individual participants promoted the effective implementation of the change. It was most helpful to the success of experiments and their subsequent diffusion when direct participants, including a large sample of assigned crew members, were given an opportunity to discuss the new organizational model and influence its details before they began operating in the new mode. This had emerged as a major industry-level lesson in Norway and Holland and among participating organizations in the U.K. Sealife Programme.

As noted in Chapter Four, Norway's Hoegh first learned the lesson when it omitted this step in the initial efforts to transfer elements of the *Multina* model to two other ships. Hoegh concluded that participative planning was an essential step in the transition of every organizational unit to the new model. In effect, this step became an integral part of the new model itself. For Hoegh planners one further implication was that they needed to allow ship-by-ship variations on the new model. This gave meaningful discretion to participants. For example, Hoegh decided not to standardize the elimination of the deck foreman, which had worked out well on the *Multina*. As a result, some of its ships opted to operate without a foreman position, while others kept the position but emphasized its training versus supervisory functions. The same applied to participative work planning. The company proposed this practice to its ships, but allowed it to be implemented in varying degrees throughout the fleet.

Sweden's Salen learned a related lesson in a change effort mentioned in Chapter Four. In the mid 1970s, top management had approved a trial in which shipboard management was delegated to its officers on four ships. When the results proved encouraging, the new practice became company policy. But when management attempted to implement it throughout the company's fleet of several dozen ships, they encountered difficulties. The officers for the experimental ships had been carefully selected for their abilities and their interest, and the shore managers who served as liaison for the experimental ships had been carefully briefed and involved in the planning. However, the company's program for implementing the change companywide overlooked the importance of these aspects of the experiment. As a result, many officers in the additional ships targeted for change were reluctant to take on the additional responsibility, and many of the shore personnel were unwilling to transfer authority because doing so threatened their current role. From this failure in diffusion, Salen management concluded that careful preparation, incuding involvement by all affected groups, was required.

Transfer of Information and Social Technology

Individuals who were effective in playing key roles in the deployment of new policies possessed the ability to tap a diverse set of sources for relevant concepts and experiences. Some ideas came from practices in other industries. For example, delegation of responsibilities to shipboard officers was a practice the large oil companies–ESSO, Shell, BP, and Texaco—first borrowed from their refining organizations. Ideas also came from shipping industries in other countries. Japan, the United Kingdom, and other countries borrowed from the Norwegian shipping experiments. Finally, ideas for new approaches came from research institutes and consultants, such as the Work Research Institute in Norway, Tavistock in the United Kingdom, and Flensberg College in West Germany.

An especially important aspect of competence in this area of endeavor is the ability to learn from others' experiences.[12] The shipping industries in our sample appeared to differ in this respect. West Germany's Ship of the Future program involved an enormous investment of resources and years of lapsed time, yet in the area of staffing the main result was to rediscover staffing concepts that were already practiced in Holland and Norway. In Sweden and Denmark as well as West Germany there was little evidence of detailed familiarity with, and interest in, the comprehensive staffing models of Norway and Holland, although these latter two countries were generally assumed to have smaller crews and the most innovative practices. Holland and Norway each benefited from the experiences of the other. The U.K. Sealife participants also used the Norwegian experiences explicitly as a point of departure. However, the most remarkable instance of intercountry learning was reported by the Norwegian shipowners' association. In 1978 a Japanese delegation visited Norway and looked closely at the Norwegian experiments and the changes in law and maritime education required for these models to continue to evolve. The Japanese returned home and within two years had made enormous progress in revising the legal framework to permit and promote advanced staffing concepts. The Norwegians were startled by the pace of change in Japan.

Even when a shipping industry was familiar with the work of another country, it insisted on its own homegrown trials rather than simply attempting to diffuse the policies proven effective in other countries. For example, the Sealife Programme in the United Kingdom wisely decided to replicate the Norwegian experiments "on U.K. ships with U.K. personnel." Even in Holland, Shell experiments were not used by the rest of the industry to evaluate the GP and semi-integrated-officer concepts. The other Dutch companies conducted industry-level trials, which then served as the basis for industry-level policymaking.

Replication of basically the same experiment served several purposes, even when the main proponents of the new experiments were already convinced of the efficacy of the changes. It provided a common experience that all of the affected parties could evaluate, especially the less informed or more skeptical. It provided a concrete basis for all parties to learn about the detailed requirements of the change process. The planning and evaluation discussions among parties provided an opportunity for them to develop a better understanding of the organizational alternatives, including their subtle effects. These discussions, like other instances of participative planning, developed commitment. How much discussion, learning, and commitment actually developed depended on the quality of the industry-level evaluation processes. A key contribution of the researchers in Norway was their role in enhancing the learning of the contact group.

The tendency cited in Chapter Eight for followers to copy only the most readily understood aspect of a complex organization model can be neutralized by greater awareness on the part of individuals. A project in the United Kingdom illustrates the tendency to focus on one aspect of the model—in this particular case the most controversial aspect of the model but not its most central feature. When in the later 1970s the Sealife Programme started the U.K. replication of the Norwegian experiment, the intention was to test such concepts as continuity of assignment and crew participation. As noted in Chapter Six, the U.K. officers, ratings, and their unions and many managers became almost exclusively preoccupied with the question of social integration. With a better grasp of the model and the Norwegian experience, participants would have seen that it was more appropriate to treat social integration in the U.K. setting as a by-product of work-role integration rather than as a central element of the planned change.

Compared to other industries worldwide, shipping interests in northwestern Europe devoted a remarkably large amount of effort to learning about organizational innovation. The many trade journals and magazines published in the region that tracked developments in the international shipping industry reported frequently, and sometimes in depth, on staffing policies and practices. Also impressive was the high quality of the research and the policy implications drawn from it. This research, focused heavily but not exclusively on the Norwegian, Dutch, and British experiences, was relevant to all the countries studied. Moreover, the conferences on innovations in shipping often were broadly international in their content and attendance. The industry's senior observers, commentators, and change agents, who are cited frequently throughout this book, were an unusually articulate and sophisticated lot. They were loyal to the industry, many of them having stayed involved in shipping over a relatively long period of time. This last point, sustained involvement, was especially important in enabling the industry to transfer technology.

Summary and Conclusions

The Role of Individual Competence in Innovative Change. I stated at the beginning of this chapter that the countries could not be ranked in terms of the competence of the actors who were managing or who could have managed innovation processes. This is particularly true for the first part of the period studied, when competence would be treated as a factor influencing the rate of change. In fact, it becomes easier to differentiate the countries toward the end of the period.

By 1980, the more innovative Norwegian, Dutch, and Japanese shipping industries were undoubtedly in the possession of more knowledge and skill relevant to the management of this form of innovation than were the other countries' shipping industries. Thus, we can be more confident in concluding that their high competence in the late 1970s was a consequence of extensive innovation activity rather than a cause of it.

The Sealife Programme presents an interesting case study of the value of experience as a teacher. Many tactical mistakes affected the degree of success or failure of a particular project and of Sealife as an industry intervention. On the one hand, the frequency of these suggested a competency gap at the time they occurred. On the other hand, the explicitness with which the participants drew the appropriate lessons from their mistakes indicated an accumulation of competence. Generally, by 1980 I judged a segment of the U.K. industry to be at least as able in managing the work-innovation process as Brostrom of Sweden and Hapag Lloyd of West Germany and more able than the other progressive firms in these two shipping industries.

Although more mistakes were made in the innovation process in the United Kingdom than in Norway, this did not necessarily mean that the U.K. sponsors were less competent when Sealife started than the Norwegian sponsors were when their earlier efforts began. The institutional context was much less favorable in the United Kingdom than in Norway. In addition, the economic environment, which emphasized attracting seafarers at the time Norway began its change, had shifted to emphasize the nastier problem of cutting labor costs by the time Sealife got under way. Thus, the situation was much less forgiving for the British pioneers than for their counterparts in Norway.

I have emphasized the role of direct experience in generating relevant social knowledge and skills for individuals in the shipping industries studied. Significant differences may have existed among at least some of the eight countries in the general knowledge and skill of managers in managing participative change processes. The strongest case could be made that the Japanese were generally better at forming consensus and enlisting participants in problem solving and planning activities. Japan also had earned a reputation as a country of learners, an attribute extremely important to the development and diffusion of innovations. But Japanese managers were not alone in having general experience in promoting social innovations of the type studied here. For example, the discussion of differences in social beliefs and social values in Chapter Six pointed out that among the eight countries, shop-floor participation was also relatively prevalent in Sweden, Norway, and the United States. It was least evident in the United Kingdom.

The conclusion to Chapter Eight reviewed the cumulative explanations for the innovation performance of certain countries, particularly those that were the least readily explained by the strength of motivational forces. Is it plausible that competence is the explanatory ingredient that was still missing after considering the first four factors?

Holland's strong institutional advantage only partly made up for its weaker social and economic forces toward change. While individuals in Dutch shipping probably had no more competence at managing social processes than their counterparts in Sweden, Denmark, and the United States at the beginning of the period in question, they gained competence once they engaged the process. Thus, we must take into account the dynamic nature of the competence factor. Once activity was initiated, for whatever reason, experience built knowledge and skills. This was similar to the finding about social attitudes. While predispositions in the Dutch industry were less favorable to participation and social integraton, attitudes became more favorable with experience.

The greatest mystery surrounded the Swedes, whose shipping institutions were consistent with their moderate innovation record, but whose strong economic incentives and positive social attitude indicated they should have been among the more innovative. Low general competence in managing social processes is simply not plausible as an explanation. The Swedes have been too effective in other spheres in sponsoring social innovations, in engineering social consensus, and in transferring social technology to discount the availability of the abilities to do these things in Sweden. However, this competence was not brought to bear on shipping. An active researcher in Sweden said he could not identify any of the prominent Swedish individuals or organizations involved in work restructuring who had taken an interest in shipping. The lower national priority for the shipping industry may help explain why these change agents, who played important roles in manufacturing and other sectors of Swedish society, did not turn their attention to this particular industry.

Implications for Action. This study of work innovations revealed the myriad tactical choices that must be made and activities that must be performed by those who manage the innovation process.

The discussion of choices in this chapter and their organization in Table 9-1 tend to characterize the innovation process as more logical and deliberate than such processes were in practice. Many choices were made intuitively, some were even made by default, and many of the positive developments were serendipitous. With learning and experience, however, more elements of the process became deliberate and intentional.

The study also confirms certain ideas about competent innovation strategies[13] that are indicated by the experience of other industries. First, the type of change studied here was more effective when it involved tentative organizational innovations developed inductively in the field, assisted by action research, than when it relied heavily on models developed deductively in research laboratories, based on traditional academic methods.

Second, innovation efforts within a company were more effective when the processes they employed were relatively inclusive—when a wide range of participants was involved in workshops that diagnosed the need for change, searched for the appropriate innovative response, and scoped the implementation issues. The workshop approach was usually preferable to a more limited involvement of members of the organization, confined to the direct participants in a sheltered pilot project.

Third, the implementation process was more effective when it involved multiple units, for example, multiple sites within a company and multiple companies within an industry.

Fourth, effectiveness was enhanced when the planning process for an innovation within an organizational unit involved as many of the actual participants from all levels of the unit as possible.

Fifth, in diffusing the social technology, an open pattern of contact between the pilot organizations and others, relying on face-to-face contact at all levels of the organization, was more effective than written information addressed to traditional gatekeepers.

Another aspect of the innovation process highlighted by the study was the potential role of third parties. In particular, the Oslo Work Research Institute provided an excellent vehicle for exploring the contribution third-party researchers or consultants can make to the innovation process. Both Thorsrud, who worked with the Norwegian industry, and his Dutch colleague Roggema, who worked in Norway, Holland, and the United Kingdom, were associated with this institute during critical periods of change. One is struck by the pervasive presence of the researchers throughout the period studied. They were involved in diagnosing the recruiting problem and redefining it in more systemic terms. They were involved in designing, implementing, and evaluating the three major project ships and went to sea on them. They helped form and participated in the interinstitutional contact group. They assisted the diffusion activities at the industry level (for example, Ship-Meets-Ship) and at the company level (Hoegh conferences). They consulted with many individual companies and with the seamen's union. They helped reshape the maritime educational institutions and worked with particular schools or colleges to adapt to the changing needs of the industry.

I mentioned earlier that these researchers played multiple roles—champion/advocate, facilitator of policy processes, and action researcher. These three roles could have readily interfered with each other. As advocates of a particular idea, they could have been suspect as either action researchers or policy process facilitators. As action researchers, they could have been accepted in their role of generating knowledge but unwelcome in the policy deliberations. How were the researchers in this case able to play all three roles actively and continuously? I can speculate.

The researchers' advocacy was not disabling because they were open about their beliefs, while they encouraged others to search out their own beliefs from experience, evidence, and discussion. From time to time their advocacy, which successively embraced different causes as they became critical factors, cost them rapport with some parties. For example, the relationships of the WRI researchers with the officers' unions were more distant and tense because on occasion they advocated changes that these unions opposed. In 1983 the researchers vocalized concerns that the shipowners were decreasing crew sizes to levels that jeopardized participation and incurred safety risks. In so doing, they risked their rapport with the shipowners.

Still, the integrity and independence by which the researchers arrived at their own views helped keep them in the policy network and helped sustain their special role in that network. Their expertise was broad and deep. Their industry involvement at different levels and with different institutions increased the information and perspective they could bring to any one situation. They could draw on experience from the shore industries and from international networks and on a deep understanding of the Norwegian shipping industry, including an appreciation of the lives of seafarers. Their long continuity of involvement was rare in my experience. This continuity was, of course, both a result of and contributor to their success as change agents.

In Chapter Twelve, I recommend the development and utilization of third-party resources to help promote innovative change in American industry and cite several third-party institutions that are presently making an important contribution.

PART FOUR

Learning from the Framework
Results and Implications

Part Four integrates the findings and derives their implications. Having analyzed in Part Three the power of each component of the innovative capacity by itself to explain the country differences (high, moderate, and low records of innovation), I review in Chapter Ten the findings country by country, asking: Which components have combined to add materially to the country's innovative capacity, and which have detracted from it? Also, how completely do the components in combination explain the relative positions of these eight countries?

Chapter Ten reviews another set of differences—those between specific innovations. For example, delegation to officers diffused more widely than officer role flexibility. The five components are drawn on to help explain this difference and several other interesting contrasts.

If the integrative summary of Chapter Ten assesses how well the theory explains the observed patterns in shipping, then Chapter Eleven examines the other side of the matter—how well the findings support the theory. Chapter Eleven also derives the implications of the findings for refining the theory and summarizes how the theory can be used as a general policy tool in a wide range of settings.

Finally, Chapter Twelve returns to the problem described in Chapter One, America's stake in strengthening industry's innovative capacity. I set forth an agenda for the attention of policymakers concerned about organizational innovations in particular, identifying the modifications in the economic, social, and institutional contexts that would promote innovation.

Chapter 10

Comparing
Innovative Capabilities
Findings from the
Shipping Industry Case

Why were some shipping countries more innovative than others? Why did some specific innovations diffuse more widely than others? These are the main questions addressed in this chapter.

Other differences in innovation patterns have been mentioned throughout the book: differences in rates of innovation from one time period to the next, differences between the shipping sector and other industries in the same country, and differences among companies in the same shipping sector. Wherever possible, we seek plausible explanations for these differences as well.

Why Some Shipping Sectors Were More Innovative than Others

The research covered a period of seventeen years, during which interest in work innovation expanded. The expansion of activity was consistent with (1) mounting market pressures, including first labor shortages and then cost pressures; (2) the development of social values favorable to the work innovations; and (3) the growing technical sophistication of the ships, which intensified the economic and social rationale for the innovations. In addition, increased innovation was consistent with the trends in the institutional framework of the shipping sectors studied toward less stringent requirements for sector-level consensus and less demand for uniformity of practices. The increase in activity was also paralleled by a tendency to utilize more comprehensive models. Finally, apart from any other trends, by virtue of cumulative experience with the changes in question, the shipping industry possessed more competence to manage the innovation process at the end of this period than at the beginning.

Inasmuch as all five components of the capacity for innovative change moved in the same direction, it was difficult to infer support for any one proposition from these broad interperiod trends for the region as a whole; however, the ebb and flow of activity in the eight countries differed, a fact that will be explored below in the analysis of differences among them.

The analysis in Chapters Five through Nine paid particular attention to differences among the eight countries and to the ability of each of the major propositions to help explain the countries' innovation records. Table 10-1 compiles the ranks in the strength of the eight countries' economic incentives, the supportiveness of their social attitudes, and the enabling character of their institutional frameworks.

Due to a lack of comparable data on the eight countries, Table 10-1 excludes ratings of actor competence. I have also excluded any treatment of the strengths of the models that guide activity in each country, for a different reason. The nature of the innovation models used by the countries correlates perfectly with the extent of the diffusion of the cornerstone innovation for most of the activity, that is, rating role flexibility. Yet, the variations in the models beg the question of what underlies the choice of particular models. The question brings us back to an analysis of the other components of innovative capacity.

The analysis starts with the six northwestern European countries—from more to less innovative clusters. Then it treats in

Table 10-1. Rank Ordering of Countries by Economic Necessity, Social Context, and Institutional Arrangements Favorable for Shipboard Innovations.

	High Innovators			Moderate Innovators			Low Innovators	
	Norway	Holland	Japan	United Kingdom	Sweden	West Germany	Denmark	United States
Economic necessity	1.0	6.5	4.0	2.0	4.0	4.0	6.5	8.0
Social context	1.0	4.0	2.5	7.5	2.5	7.5	5.5	5.5
Institutional arrangements	2.5	2.5	1.0	6.0	5.0	4.0	7.0	8.0
Totals with all factors equally weighted	4.5	13.0	7.5	15.5	11.5	15.5	19.0	21.5
Totals with institutional factors double weighted	7.0	15.5	8.5	21.5	16.5	19.5	26.0	29.5

considerably more detail the shipping industries of Japan and the United States, which are polar opposites on many of the components.

Northwestern European Countries

Norway. Norway's innovation record over the two decades is readily explained. It possessed the strongest set of economic incentives, one of the two more favorable social climates, and a relatively good institutional environment. It also benefited from the activities of an especially competent third-party resource. Its major shortfall—its inability to implement officer role flexibility—is related to the opposition of fragmented officers' unions.

Although Norway had pioneered the comprehensive innovations in the early 1970s and spread them throughout the 1970s, it lost momentum in the 1980s. I assume that social attitudes and competence continued to develop in a way helpful to innovation; therefore, the explanation for a tapering off of activity must be explained by other factors. In fact, economic incentives changed. As economic pressure continued to mount, the government made it easier for shipowners to flag out, relieving some pressure that might otherwise have fueled the change efforts. Moreover, whereas forums had become more active and the requirements for institutional consensus had been lowered through most of the 1970s, the forums declined in use in the late 1970s, and the government bypassed them almost completely in the 1983 staffing regulations. These developments helped to explain the decline in new innovation initiatives.

We can gain additional insight into the factors influencing innovation by comparing the shipping sector with other Norwegian industries. While Norway's manufacturing industry is relatively innovative, the shipping sector clearly is more advanced than is manufacturing. The reasons for this include the high national importance of shipping combined with the cohesiveness of the shipowners' association and a general sense of community within the industry. The importance of the industry influenced both the sector-level support for ship operations and research and development by industry and government and the priority given to the industry by social science researchers. The coherence and community within the shipping industry underlay the more enabling institutional relations.

Holland. Holland is the overachiever, in the sense that its record of innovative performance exceeds the favorability of the social, economic, and institutional factors as I assess them. Its good innovation performance was facilitated by an industry structure that permitted Shell B.V. Tankers to innovate on its own and enabled subsequent innovation and diffusion in the rest of the industry. The simpler institutional structure—one union for all ratings and one for all officers—made reaching consensus about role flexibility an easier task in Holland than in any other country except Japan. Although individual seafarers may have been initially opposed to the innovations, the institutional support for the innovations from government and shipowners and acquiescence by if not support from unions were important developments. Holland achieved diffusion of comprehensive change despite initial attitudes generally less favorable to two key elements, participation and social integration, than in those found in the three Scandinavian countries and Japan. This achievement is even more remarkable considering that Holland also had a generally weak set of economic pressures promoting work innovations.

The pacing of innovative activity in Holland contrasts sharply with Norway's pattern. Holland started innovating later and was continuing on a trend of accelerated change in 1983. The surge in the late 1970s and early 1980s was more related to improving institutional forces than to changing economics. Also, while there was acceleration in trends of social attitudes in society, there was a favorable trend within the Dutch shipping industry based on their direct experience.

Sweden. Sweden was an underachiever. It had moderately favorable economic incentives and one of the social contexts more favorable to the new organization. Moreover, because of the amount of similar social innovation in other sectors of Swedish society, we can assume that the competence to innovate in shipping was available. A weaker link in the Swedish case is the institutional framework, but it still ranked intermediate in enabling attributes.

In particular, the comparison of Sweden and Holland supports our conclusion that institutional factors were more important than either social or economic motivation in this industry during this period of time. At the end of the period studied, Sweden remained the most fertile ground for major progress in diffusing the flexible shipboard organization.

Another comparison—this one between Sweden and Norway—is instructive. In both countries their shipping sectors differed significantly from their manufacturing sectors in terms of progress toward innovative organizations. Norway's shipping sector led, while Sweden's lagged. Sweden was the most active in northwestern Europe, implementing the types of changes studied here in its manufacturing and service industries, yet it lagged in shipping. The lower national priority of shipping may help explain why change agents promoting work reform in Sweden did not attend to shipping. In Norway the importance of shipping helped attract the attention of social scientists in the late 1960s, who became part of the contact group that facilitated innovation. Nothing of this sort occurred in Sweden. There was a striking lack of awareness about the shipping sector and its organizational problems and opportunities compared with the high attention paid to automobile manufacturing and other industries seen as more important to the country.

The United Kingdom. The results and the causal factors are complicated in the case of the United Kingdom, but they are not difficult to interpret. Recall that apart from delegation to officers there was little else in the way of industrywide change. A few U.K. firms featured totally revamped shipboard organizations, but the industry as a whole was disinclined to innovate with ratings.

Economic necessity was the element most favorable for innovative change in the United Kingdom. Shipowners and seafarers had intermediate to strong incentives to change staffing practices to enhance competitiveness. However, the enormous pressures on the industry were partly neutralized as drivers of innovation by the flight of British ships to flags of convenience. Also, while according to our indexes the industry was objectively important to the U.K. economy, it was not treated as such by public policy or concerted industry action. This brings us to the forces limiting the United Kingdom's innovation record: social dissension and institutional fragmentation.

The U.K. industry undertook in the Sealife Programme a major change effort, but it was wracked with controversy. The prevailing attitudes toward a change in the role of ratings and social integration in the shipboard organization were by far the most unfavorable found in the eight countries. The institutions were too fragmented to permit any systematic effort to transform the industry. The unions were at each other's throats; the shipowners' association was large, diverse, and weak; and government agencies were a fragmented lot, without any prescribed role for revitalizing the industry.

Thus, the initial surprise was that the U.K. industry compiled a record as a moderate innovator (with Sweden and West Germany) rather than as a low innovator. When one examines the particular pattern of innovation that helped us rank the United Kingdom as a moderate innovator, the mystery disappears. The major industrywide innovation in the United Kingdom, delegation to officers, was one that was responsive to the positive economic incentives but was not affected by the negative social attitude toward changes in the status of ratings. In addition, it was not subject to institutional decisions. Where bold comprehensive innovations by several individual companies did occur, it was possible in part because of the lower requirements for consensus among sector-level institutions. The innovations were as much an expression of the diversity and fragmentation of the industry as they were actions taken despite the fragmentation.

While the United Kingdom's innovation activity was never as vigorous as Norway's, the United Kingdom experienced a decline in new activity after 1979 as sharp as that of Norway. This can be attributed in part to frozen social attitudes, to a worsening institutional climate, and to a growing appreciation of the negative effect of those two factors on innovation projects in the United Kingdom, an appreciation sharpened by the Sealife Programme experience. Other factors certainly were depressing the amount of innovation activity in 1983: the rapid decline in the flag fleet, the ease of flagging out, the absence of any government policy or action to stem the decline, and the deep pessimism among shipowners about the British shipping industry's future.

West Germany. West Germany, in the middle cluster of innovation results, was an uncomplicated case and readily interpretable. West Germany was placed in the intermediate range in economic necessity and institutional factors and in the lower range on social attitudes. Its institutional arrangements were similar to Sweden's but somewhat less pressing for innovative change, primarily because of West Germany's liberal flagging-out pattern. Even the individual aspects of West Germany's economic context were mainly in the middle range, including staffing costs, rate of decline of the flag fleet, and government assistance. Two factors were more extreme. West Germany had the second-highest rate of flagging out, which subtracted from the pressure to change on West German shipowners. The employment threats faced by labor were also the second highest, which added pressure to change on West German seafarers.

West Germany's shipping institutions had less capacity to engineer labor and management consensus than is characteristic of West Germany. They imposed on themselves moderately high requirements for consensus at the same time that they were handicapped in achieving consensus by rivalries within the shipowners' association and between the two seafaring unions.

Denmark. Denmark was similarly uncomplicated. Its standing as a low innovator can be explained by one of the least favorable economic contexts for innovation and one of the least enabling institutional arrangements. It had relatively low labor costs. Moreover, it received relatively more government assistance and had experienced less decline in its flag fleet, which ameliorated the urgency felt by shipowners. Significantly, because its practice of cushioning the impact of declining employment on domestic seafarers was not contingent on labor participating in staffing reforms, it blunted labor's incentive to consider change.

The institutional context placed many obstacles in the way of efforts to reach consensus. The shipping-sector unions were fragmented (with seven separate unions) and strong, and many of them tended to be highly adversarial. The seamen's union in particular blocked role flexibility and a move from casualism (through the union-controlled hiring hall) to permanent employment. To make the institutional context even worse, the shipowners' association was relatively weak.

Finally, the social context was intermediate in terms of receptivity to the work innovations, but that fact was little help in the absence of stronger economic drivers and favorable institutional factors.

Japan

By 1983 it appeared that the Japanese could soon claim to be the most advanced country in shipboard innovations. Indeed, a spokesman for the Norwegian shipowners' association had already proclaimed Japan's leadership. The vision guiding Japan's innovations was of the same sort as those of their predecessors—the Norwegians and Dutch—but more ambitious. Representatives of the Japanese modernization committee emphasized that they were deliberately planning no more than gradual change. Yet the rate of change they had planned was the most rapid. The changes included not only the implementation of experimental ships but, equally important, the complete overhaul of the controlling legal framework and sector-level programs for educating, training, and certifying seafarers.

Why did Japan emerge as one of the leading innovators and appear to be on a track to becoming the leader? There were many reasons. Japan's performance, like Norway's, was overdetermined in that Japan scored positive on all five components of innovative change and strongly positive on several of them.

First, Japan's new shipboard-organization model was more radical than the advanced European versions. The Japanese also had the highest aspirations for technological advances in the sense of applying, if not developing, automation technology. They talked seriously about ten-person crews, while the most farsighted Europeans contemplated twelve-person crews. Perhaps the radical form of their work innovations was related to the ambitiousness of their vision of future technology. In any event, the Japanese staffing model represented further departure from the past along several dimensions of change. It provided more flexibility in the assignment of tasks—vertical integration (ratings standing watch in place of officers) as well as interdepartmental integration (at both rating and officer levels). It envisioned a more dramatic decrease in status differentials to promote social integration—the shared vision of an all-officer crew. It also incorporated the strongest guarantees of employment stability—lifetime employment. The model provided for power sharing with ratings but not delegation from shore to ship. Ambitious as the individual policy elements were, they were internally consistent and mutually reinforcing. Ambitious as the innovative model was in terms of the economic benefit it sought for the enterprise, it was also very attentive to the economic and social concerns of those affected. In sum, it was a very strong model.

Second, economic necessity contributed to Japan's innovation record. As in most of our other countries, actual declines in the Japanese fleet had made the competitive threat of the newly industrialized countries a clear and present danger. As in Norway (but not the United Kingdom), the higher national economic importance of shipping favored innovation, especially because it stimulated some of the activity that must occur among institutions at the sector level. Japan's second-highest crew costs were also part of the mix of positive incentives, but we know that this factor itself was not decisive because the United States and Sweden, countries ranking first and third in crew costs, were not among the more innovative.

The economic incentives affecting labor differentiated Japan from other countries in our sample and helped explain labor's support and hence Japan's achievements. Japan's policy inducements involving employment assurances were the most impressive. In return for labor's support of the modernization program, shipowners agreed to consult the union prior to removing a vessel from the flag fleet, with the understanding that they would make every effort to replace the vessels on a one-for-one basis. Shipowners reaffirmed their lifetime employment policies and were committed to finding employment on shore or FOC ships for any of their seafarers displaced from a flag vessel by the modernization program. Japan's shipowners also agreed to a number of other improvements for seafarers, including training for upgraded positions, promotional opportunities for existing seafarers, and additional pay.

Third, institutional arrangements were uniquely favorable for Japan and played a major role in explaining Japan's innovative performance. Particularly helpful was the single union for all seafarers. Because officers and ratings were represented by the same union, it was politically feasible for the union to accept a proposal that certain tasks performed by officers—for example, watch standing—could be transferred to a newly qualified classification of ratings. The single union also made it easier for labor to enter into policy deliberations with other groups.

The mechanism devised by the Japanese to chart the future seafarer system, the modernization committee, was itself an impressive innovation. An instrument for planning and managing industrywide change, it included labor, shipowners, government, and a representative of the public. It enabled members of the tripartite-plus-public committee to learn from other countries, negotiate the issues, and discuss proposals with their constituencies. The modernization mechanism was feasible for the Japanese because of institutional relations, mechanisms, and norms that had already developed in the industry by the mid 1970s.

Fourth, Japan's social values were favorable to the shipboard innovations implemented in the late 1970s, partly because of prior practices. The high attachment of Japanese seafarers to their companies, resulting from the lifetime employment policy and a considerate management style, was accompanied by a high amount of shipboard teamwork. This experience made seafarers more receptive to the innovations proposed in the late 1970s. Moreover, because seafarers were already attached to companies, management could invest in their training.

Fifth, it is at least arguable that participants in the Japanese shipping industry had as much competence as their counterparts elsewhere in managing the type of social-innovation process required. They appeared to be adept at learning from others, imaginative in developing institutional forums, and skillful in resolving the differences among stakeholder groups. Although I have less evidence to go on, I assume the competence factor was also on the asset side of the ledger in Japan.

The United States

The United States not only produced as little innovation as Denmark, the least innovative country in northwestern Europe, but also reduced staffing less by traditional means than the least changer in Europe—the United Kingdom. The U.S. crew reductions during the period studied were the smallest, even when the comparison involved the newer, comparably equipped ships. Why this poor record of innovation and noninnovative change? Conditions were unfavorable or very unfavorable in four of the five components.

First, during the period to 1983 the only vision of alternative staffing patterns being discussed was reduced staffing. Innovations were not considered by anyone in the industry except for a few individuals in the MarAd organization, who had become familiar with developments in Europe and Japan. The absence of a viable model was a consequence of many other factors, including the average age of U.S. ships, the level of technology, the size of crews, and the nature of the economic incentives and institutional forms discussed below.

Second, while the highest staffing costs in the world gave U.S. shipowners strong incentives for change and innovation, other factors completely neutralized the incentives. Shipowners could deal with the strong cost pressure in several ways. They could qualify for the operating differential subsidy program, which provided direct subsidies to cover cost advantages of foreign-flag ships operating on the same route. They could bid for business that U.S. shippers were required by law to transport on U.S. vessels; in this business they competed only with other American shipping companies paying American wages to American seafarers. Another option was to transfer ships to a flag of convenience and participate in the competitive world market. Two facts indicate that U.S. shipowners fared better during the period from 1973 to 1983 than their extremely high labor costs would suggest: (1) the heavily subsidized U.S.-flag fleet increased its tonnage capacity by 57 percent over the decade (compared to Japan's 9 percent increase and a 49 percent increase worldwide) and (2) the fleet of American-owned ships registered under flags of convenience and competing in world markets was the fourth largest in the world. Thus, shipping companies were hurting less than one might expect.

U.S. seafarers were also less affected than one might expect. They were potentially vulnerable to declines in employment in the period from 1973 to 1983 for several reasons. The severe declines in employment in the previous decade had already created a pool of unemployed, and most seafarers in the United States, like those in Japan but unlike those in European countries, were committed to the occupation for their entire careers, making declines in available jobs very painful; also, the U.S. fleet started the period with an all-national work force, like Japan and unlike European countries. The latter had in 1973 a number of foreign workers, who could be and often were repatriated to cushion the impact of declining jobs on nationals. But the potential pain never came to pass. The subsidy program made the size of the flag fleet relatively insensitive to labor costs. The number of ships thus declined only modestly— 10 percent from 1973 to 1983—and by sharing work more widely through their hiring halls, unions reversed the decline in the number of active seafarers. The unions were relatively successful in slowing down crew reductions, even on ships where automation explicitly designed to allow a reduction in billets was already installed.

Other economic conditions discouraged U.S. work innovations. One was the fewer number of new ships constructed during the decade before 1983 (39 percent for the United States versus from 57 to 77 percent for the other countries), which removed one uniquely favorable situation for negotiating new staffing schemes with labor. The second was the large unfunded liabilities that characterized the union pension funds. Any innovation that decreased the number of active seafarers under one of these pension schemes would exacerbate the funding deficiencies, to the consternation of both employers and seafaring unions.

The third component, institutional arrangements, was even more unfavorable for work innovations than the economic context. As in Europe and Japan, a number of laws specifically prescribed roles and assignments that precluded the work innovations, but changing the rules and regulations appeared to be a more difficult task in the United States. U.S. unions were highly fragmented.

Eleven unions competed to represent combinations of nine separate craft groups. Rivalry, even bitterness, prevented collaborative planning within the union movement. Several separate national associations represented U.S. shipowners, and they did not engage in joint planning. Labor and management attitudes toward the government agencies that served the industry included an awkward sense of dependence and deep-seated resentment. The climate was not conducive for either the Maritime Administration or the Coast Guard to play a catalytic role in facilitating innovations.

Fourth, social forces, though mixed, were more unfavorable than favorable to innovation. During the 1970s and early 1980s America's manufacturers gained a growing appreciation of advantages to increased worker involvement and flexibility. Indeed, the appreciation was stronger in the United States than in most of the countries in the sample. But the generally favorable social climate was more than offset by several decidedly unfavorable factors in the shipping industry. One was the advanced age of active seafarers, who averaged fifty-four years, making them ten to twenty years older than the seafarers in other countries.

Another social factor was a strong commitment by the U.S. unions to preserve the primary, if not exclusive, attachment of seafarers to the unions. Thus, they were opposed to the idea of replacing casual hiring with permanent employment. The union hiring hall served another of the union's social objectives—wider distribution of scarce work among its members. Wider distribution of jobs was seen by union leaders as fair and also preserved a larger active membership.

The fifth element, competence, was a neutral to positive condition in the U.S. case, in my opinion. I allow that shipping-industry participants in Japan and Norway—both countries were innovative socially as well as technically—may have been better equipped with the knowledge and skills relevant to managing work-innovation processes than their counterparts in the United States, but I cannot argue that any of the other five countries were better endowed than the United States. I should note, for example, that U.S. shipowners pioneered major innovations in offering intermodal services—containers transported by rail, truck, and ship.

The analysis of the factors affecting the prospects for innovation in the United States suggests a number of contrasts and comparisons. Japan and the United States had the two highest crewing costs, but the similarity ended there. The high national economic importance of shipping for Japan contrasted with its modest importance for the United States. In Japanese shipping, the single trade union, unified employer groups, and existence of a constructive climate at the sector level for articulating and integrating stakeholder interests stood in contrast to American shipping, with its highly fragmented union structure, several shipowners' associations, and adversarial relations among labor, shipowners, and government. The U.S. institutions were most like those of the United Kingdom (low on noninnovative change) and Denmark (low on innovation).

The United States was also distinguished as the country with the largest percentage of ships owned by nationals but registered under foreign flags. Japan and West Germany were also high relative to the rest. Japan was a high innovator, West Germany a moderate innovator, and the United States a low innovator, a diversity of performance that discourages us from drawing too much significance from this factor by itself.

The factor in which the U.S. shipping industry was unique among the eight countries was in the nature and effects of the operating differential subsidy and requirements for U.S. shippers to utilize U.S.-flag vessels to transport certain goods. The effects of these provisions appeared to be significant in explaining the lack of staffing reductions by conventional or innovative means. Another unique aspect of the U.S. context for innovation was the seventeen-year average age of its fleet, compared with seven to ten years for the other seven countries. The fleet age was largely a consequence of the other U.S. conditions, but the lack of new construction did have its own effect in further depressing change and innovation.

Let us consider the overall explanations for intercountry differences (see Table 10-1). Weighting the three components equally produces a rank order generally consistent with the actual observed differences in innovation. However, it would lead one to expect somewhat worse performance by the United Kingdom than was actually observed. It would also fail to fully anticipate Holland's strong pattern of innovation and Sweden's somewhat weaker pattern. The chapter-by-chapter analysis suggested that institutional differences were more influential than either economic incentives, social attitudes, or both of these combined. When the institutional ranking is double weighted, then the three components combined produce an ordering in which Holland's position is more understandable.

Why Some Innovations Diffused More Widely than Others

The comprehensive model embraces all four types of innovations and involves changes in the roles and relationships of ratings, officers, and shore staff. In practice, the comprehensive flexible organization was still the exception in our example. Even in the three countries where it guided innovation activities, some specific innovations that comprise the model were more widely diffused than others. Differences observed in the rates of diffusion of specific innovations include the following.

1.   Continuity of both employment and assignment was more widespread for officers than ratings.
2.   Role flexibility was less widespread among officers than ratings.
3.   Delegation/participation trends (which empower employees) affected more officers than ratings.
4.   Role flexibility for officers was less widespread than delegation for officers. In contrast, role flexibility for ratings diffused more widely than participation by ratings.

How does the theory help us explain these differences? I found that one or two of the five facilitating elements applied more than the others to certain types of innovation (see Table 10-2). I discuss below how diffusion of particular innovations is explained by patterns of salience of economic necessity, social approval, and institutional arrangements. The strength of the model, which includes a recognition of the interdependence among the specific innovations, is by definition salient to all of them, and the

Table 10-2. Salience of Enabling Factors for Diffusion of
Specific Shipboard Innovations.

Specific Innovations	Enabling Factors		
	Economic Necessity	Social Context	Institutional Arrangements
Role flexibility (ratings)	xx	x	xxx
Role flexibility (officers)	xx	x	xxx
Participation (ratings)	x	xx	
Delegation (officers)	xxx	xx	
Employment continuity			
Ratings	xx	x	xx
Officers	xxx	x	xx
Assignment continuity			
Ratings	x	x	x
Officers	xxx	x	x
Equalized perks	xx	xx	x
Social integration	x	xxx	x

Note: x = low salience; xx = medium; xxx = high.

particular interdependencies (for example, between continuity, role
flexibility, and participation) have been emphasized repeatedly
throughout this book. Similarly, individual competence in
managing the process was relevant to implementation of all the
innovations but probably most relevant to delegation/participa-
tion. Competence was more relevant to role flexibility and social
integration than to continuity policies and equalized perks because
the latter are more straightforward administrative changes. We now
turn to an analysis of the four differences listed above.

1. The greater stability of employment and assignment
sought by shipowners for officers more than for ratings is a direct
reflection of the greater expected economic benefit from the former.
The social attitudes toward the innovation were not strong, and
they did not vary much between the two groups. There were not
important institutional differences affecting ratings versus officers.

2. Role flexibility for both ratings and officers seems to be
more sensitive to institutional and economic factors and less
sensitive to social attitudes (see Table 10-2). Social attitudes can be
ruled out as an explanation for less officer role flexibility because
the attitudes of ratings and officers toward the innovation were

similar for both groups, with initial mild opposition. The economic rationale for shipowners to pursue role flexibility with both groups was equally strong.

Two other conditions must explain the slower diffusion of officer flexibility: (1) the slightly weaker economic incentives for officers to accept role flexibility and (2) the somewhat more fragmented union structures representing officers. The economic disincentives for officers to accept role flexibility outweighed their incentives. The officers' unions opposed role flexibility as a step toward heavier work loads and fewer officer billets. If costs forced the shipowners to flag out, they usually would still use some nationals in their officer billets. In contrast, the ratings had to be concerned not only about fewer billets per ship but also about reducing costs to avoid reregistration of ships, because the rating jobs on FOC ships were invariably lost to foreign labor. Thus, the ratings' employment incentives were slightly more aligned with those of shipowners.

Officers were more often represented by multiple unions than were ratings. Only in the United States and Denmark were engine-room and deck ratings represented by different unions. In Denmark this may have been the decisive factor in constraining role flexibility among ratings. In most countries the common union made institutional consensus about role flexibility much easier to achieve. In contrast, in half of the countries engineers and deck officers were represented by different unions. In the two countries in which officer role flexibility was implemented, Holland and Japan, deck officers and engineers were members of the same union.

In summary, not only were economic necessity and institutional arrangement the more salient factors for role flexibility, but also they varied significantly between ratings and officers in terms of how favorable they were for this type of innovation.

3. Delegation/participation affected greater numbers of officers than ratings. These innovations are similar in two respects. First, the empowering of middle and lower levels of the organization was opposed in both cases by the groups that were expected to share power—the shore staff, whose functions would be delegated to officers, and the officers, whose decisions would be open to rating influence. Second, as shown in Table 10-2, the institutional

framework had virtually no relevance for either form of power sharing. (Paradoxically, the importance of institutional factors may in this study be understood better by examining innovations that are not subject to institutional approval.) The difference between them results from a particularly interesting interaction between economic and social motivations.

Consider first shipboard management—the delegation of authority from shore to ships' officers. It was driven primarily by the expectations of economic gain; it would attract better talent, motivate officers, and produce better decisions. But the potential gains were not universally expected. We can infer they were expected by large numbers of shipowners in Holland, Norway, and the United Kingdom; a few in Sweden and the United States; one in Denmark; and none in Japan and West Germany. Whether the economic gains were expected depended on the shipowners' social beliefs—beliefs about officers' responses to greater autonomy, responsibility, and influence.

A slightly different mix of economic and social motivations affected the trend toward rating participation in work planning. With the one exception of Japan, shipowners could see less direct economic benefit from enlarging the influence of ratings than from expanding the autonomy of officers. In the absence of direct experiences, ratings themselves often were skeptical about participation, while officers were usually enthusiastic about the idea of shipboard management. With experience, both groups tended to become positively disposed.

Thus, I conclude that delegation to officers occurred more frequently than participation involving ratings for two reasons. Economics was the major driving force for change, and the delegation practice offered more apparent economical benefit. Social approval by the recipients of additional influence, although a weaker force, also was more uniformly positive from the outset in the case of officers.

4. The conditions already discussed explain why role flexibility was less common than delegation among officers, while the opposite was true for ratings. Shipowners had an economic rationale for considering officer delegation and role flexibility. However, they found officers favorably disposed toward delegation

for social reasons and opposed to role flexibility for economic reasons. Moreover, owners confronted no institutional constraints on delegation and major constraints on role flexibility, involving union and government approval and changes in the curricula of maritime academies.

The fact that among ratings role flexibility was more common than participation can be explained by the fact that the economic advantages to shipowners were obvious for rating role flexibility but not for rating involvement in work planning. Moreover, the economic implications of role flexibility for ratings were mixed, and the institutional barriers to role flexibility were less difficult to overcome because of the relatively unified structures for ratings.

To review, we find that the progress on some innovations depended much more heavily on one or two of the components, and sometimes did not involve all three of them. Economic necessity affected all of the innovations, but while it was a strong influence for role flexibility, continuity policies, delegation to shipboard management, and equalized perks, it played a weaker role in participative planning and social integration. Social motives provided only weak support for or opposition to role flexibility, employment continuity, and assignment stability. It was a strong factor in the officers' support for any proposal for shipboard management; moreover, social beliefs of the shipowner determined whether it was offered in the first place. Social motivations also were strong—stronger than economic motivations—in participative planning and social integration. Institutional arrangements were crucial for the cornerstone innovation of role flexibility, important for employment stability, and relevant for continuity policies and social integration. Institutions were not relevant at all for shipboard management and participative planning.

Postscript: Developments After 1983

After 1983 the world shipping industry continued in a state of overcapacity, with strong downward pressure on freight rates affecting all of the countries studied. Japan followed the trajectory of change established in prior years, and the patterns of work innovation observed in Europe in the early 1980s generally continued through 1986. Although the United States remained in the low-innovation cluster, its situation became more promising. Several American shipowners initiated efforts to reduce staffing by conventional methods, and two others began experimenting with advanced staffing concepts. Two developments help explain this new activity: decreased subsidies and increased exposure to the European and Japanese staffing developments.

The largest U.S. liner companies—Sealand, U.S. Lines, and Lykes, each with two to three dozen ships—negotiated sharply reduced crews on their newly constructed ships. Instead of normal crew sizes in the high thirties, they were seeking crews in the low twenties. They encountered difficulties, but the commitment of American shipowners to this magnitude of change was itself an important first step. They were not yet prepared to introduce role flexibility or other shipboard organization changes.

Two other U.S. companies had attempted to introduce innovations with a view toward comprehensive change of the type observed in Europe. One firm was the American President Lines (APL), the fourth-largest liner company, with about two dozen ships. When the APL management agreed to purchase two modern containerships, it decided these ships would be "projects" to try new shipboard concepts and to provide an experience base for subsequent change throughout the entire APL fleet. APL management envisioned intra- and interdepartmental role flexibility, shipboard management teams, crew participation, crew assignment continuity, and social integration. The goals of these changes were reduced crew sizes of about twenty-one, high crew morale, and safe ships.

American President Lines secured approval for role flexibility from each of the six unions affected and began the project in 1984. The strategy for achieving consensus among the many stakeholder groups followed the best practice observed in Europe. Defining its projects as "participative action-research," APL acknowledged that "objective-setting, planning, and evaluation will have to involve a number of parties (management, unions, government, and the employees affected)." The design and implementation of the projects included the formation of a steering committee of senior management and union officials, an internal company committee to deal with the operational aspects of the project ships, and participative structures on the two vessels themselves "through which all crew members play a role in planning and evaluating the experimental changes."

The sequence of changes in APL staffing practices was distinctly American. In almost all other countries, rating role flexibility had been conceived as the cornerstone change and had either preceded or accompanied any other changes targeted at ratings. APL's strategy was to introduce delegation and participation first, accompanied by progressive increases in continuity and social integration. When these changes had promoted a high-commitment shipboard culture, role flexibility would be introduced. This sequence conforms to the prevailing practice in other U.S. industries.

The APL projects at implementation encountered problems similar to those encountered in many northwestern European trials. For example, the company achieved stability among officer personnel on the project ships but continued to experience continual turnover among ratings. Therefore, officers, who themselves were learning new roles and procedures, had to train a fresh complement of ratings for the new system on each voyage. Nevertheless, the overall progress of the trials was sufficiently encouraging that it strengthened management's commitment to the program of change.

A second company, Pacific Gulf Marine (PGM), embarked on a two-ship innovation project in 1985. PGM had five ships and planned to expand its fleet. Its initial plan placed more explicit emphasis than that of APL on role flexibility and other work-assignment patterns. However, after the initial voyages of its two trial ships, the *Eagle* and the *Condor*, management concluded that more preliminary work was required to develop participative processes before role flexibility could be effective.

Chapter 11

Dynamics of Innovative Capabilities
Implications for Theory and Diagnosis

Chapter Ten concluded that the propositions about the capacity for innovative change helped explain why some countries were more innovative than others, and why some specific work innovations diffused more widely than others. Now we turn the tables and ask in what way the shipping findings support and elaborate the theory outlined in Chapter Two, examining the role of the five components of innovative change, their internal dynamics, and the effects on them of external forces. Wherever appropriate, I will note how the findings and the underlying theoretical concepts support or fail to support previous studies.[1] I conclude the chapter with a discussion that extends the approach to diverse social innovations in the computer industry.

Support for the Five Basic Components

I proposed that the capability of a social system (plant, company, industry, or country) to develop and diffuse organizational innovations that help it compete depends on a combination of five interacting components. While the findings support the five elements taken as a whole, they provide varying levels of support for the influence of particular elements in this setting.

1. *Sound models:* The shipping study could not have provided stronger support for the advantages of a sound model. In the six countries with moderate or high innovation records, the directions of change were remarkably similar, but the guiding models varied in their strength as I had defined it. The more comprehensive and integrative models were more robust than the limited rating model and were associated with the more successful diffusion records.

2. *Social context:* While social values seemed to play a role in relation to the diffusion of specific innovations, they did not influence decisively the overall patterns of innovation. I found only a moderate correspondence between the countries' innovation records and the initial support for the innovations provided by their social contexts. I found as much evidence of a tendency for innovation activity to influence social assessments of the innovation, a direction of influence discussed below.

3. *Economic necessity:* Economic incentives for innovative change in shipping included many separate forms of market pressure as well as other conditions, such as longer planning horizons, that enabled investment in innovation activity. The composite of economic incentives was slightly more helpful than the social context in explaining the innovation rankings. Some specific findings were especially interesting. The most obvious form of market pressure, the size of the labor cost disadvantage, did not by itself help explain the eight countries' records, nor did any of the following factors: flagging-out patterns, government assistance, and new-construction rates. Each factor did, however, exercise an important influence in one or a few specific countries. National economic importance of the shipping industry was a significant consideration for two of the three high innovators, Norway and Japan. However, for the third, Holland, national economic importance was low. One economic factor that had considerable explanatory power was the introduction of policy inducements for labor to accept change. An alignment of economic incentives for

shipowners and the union appeared to be more important than the magnitude of the incentive for the shipowner.

4. *Institutions:* The proposition about institutions was strongly supported by comparisons of countries and of specific innovations. Institutional forums influenced learning from the innovation process, for instance, by providing mechanisms for monitoring pioneer efforts. Institutions determined the net capacity for consensus, which results from the requirements for agreement compared with the difficulty of achieving it. As expected, innovation was promoted by less stringent consensus requirements, for example, when shipowners could experiment without detailed agreement by labor and government. Innovation was also assisted when consensus was made easier to achieve by such factors as unified labor and cohesive employer associations. In fact, no other single factor influenced the capacity for innovative change more than fragmentation of the union structure, ranging from a single seafaring union in Japan to eleven in the United States.

The findings just summarized are about the effect of institutions on the innovation process. Institutional arrangements affected innovation by other routes as well. Apart from complicating the innovation process, internally fragmented groups and adversarial relations among groups also injected political concerns that in some cases reinforced union opposition to particular innovations, for example, role flexibility and regular company employment. Fragmentation and adversarialism also prevented government and employer policies that could enhance the incentives for change.

In countries with unified and mutually reliant shipping institutions, these institutional patterns had developed because social beliefs made them legitimate. In the United States beliefs in individualism, limited government, and arm's-length relations among labor, management, and government acted to inhibit institutional arrangements in shipping that would enable work innovations.

The strong influence of shipping institutions lends credence to the recent resurgence of interest in institutional factors among political scientists, reported by March and Olsen and cited in Chapter Two. The findings about the constructive influence of

internal unity, problem-solving forums, and cooperative orientations among shipping institutions on the adaptive process reinforce
and extend the findings of Katzenstein, Reich, and Badaracco summarized in Chapter Two. My findings, which took the national
industry as the primary unit of analysis, are also remarkably
consistent with the results of the studies by Kanter and Pettigrew
(also reviewed in Chapter Two), which focused on innovation and
change activities inside the corporate organization. The disabling
effects of fragmentation in shipping institutions and the adversarial
relations among them are directly analogous to the way innovative
behavior is inhibited by organizational segmentation within
corporations.

5. *Competence:* Without the comparative data to determine
whether the countries that had posted better innovation records
were also those endowed with more competence in managing
social-innovation processes, I nonetheless found an abundance of
anecdotal evidence that knowledge and skill often made an
important difference in the success of specific innovative efforts.
Moreover, the findings indicate that if the willingness to innovate
is present and leads to action, the specific knowledge and skills will
develop with experience. I will discuss this feedback effect of
experience on competence later.

The findings of this study help place some earlier studies on
work innovation in a different perspective. Prior research,
including my own, usually has emphasized the importance of
competent choices in managing the change process.[2] Yet the
shipping study could explain differences in the innovation records
almost completely without reference to any differences in the skill
of managing the process. This raises the question whether earlier
studies may have ignored the effects of certain contextual and
structural factors. In any event, it suggests that while process
competencies of the type described in Chapter Nine may play a
more decisive role in explaining the amount of change in specific
plants and companies where change is initiated, this type of factor
becomes less important when attempting to understand broader
differences, for example, when comparing countries participating
in the same world industry or different industries in the same
country.

Why Components Have More or Less Influence. Why were a few of the components proposed in Chapter Two much more influential than others? Institutional differences in particular played the heavyweight role in this industry and prior social attitudes and beliefs about the innovation only a minor role. However, the relative weightings of the five explanatory elements, which appear consistent with the overall innovation records of countries, cannot be generalized blindly. Even within the shipping industry, different relative weightings are required to account for the observations that some specific shipboard innovations diffused more widely than others. For example, whereas both economic and social motives were required to explain the fact that delegation/participation affected greater numbers of officers than ratings, only economic incentives were needed to explain the finding that continuity of vessel assignment was practiced more extensively among officers than among ratings. There is even less reason to expect the relative weightings found in this study to hold for other innovations in other industries. Based on the shipping study, the actual weight of a component appears to be determined by two of its attributes: its salience and its variability.

The first attribute is the inherent salience of the component for the innovation: Does the innovation require a complex and demanding change process and therefore become sensitive to differences in skills? Does the innovation by its nature have strong, moderate, or weak implications for economic stakes of the stakeholder groups? Does the innovation require institutional decision making? At how many levels? For example, in an institutional setting with fewer rules negotiated by labor and legislated by government than I found in the shipping industry, the institutional factor would be less important. In sum, the higher the salience of each component, the more likely it is to play a differentiating role.

The second attribute is the variability of the component in the population in question. Does the strength of economic incentives vary from country to country? How much actual variation is there in social attitudes, institutional forms, and competence? For example, I found more variation in the form of shipping institutions among the eight countries than in their social attitudes toward the innovations. In explaining different diffusion records of companies within one country's shipping industry, the institutional forms would vary less, and social attitudes would vary more. Components that vary over a wider range are more likely to explain different patterns of innovation.

Why Country, Industry, and Enterprise Levels Vary in Influence. The shipping study also confirms the need for the explanatory theory to consider conditions at all three levels of social analysis—country, industry, and enterprise. The social attitudes and beliefs of a company's seafaring employees were shaped by societal trends, shipping-industry practices, and the philosophies of individual shipowners. The overall economic necessity for a shipowner was influenced by national wage levels, the industry's subsidies, and the options the company exercised in hiring foreign labor and in reregistering vessels to flags of convenience. The institutional context within which a shipowner must initiate change included the societal pattern of relationships among unions, management, and government and the regulations covering employment relations. It also included the industry-specific regulations, labor unions, and management associations. Finally, it included company-level union-management agreements and relationships.

The variations in the relative importance of the three levels depend on both the industry and the innovation in question. The industry level—the intermediate level—was extremely important in shipping because industrywide institutions and economic policies targeted at the industry were highly salient to certain work innovations, and because these industry-specific conditions varied significantly among the eight countries. Seafaring unions were organized on an industry basis, shipowners' associations were active at the industry level, specialized government agencies dealt with shipping matters, and training for seafarers was provided by industry-level institutions. Moreover, the government targeted specific assistance to the shipping industry in many forms, ranging from research and development to construction subsidies. Finally, and most importantly, industry-specific laws and regulations had a pervasive effect on shipboard practices.

The industry level varies widely in importance among U.S. industries, due in part to the organization of labor. All organized workers belong to the same union in autos and basic steel but not in aircraft manufacturing and chemical processing. Collective bargaining traditionally has been conducted on an industrywide basis in steel, coal, and trucking. It has taken place on an enterprise or plant level in autos, rubber, and electrical equipment.

Insights into the Internal Dynamics of Innovative Capability

Two types of findings in shipping illustrate how the relationships among and between the components and innovative results affect the capability for innovative change.

One type of finding relates to influences among the five elements—guiding models, social approval, economic necessity, institutional forms, and individual competence. I proposed that the choice of models would be explained in part by the pattern of motivational forces, an idea that received only modest empirical support. Translating this idea into the specifics of the shipping study, I expected that where values were more sympathetic to the socially sensitive innovations, namely, participation and social integration, the models that emerged to guide practices would incorporate them. Sweden and Holland were the major anomalies. Sweden should have adopted the comprehensive model, but it did not. Holland did but should not have, according to the logic of this proposition and the data. I am not inclined to abandon the proposition; rather, I simply acknowledge that in this instance prior social assessments of particular innovations were a weak determinant of the content of the guiding vision compared to other factors.

I also proposed that the development of strong models is influenced by aspects of the innovation process. Specifically, a process that allows multiple stakeholders to exercise influence, and that is capable of considering social as well as economic effectiveness criteria, is more likely to produce stronger models. Indeed, I did find that the emergence of the more comprehensive shipboard innovations could be systematically related to aspects of the innovation process, most notably the consensus capability of a country's maritime institutions.

I found another important influence—the influence of institutions on the development of economic incentives for change. The analysis of economic necessity identified favorable labor policies in just three countries. The next chapter, on institutions, found that these same three shipping industries had the most favorable institutional structures and relationships, helping to explain why the labor policies had developed.

A second type of dynamic relationship confirmed by the analysis is the interaction between the outcome I was trying to explain, the amount of innovation, and two of the explanatory factors: social attitudes toward the new work forms and competence in managing the innovation process.

Initial social attitudes by officers and ratings toward several innovations—specifically, role flexibility, participative planning, and social integration—tended to change substantially on the basis of actual experience when these innovations were part of a comprehensive change in the shipboard organization, but not when they were introduced as separate policy changes. Holland provided the strongest evidence on this point.

The tendency for initial social attitudes and beliefs to change with experience is extremely important. Even when initial attitudes are negative, if the model is sound (especially if it is integrative), and if the process is managed competently (especially participatively), then participants will have an opportunity to discover and influence the ways in which the innovative organization serves their needs.

The parties learned through trial and error a number of lessons about the management of innovative change, including, for example, the importance of participation in the planning of change. The U.K.'s Sealife Programme offered the most detailed evidence of experience as teacher. In addition, the Work Research Institute in Norway showed that competent and credible third parties can play a key role in the management of the innovation process.

This important reciprocal and dynamic relationship among social beliefs, organizational forms, and experience is allowed for but not emphasized in the theory proposed in Chapter Two. Nor has it been given sufficient recognition in previous studies making cross-cultural comparisons of managers and organizational forms, including the classic studies, cited in Chapter Two, by Dore, Hofstede, and Laurent.

Understanding Environmental Trends and Metacompetence

The shipping study confirmed that the economic, social, and institutional components and hence the innovative capability itself could be modified by two types of external forces: environmental trends and the exercise of metacompetence.

Chapter Three showed that the specific innovations were responsive to three general trends since the late 1960s—social, economic, and technological. The economic trends involved labor shortages followed by cost pressures. The social trends were toward participation and egalitarianism. The technological trend made smaller crews feasible and increased the technical sophistication of ships, both of which intensified the economic and social benefits of implementing work innovations.

By coincidence, I believe, labor market shortages before 1973 and labor cost pressures after that had directionally similar effects on these particular innovations, especially in the pioneering countries. The particular sequence of these two pressures helped promote innovation. Labor shortages sensitized the shipowners in some countries to the social aspects of shipboard reforms, and many of the owners continued to take these aspects into account even after the major driver of change became cost reduction.

Several findings reported in Chapters Five through Nine support the idea that metacompetence can enhance the capacity for innovative change. Some contextual changes exemplify this strategic form of competence. The policies that cushioned labor from employment effects in return for its support for shipboard organizational reform were a policy innovation. The tripartite-plus-public mechanism for planning and implementing the Japanese modernization program was an institutional innovation. The Ship-Meets-Ship network for supporting change at the grass-roots level in Norway was another institutional innovation.

Similarly, the decentralization of some of the decision making about shipboard organizational matters, from the industry to the company level in many countries during the 1970s, was an adaptive reform. These innovations and reforms were explicitly designed to change or elaborate the context for work-innovation activity.

The Framework as a Policy Tool: Going Beyond Work Reform

I emphasized in Chapters One and Two that the framework is both a theory and a policy tool; that it applies not only to distressed industries such as shipping, autos, and steel, but also to growth industries; and that its relevance goes beyond work reform to a wide range of social and organizational innovations.

The broader range of social and organizational innovations, which can help American industries become more competitive in the world economy, include the structuring of new long-term relationships between manufacturers and select suppliers; new forms of cooperative research and development and technology transfer among U.S. firms, who also compete with each other; new forms of relationship between industry and academic institutions to enhance the relevance of research and training to America's competitiveness; and new corporate strategies and relationships with the financial institutions to permit longer-term planning and investment, comparable to the practices of other world competitors. Some innovations may require government to play a catalytic role and may involve the government in new relationships with industry and labor.[3]

The computer industry, one of the most strategic industries in the U.S. economy, illustrates some of these requirements for innovative change. It also provides a basis for summarizing how the framework can be used as a general policy tool for improving the innovative capabilities of this and other industries.

Computer companies must learn how to compete increasingly on a cost and reliability basis as well as how to continue to maintain a technological edge over increasingly inventive world competitors. This requires innovation affecting several external relations as well as internal organizational changes.

First, companies need to learn how to manage the cooperative industry-level research venture, the Macroelectronics and Computer Technology Corporation, involving twenty-one U.S. companies. This cooperative venture was a response to a collaborative effort in Japan among five mainframe computer manufacturers and the Ministry of International Trade and Industry. What can the U.S. computer industry learn from the Japanese venture and from similarly inspired efforts in other countries and in other industries in this country? Which economic forces, social attitudes, and institutions help and which hinder effective management of this cooperative industry effort?

Second, the electronics companies individually and collectively must address the shortages in the industry of electronic engineers, computer scientists and engineers, software programmers, and technicians. Addressing these shortages may involve change within academic institutions and in their relationship to companies or to a specific industry. It will also involve innovations in company policies for recruiting, organizing, assigning, compensating, developing, and advancing talent. How much capacity does the industry have to develop innovations at the industry level and to develop and diffuse effective practices at the company level?

Third, many computer companies are finding that traditional arm's-length, short-term relationships with many suppliers are no longer appropriate. They are entering into closer, more complex, and longer-term relationships with one or a few suppliers. These relationships involve new interdependencies in their internal information systems, market intelligence systems, research and development expenditures, and manpower development programs. Clearly, these new intimate forms of relationship between separate firms require new attitudes and skills; differently formulated commercial objectives; and the invention of new techniques, structures, and processes. How much capability does the industry have for developing these new solutions and diffusing them? What factors enhance the capability and what factors limit it?

Diagnosis as an Aspect of Metacompetence. Consider a policymaker concerned about the computer industry who perceives a gap between the need for the social innovations, mentioned above, and practice. The sense of a problem or an opportunity may be triggered by any of a number of comparisons—for example, comparing U.S. practice with the developments in Europe, Japan, and South Korea; comparing practices in the target industry with progressive developments in other U.S. sectors; or comparing practices in the average company with developments in the leading U.S. computer companies.

The diagnosis involves a search backward from outcomes to causal elements (from right to left on the diagram of the theory) presented in Chapter Two (see Figure 2-1). The framework helps the policymaker or policy analyst ask the right questions. Where are the bottleneck factors? Is there inadequate motivation to change organizational forms, relationships, or policies? Is there a lack of viable alternatives to the current ones? Is there a lack of capabilities for managing change?

If the net motivation is inadequate, why? Weak competitive pressure? Policies or practices that protect all U.S. companies (or the leading ones) from market forces? Options that enable them to escape or minimize effects of pressures, such as going overseas or entering into joint ventures? Social beliefs that are arrayed against the innovation, such as individualism? Lack of alignment of economic and/or social motivations of the stakeholders?

If there are not viable alternatives to the current organization, relationships, or policies, why? If some experimentation has occurred but has not proved as effective as expected, is the innovation too limited, not incorporating changes in policy required to support the focal innovation? Does the innovation represent more a compromise than an integration of stakeholders' interests? If the current vision of the industry is too limited, is this fact explained by the prevailing social beliefs of stakeholders or by the limited capacity of the existing institutional arrangements to deal with more complex innovation models?

If there appear to be generally adequate economic incentives and reconcilable social attitudes on the part of the stakeholders, and if there appears to be an adequate vision to guide innovation but an inability to promote the innovation processes, is it because of a lack of strong, credible sponsorship, a lack of the requisite consensus to enable progress to be made, or a lack of information and other aspects of social technology transfer? Do the identified deficiencies relate to constraints born of institutional arrangements or to an absence of knowledge and skills relevant to the management of the social-innovation process?

The preliminary phases of the diagnosis identify the problematic areas, and the subsequent phases investigate those areas in more detail.

Strategic Action Taking as an Aspect of Metacompetence. The discussions of both the explanatory theory and the framework as a diagnostic tool conclude with consideration of the same topic— the action role played by metacompetence. It is not only necessary to call on this type of competence to explain some past improvements observed in the capacity for innovative change; it is a requisite capacity for a social system if its members are actively to manage the future.

The comprehensive diagnosis outlined above is half of metacompetence. Strategic action to alter the context of an industry is the second, more important, half. The theory can also be used to plan how to strengthen the elements that enhance the innovative capability of the industry and modify the ones that limit the capability.

Once a diagnostic understanding of the role of economic, social, institutional, and competence factors promoting or inhibiting innovation has been achieved, then the inhibiting conditions can be analyzed in terms of whether they offer action levers. Which of them can be modified? By whom? Within what time frame can they be modified and have an effect on innovation behavior? How much leverage will they have? What combinations of changes in economic incentives, social values, institutional arrangements, and knowledge and skills will be sufficient to promote the innovation required?

Metacompetence includes mastery of the policy-changing processes, especially those affecting the strength and symmetry of economic necessity for the stakeholders. It includes such matters as changing the forms of employment assurances from those that weaken employees' interest in adaptive change to ones that strengthen it. If government assistance or protection is blunting the incentives for companies to adapt, the task is to modify government policies so that they sharpen the incentives. Metacompetence also includes changing the legislated rules of the game. For example, if antitrust rules are preventing cooperative research and development among American companies, the task is to review and modify the rules when it is in the public interest to do so.

Metacompetence includes the social skills to examine prevailing beliefs and to bring them into line with changing realities, as well as the social norms to support the examination and the change. This applies, for example, to beliefs about what distribution of power and authority produces the most effective work units. It also applies to beliefs about the appropriateness of adversarial relations between employees and management and about strictly arm's-length relations among American firms in the same industry. Metacompetence also includes the ability to create experiences and mechanisms by which the new ideas that challenge prevailing beliefs can themselves be tested and objectively evaluated. Thus, experiments and mechanisms for monitoring and assessing trials as well as the norm of suspended judgment support this strategic competence.

Perhaps most importantly, strategic competence includes adaptive institutions. Institutions, whether business, labor, or government entities, tend to take on a life of their own, developing many self-preserving processes. Metacompetence involves avoiding these tendencies. It is based on a view of institutions as problem-solving devices, and it therefore seeks to change the missions and structures of institutions where major shifts occur in the problems that need to be solved. The ability to invent and modify institutional arrangements appears to be the most crucial aspect of strategic competence because, as the shipping study shows, institutions not only can affect the innovation process directly, but they also influence the types of economic policies that are enacted and the models that emerge to guide innovation.

Obviously, any particular policymaker—whether company, government, or labor—will be able to influence some subset of the factors and not others. A key implementation task in almost every case is to engage multiple stakeholders in the diagnosis-and-planning process. Each stakeholder can add some bit to the strategic competence of the system in which they are members.

Metacompetence is the ability to diagnose the many components of a social system's capacity to develop and diffuse work reforms. It also is the ability to bring about change in the institutions, policies, and social beliefs that limit the system's capacity to innovate. In the next chapter I discuss in more detail some major aspects of the context for innovative change in American industry that must be managed.

Chapter 12

Guidelines for Planning and Implementing Innovative Change in American Industry

Chapter One discussed a general concern about improving the innovative capacity of American industry, reviewing in particular a need to accelerate the development and diffusion of work innovations already initiated in such industries as automobiles and steel. The subsequent review of shipping identified a similar need in U.S. shipping. This chapter returns to a direct consideration of innovation in these and other domestic sectors.

The focus is on managing the context for social innovation, in effect, the exercise of metacompetence. I identify the strategic action issues requiring the attention of the leaders of American institutions with a stake in the country's competitiveness.

The emphasis here on managing the context does not minimize the importance of managing the innovation process itself, as described in Chapter Nine. Certainly, if innovative efforts are to succeed, they must be based on wise tactical choices to sponsor change, engineer consensus, and transfer information relevant to specific innovations. However, I conclude the book by treating the strategic tasks of making policy innovations and institutional reforms for two reasons. First, choices about policies and institutional forms can make significant differences. Second, the strong influence of contextual factors is less well understood and has received less attention in previous discussions of the development and diffusion of work reforms.

The idea of context is relative, depending on the scope of the system being considered. Throughout the book, I have emphasized the capacity for change of an entire national industry, such as the Norwegian shipping industry. I have claimed that the concepts could be applied to discuss the innovative capacity of a particular company within an industry or even a plant within a company. The discussion in this chapter includes action implications for policymakers concerned about a particular enterprise and policymakers concerned about the competitiveness of an entire industry. Those who make or influence policy can include business executives, labor officials, and government officials who are concerned about the economic health of a particular industry.

After discussing certain types of desirable changes in the motivational and institutional contexts, I will treat their implications for the prevailing assumptions in the United States about the appropriate roles of management, labor, and government. These subjects are interrelated. The development of policies to provide more favorable incentives often depends on first structuring a more enabling institutional framework. Institutional reform depends on modifications in the underlying premises about the roles of different groups in society.

Managing the Motivational Context

Many motivational forces are better than fewer ones. We cannot rely on raw market forces alone, even when they are powerful, to provide sufficient incentives for change. Leadership in government, management, labor, and academia must articulate the need for change. More importantly, they must devise ways to translate the market pressures into positive economic incentives for all of the stakeholders and invent means to respond to other independent social forces in the interest of adaptive change.

Harnessing Social as Well as Economic Motives. Successful innovative efforts in many shipping countries and in many U.S. industries were effective in part because they harnessed social as well as economic motives. Often their planners took advantage of the coincidence of two types of crises or environmental threats and developed reforms responsive to both.

In shipping, the manpower shortage that prompted European shipowners to enhance employment conditions in seafaring was followed shortly by pressures to increase labor productivity. Fortunately, some means for making seafaring more attractive to recruits were among those required to improve productivity. Unfortunately, only a few shipowners and their union counterparts perceived and acted promptly on the opportunity presented by the close historical sequence of these two types of pressure in the mid 1970s. It is interesting to note that Japan's shipping industry was not among the early pioneers, although the Japanese showed an extraordinary capacity for innovative change once they achieved industry-level recognition of the problem and opportunities for shipboard change.

In American manufacturing and service industries, a similar sequence of crises created equally advantageous conditions for social innovation. In the late 1960s and early 1970s a crisis of worker confidence in management developed. At stake was the very legitimacy of management's authority. Influenced by the same forces that created rebellions in urban areas and disruptions on college campuses, workers increasingly defied supervisory authority and acted in ways that subverted the interests of their employers. They also grew increasingly unresponsive to the union establishment. The disaffection itself was dubbed by the media the "blue-collar blues and white-collar woes." The constructive responses to the disaffection, often called quality-of-work-life (QWL) activities, helped meet the rising expectations of the work force for personal dignity and direct influence. In doing this, QWL helped restore legitimacy to management.

Before American industry had proceeded far along the track of dealing with this crisis of confidence in management, it was faced with an even more ominous threat—formidable competition from foreign manufacturers. The special opportunity created by the combination of two problems is described by Sam Camens of the United Steelworkers of America.

> From its inception the steel industry has operated as an autocratic industrial institution. Simply put: workers were hired to do exactly as ordered by their foremen. No questions, no back talk. A good worker was one who showed up every day on time, did as he was told, and did not complain. Thus, a steelworker learned quickly that he was just a check number, hired to labor, with no right to use his experience, mind, or desires to be involved in any decision-making process on matters on which he has knowledge. . . .
>
> The problem has become more acute due to the fact that steelworkers hired in the last two decades are part of a new generation with changing cultural attitudes. Asking more out of life than just a well-paying job that strips them of their self-identity, they seek satisfaction for personal input and a feeling of having contributed something more than just their guts and sweat in the work process.
>
> Ironically, the present steel crisis gave the Union an opportunity to take an important step forward. Steel management finally concluded that it could not successfully compete in a new market stressing quality and plant efficiency without the active assistance of its employees. And it could not use autocratic methods to make people conscious of the need for quality and productivity.[1]

Similarly, AT&T and the Communications Workers of America (CWA) both became concerned about morale problems and high levels of stress among workers in the late 1960s and early 1970s. AT&T management was concerned because these workplace attitudes affected the quality of service delivered to subscribers and complicated its ability to manage the vast corporate organization. The leaders of CWA were concerned because the membership was increasingly agitated by job pressures related to new technology, close supervision, and electronic monitoring, problems the union leaders found they could not handle effectively through traditional negotiation and grievance procedures. In the early 1970s AT&T created a Work Relationship Group in its headquarters to analyze and address the morale problems; the CWA established a Job Pressures Committee to study these problems. The two parties agreed in 1980 negotiations to establish a QWL mechanism to jointly work "to improve the quality of work life of employees and enhance the effectiveness of the organization."

The developments in steel and in AT&T occurred after GM had pioneered its joint effort. Irving Bluestone, head of the GM department of the UAW, was the first labor leader to perceive in the problems of the early 1970s the opportunity for the labor movement to make the workplace more democratic.

While the duality of social and economic motivations has enabled progress in the situations cited, work is required to broaden the motivational forces. Even in industries where change is well under way, the vast majority of workers, union officials, and managers have not yet been enlisted. And many of them will not be enlisted as long as they view the change agenda as oriented exclusively to increasing productivity, regardless of the strength of competitive pressures.

Thus, one task of strategic management is to identify multiple opportunities or problems (including problems that have not yet become acute), recognize the possibilities for combining them in the same agenda for innovative change, and effect policy changes that give all stakeholders a strong incentive to support adaptive changes. This sets the stage for the tactical management of the innovation process, which includes mobilizing these multiple sources of motivation and applying them to the development and diffusion of specific innovations.

The desire to harness social as well as economic motives should be reflected in statements by policymakers about the objectives for change as well as in the machinery they set up to implement it. It is especially important for union leaders to emphasize the role of productivity in securing the future of the industry or a particular enterprise. It is equally important for business executives to emphasize human development and the importance of mutual commitment between the organization and employees in promoting a viable industry or enterprise. Their actions, of course, must match their words. Government officials, who must concern themselves with the competitiveness of whole industries rather than specific American companies, should gain a firsthand understanding of the potential power of dual social and economic motives in driving adjustment processes.

Giving Labor as Well as Management an Economic Stake in Change. Labor usually requires more from work innovations than the social gains described above. The economic concerns of labor and management must be addressed. Indeed, symmetry in the economic motivation of labor and management appears to be more important than the strength of the motivation of management for innovative change, even though management must initiate the work innovations.

One pressure on labor to accept innovative change simply parallels the pressure on management: changes that preserve market share also preserve jobs. This force was present in many countries' shipping sectors and in the other U.S. industries discussed in this book. While marketplace pressure may induce labor to accept give-backs in wages and work rules, it usually is not a sufficient condition by itself to enlist labor in innovative change.

An additional inducement was present in the more successful innovative change efforts in shipping. They were distinguished by policies that provided employment assurances for labor in return for labor's support. These policy inducements took various forms, ranging from preserving jobs for nationals at the expense of those for foreigners to enlarging employment by lengthening shore leaves and the more encompassing employment assurances made by Japanese shipowners. The policy assurances resulted from bilateral negotiations between employers and unions in Japan and among employers, labor, and the government in Holland.

If the U.S. fleet is to implement shipboard innovations, the parties must heed the lessons of Japan and Holland. They must improve the economic incentives for labor to cooperate. The U.S. seafaring unions have had strong economic reasons to oppose role flexibility and crew reductions. I refer to the large pool of unemployed seafarers firmly committed to their occupations and the large unfunded pension liability hanging over the industry. These problems also reinforce union opposition to employment continuity and assignment continuity because the reforms would bypass the hiring hall, an institution that enables the union to distribute limited work among more of its members. As noted earlier, the wider distribution of work is viewed as equitable, preserves a broader active union membership base, and keeps more active seafarers contributing to the underfunded and vulnerable pension schemes. Therefore, unions should not be expected to support role flexibility and employment continuity unless the other stakeholders—in this case, probably the government as well as the employers—join with labor to address the problems of unemployment and the unfunded pension liability. The problem of the unfunded pension liability will require ingenuity, resources, and concessions to solve. Indeed, it could serve as a catalyst for union-management-government planning because it adversely affects all groups in the industry.

The issue of employment security is a major obstacle limiting the rate of innovative change in U.S. industry in general. In steel, for example, the continued threat of plant shutdowns remains a major deterrent to innovative change. According to a USWA official,

> So long as the problem of job insecurity remains a viable threat, workers will hold back. Even though they might agree that the LMPT (labor-management participation teams) process is a good one, they will be reluctant to support it if they believe their jobs are not secure in their plant. If workers perceive that greater plant efficiency and production do not enhance their job security but lessen it, LMPTs will not succeed.

The economic plight of the steel industry and its present crisis are a hindrance and a bar to all-out efforts. The problems of imports and government policies must become a major concern for the steel industry and the union, followed by a joint effort to address it and make it our number one concern.[2]

The progress that has been made in addressing employment insecurity in autos has promoted innovative change. After making some headway on the issue in 1982, GM and the UAW made more dramatic progress in the negotiations that started in the fall of 1984. The negotiations created the Job Opportunity Bank Security (JOBS) program.[3] The parties agreed that no GM worker with one year of seniority will be laid off as a result of the introduction of new technology, consolidation of component-production activities, outsourcing of work, or negotiated productivity improvements. Workers who are made redundant by these developments will be retrained at full pay and benefits, used to replace other workers who are in training, or reassigned to another GM plant. Workers can be assigned to a wide range of work. The program, agreed to for a period of at least six years, is backed by a $1 billion financial commitment and is jointly controlled by labor and management at the local and national levels. Ford and the UAW agreed to a similar program for Ford workers. More work on employment stability is required in this industry, but some first steps have been taken.

The Work in America Institute has reviewed the large number of policies that have been devised by American companies to deal constructively with the problems that cause employment instability and those that are created by it. Their reports indicate that American companies have been inventive in developing a large number of helpful tactics, but that diffusion of these practices has been very limited.[4]

Companies have used a variety of policies to give plants—plant managements and unionized work forces—an incentive to promote work reforms. A consumer products company allowed its plants to bid on new products that could be placed in any of several plants located in the same geographical region. General Motors made decisions about which plants would start up second-shift operations during an upswing based partly on the quality of their recent performance. Both of these policies aligned and strengthened interest of labor and management in work reforms. Similarly, General Electric made decisions whether to locate highly automated factories in militantly unionized locations based on a prior understanding with their labor unions that the latter would support radical changes in work structures.

Emphasizing the National Stake in Competitiveness. When the country as a whole has a stake in the survival and prosperity of an industry, actively emphasizing this national stake can enhance the capacity for innovative change. The idea of identifying the national importance of a competitive industry and using this concept constructively in the innovative change process requires that the parties consider not only their mutual interests, for example, in preserving jobs and market share, but also their joint responsibility to the larger society to preserve and enhance a national asset.

In Japan's shipping sector, the importance of the industry to the national economy was recognized by every stakeholder and was part of the rationale for their shared vision about the new employment system for seafarers. The Japanese union (which had struck the industry in the early 1970s, and which maintained its own preconditions for cooperation in the modernization program) reminded its members that this national stake was an important reason to support modernization.

Norway also benefited from a widely shared commitment to the national importance of shipping. In Norway the commitment based on the economic importance of shipping to the national economy was reinforced by a strong cultural attachment to shipping.

The shipping sectors in Japan and Norway illustrate the benefits of emphasizing the national economic importance of the industry. This can take many forms. (1) It can, as the case of Japan illustrates, become a superordinate goal for labor and management, encouraging and justifying collaborative efforts to strengthen the industry's competitiveness, including work innovations. (2) It can cause the government to review its policies toward the industry to ensure that these policies act to strengthen the competitiveness of the industry and not merely to preserve its physical capacity, as occurred in U.S. shipping. (3) The national economic importance of shipping can also attract the attention of the media, researchers, and third parties, who can play a catalytic role and perform other supportive functions in the innovative process, such as those performed by the Work Research Institute in Norway.

The U.S. and U.K. shipping sectors provide dramatic contrasts with those of Japan and Norway in this respect. Neither the United Kingdom nor the United States used the economic importance of shipping as an asset for innovative change. In the United Kingdom it was objectively important relative to the gross national product (GNP). In the United States it was becoming more important as international trade doubled as a percentage of GNP during the 1970s. Nevertheless, in the United States the national importance of shipping was perceived primarily, if not exclusively, in terms of national defense. Ironically, the policies to protect the industry for defense purposes insulated it from the market pressures that would have helped promote innovative change, technically as well as socially. The result is a U.S.-flag fleet that is old (about twice as old as the fleets of the other seven countries), technically backward, slow, and expensive to operate.

It is not surprising that the national security importance of the U.S. fleet was recognized and given policy support (ill-advised though the support may have been). It is equally understandable that enhancing the national economic importance of the U.S.-flag fleet did not become a policy objective of the U.S. government, given the prevailing assumption that the government can have a defense plan but not an industrial strategy.

The observations about U.S. shipping also apply to other sectors of the U.S. economy, including steel and autos, which have an economic importance to the U.S. economy and industrial base that has not been used to mobilize cooperative efforts. The representatives of labor and management responsible for initiating and managing innovative change in these industries have an opportunity to develop this potential superordinate goal. As mentioned above, this can add incentive for their search for

integrative solutions and can be part of the rationale they provide
their members for expediting the diffusion of innovative forms.

Something in this spirit motivated the Carter administration
to create tripartite machinery for the steel industry, which permitted
the parties to deal with a set of interrelated policies. For example,
if a delay of the effective date for certain pollution standards reduced
the demands placed on companies for new capital equipment, the
union's position was that the released capital should be invested in
improving competitiveness. For its part, the union recognized the
need for plants to be closed in order to bring capacity and market
demand into closer alignment. Interestingly in this case, the
concerns of the union and the basic steel companies included
strengthening the competitiveness of the unionized sector of steel
vis-à-vis the nonunionized mills.

While in many respects the Reagan administration has not
encouraged this particular type of venture, a number of other
initiatives by governmental entities have helped to raise consciousness about industry competitiveness and to promote some innovative solutions. The Cooperative Research and Development Act of
1984 is an example. It attempts to promote cooperative research and
development ventures among U.S. companies that also compete
vigorously in the marketplace.

Thus, to use the national economic importance of an
industry as a rationale for revising government policy and
modifying the labor-management-government institutional
framework, we Americans would first have to modify our prevailing
assumptions about the roles of government, management, and labor
and about their responsibilities to the larger community. I will
discuss this in more detail later.

Avoiding Too Much as Well as Too Little Pressure. Efforts
to manage the motivational context should be guided by an
understanding of the effects of the amount of economic pressure for
change. There can be so little pressure that it fails to mobilize the
stakeholders; there can also be so much threat that it immobilizes
them, particularly in terms of innovative change. Severe threats may
induce change, but it is likely to be conventional cost cutting, not
innovative adaptation.

A classic case of too little economic pressure for change, even while an industry was declining in its relative performance capabilities, was the highly protected U.S. shipping industry during the 1970s and early 1980s. The postscript to Chapter Ten reported promising developments in U.S. shipping between 1983 and 1986. These developments and reasons they occurred underscore the importance of managing contextual factors, including the level of economic pressure on the industry.

The U.S. operating differential subsidy long blunted shipowners' incentive to attack high crew costs. However, in recent years the cost disadvantages of U.S. operators have increasingly exceeded the upper limit that MarAd is permitted to cover, and operators are therefore becoming more concerned about costs. Moreover, since the study was completed MarAd has become increasingly diligent and imaginative in administering the program to sharpen the interest of shipping companies in becoming more cost-effective.

The restriction that only U.S. ships can serve the coastal routes and offshore territories continues to insulate this segment of the shipping industry from foreign competition, but it does not preclude stiff domestic competition among U.S. shipowners and from other modes of transportation in the United States. Further analysis would be required to identify all the factors encouraging or discouraging innovations to increase cost-effectiveness. Certainly, however, at the present time the unions have even less incentive to work toward work innovations in domestic than in foreign trade, where the overall U.S. fleet may decline from a lack of competitiveness.

If some economic threat has constructive influence on the change process, it does not necessarily follow that more threat is even better. An instructive case of too much economic pressure for change is that of shipping in the United Kingdom by the early 1980s. The precipitous decline in British shipping created threat and uncertainty to shipowners so great that their planning horizons became too short to justify the investment required to develop and diffuse innovations that could only pay off over many years.

A similar dynamic may have been operating in the U.S. auto industry. One reason suggested why neither Chrysler nor American

Motors followed the lead of GM and Ford in introducing joint programs of work reform was that the former faced more extreme financial situations, and their managements concluded that the payoff was not quick enough to justify the investment for the start-up of the programs.[5]

The U.S. government has provided significant measures of protection for the domestic automobile and steel industries. Because these measures reduced the threat but have not removed it as a source of motivation for change, they have contributed to a degree of stability that probably is conducive to innovative change. However, public policy could be better tailored to support innovative change if those who shaped it recognized the idea of an optimum level of threat and uncertainty.

Policies of avoiding too much as well as too little pressure are often thought of as merely temporizing—giving symptomatic relief from but not mobilizing an attack on the underlying causes of industrial weaknesses. Indeed, temporizing is an apt term for referring to what happened in shipping in Sweden and Denmark, where the measures providing relief from employment threats were not made part of an understanding about seafarers' cooperation in adaptive change.

Promoting Modernization as a Catalyst for Social Innovation. The renovation and construction of new plants and equipment provide unique opportunities for work innovations. Therefore, the policies of government, management, and labor that encourage modernization also often encourage social innovation.

Modernization promotes work innovations in several ways. When a facility represents an incremental investment, management can decide to make the investment contingent on the union agreeing to the work innovations. Moreover, the union leadership can better justify the change to its members if they can point to new investment, with its symbolic and practical implications for the industry's future. In addition, the new facility, which lacks an established set of attitudes and habits, facilitates the implementation of new organizational forms.

The beneficial effect of modernization was abundantly illustrated in the shipping industry, ranging from the purchase of six vessels by the Swedish shipowner Brostrom to the industrywide modernization program in Japan. It has also begun to be felt in U.S. shipping in recent years.

The historical requirement that only ships bought from American shipyards could be operated under the U.S. fleet had increasingly discouraged shipowners from acquiring new vessels because construction subsidies increasingly failed to offset the much higher cost of American ships. In 1982 the Reagan administration gave U.S.-flag operators the latitude to include foreign-built ships in the U.S. fleet. By freeing shipowners to shop abroad for advantageous terms for new ships, the policy facilitated new construction, in turn creating more favorable opportunities for negotiating and implementing change. Other economic policies that encourage fleet modernization, including depreciation and other tax policies, would also promote the development of more competitive staffing policies (a secondary effect that policymakers may fail to appreciate).

The use of new facilities, even new companies, to introduce new organizational forms designed to elicit high commitment from employees has been an important feature of work reform in U.S. manufacturing and service sectors. New airlines, such as People Express, and new mini-steel-mill companies, such as NUCore and Chaparell, have pioneered innovative organization and management strategies. Similarly, in most major American corporations experiments with bold forms of participation and flexibility were first conducted in newly created organizations.

GM's plant organization, based on self-managing teams, was first tried out in new nonunion plants opened in the South. Later the teams were planned and implemented jointly with the UAW in renovated plants in the North. Ford has made much less use of this type of comprehensively redesigned organization, in part because it was not opening or refurbishing facilities to the same extent as GM.[6]

Managing the Institutional Context

The policy incentives described above and the institutional arrangements treated here are complementary. Most of the policies favorable to innovative change become more likely when institutional groups are cohesive internally, and their relationships with each other are collaborative. Conversely, institutional collaboration is fostered by the contexts that emphasize the national stake in competitiveness and harness social as well as economic motives for innovative change. These and other complementary relationships are reflected throughout the chapter.

Influencing the Power and Orientation in Labor Relations. An important aspect of the institutional context discussed in Chapter Eight is the particular combination of power and orientation that characterizes labor relations. The possible combinations of high to low power and adversarial to cooperative orientation of labor relations are portrayed in Figure 12-1.

While the power of seafarers in all countries studied was high and did not vary significantly, the orientation of their relationships did. Shipowners faced with strong unions could pursue two contrasting strategic choices. One strategy was pursued by Japanese shipowners beginning in the mid 1970s. The strategy was to recognize and accept the power of the union and attempt to restructure the relationship with labor to emphasize more mutuality. An alternative strategy would have been to attempt to decrease the power of seafaring unions. This happened to a minor degree in Norway, when the government unilaterally imposed changes favorable to shipowners.

Unlike the shipping sample, where there were no examples of strongly aggressive attempts to weaken unions, both of the contrasting management strategies are found in U.S. manufacturing today. Since the late 1970s GM, Ford, and most of the basic steel companies have been attempting to modify their labor relations toward a more cooperative basis without threatening the traditionally strong power of the unions with which they deal. Other U.S. companies, for example, Continental Airlines, Phelps Dodge, and Greyhound, have, like the Thatcher government in Britain, engaged in aggressive efforts to weaken labor's power. Many other companies, such as General Electric and TRW, Inc., have pursued mixed strategies, attempting to weaken the unions in some locations and structure cooperative relationships in others.

**Figure 12-1. Power and Orientation in Labor Relations
and Their Implications for Change and Innovation.**

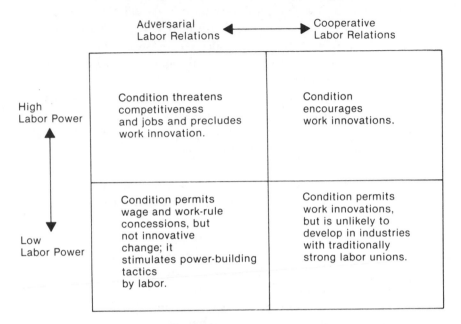

	Adversarial Labor Relations ⟷ Cooperative Labor Relations	
High Labor Power	Condition threatens competitiveness and jobs and precludes work innovation.	Condition encourages work innovations.
Low Labor Power	Condition permits wage and work-rule concessions, but not innovative change; it stimulates power-building tactics by labor.	Condition permits work innovations, but is unlikely to develop in industries with traditionally strong labor unions.

Common to all the strategies just cited is their attempt to escape the combination of high labor power and adversarial labor relations. Increasingly, this combination is no longer an acceptable one because of its adverse effect on the ability of industries to compete in world markets.

From the company's perspective, management must either lower the power of labor or replace adversarialism with mutual reliance. If management attempts to reduce labor's power and succeeds, it can achieve change in traditional terms, that is, wage and work-role concessions, but it will intensify the adversarial orientation of labor, which will severely limit the amount of innovative change management can implement effectively.[7] Taking the other choice, attempting to promote a more collaborative relationship, may complicate management's decision-making process but creates conditions more conducive to innovative change.

From the perspective of labor that already has power and is in an adversarial relationship, the good options are even more limited. If a union does not restructure its relationship with management toward greater cooperation, it will be forced to fight to defend its power. And even if it succeeds in preserving its power, the effect of increased adversarialism on competitiveness threatens the jobs and standard of living of workers.

The most prevalent view expressed by labor leaders is that it is up to management to create the conditions making it possible for labor to cooperate in innovative change. According to AFL-CIO Secretary-Treasurer Thomas R. Donahue:

> For our part, we'd like to see the fullest degree of labor-management cooperation in this country, but we'd like to see it based on mutual acceptance of the other side's right to exist, of the bona fides of the other side; based on an acceptance of corporations' needs to be productive and to generate capital for investment, production, payroll and profit; and based on an acceptance of worker needs to be undisturbed and unintimidated in their rights to form unions or to be participants in forms of industrial democracy which would guarantee their dignity and the decency of their living and working conditions. But until those things are an accepted part of the labor-management scene, it seems to me silly to speak about labor-management cooperation other than as an abstract principle.[8]

The American unions are angered by the activities of the National Association of Manufacturers and the National Chamber of Commerce to promote a union-free environment. John T. Joyce, president of the bricklayers' union, said, "The leadership of American labor has yet to recover from the shock of discovery, during the labor law reform effort of 1978, that the acceptance by American labor of private enterprise is not reciprocated by management."[9] He and others were incensed that managements, including many who "preached cooperation," would promote a legal framework that frustrated union organization efforts.

Managers of American companies with unionized work forces may prefer weak and cooperative unions, but I believe that in practice most of them must choose between strong cooperative unions, with all the risk that entails, or a continuing power struggle in an adversarial relationship that is bad for competitiveness.

Promoting Cohesion in Stakeholder Groups. It is usually advantageous to promote unity within the stakeholder groups. No single aspect of the shipping industry had more effect on the capacity for innovative change than the internal unity or fragmentation of major stakeholder groups, especially labor. Cohesion or unity does not necessarily imply central hierarchical control of innovative activity, a subject addressed in the next section. Unity may refer to structural unity: Japan, with its single union representing all seafarers, provided an institutional framework significantly more favorable to innovative change than Denmark, with its seven craft unions. Unity may refer to the degree of policy agreement: The lack of tensions between ratings' and officers' unions in Holland, compared with the tensions that existed in the United Kingdom and Norway, was a favorable factor for innovative change. Similarly, Norway's more cohesive employers' association was more favorable than Britain's loose and divided association.

Fragmentation can affect innovative change by a number of routes. It complicates the consensus process merely by increasing the number of separate organizations that must agree. Some issues, for example, social integration, may pit one set of employees against another. Other issues, for example, flexibility, may threaten the affected unions as institutions, because if the tasks of their members are combined, the unions cannot continue as separate institutions.

This issue of fragmentation must receive priority attention in the U.S. shipping industry. Interestingly, the fragmentation of the U.S. seafaring-union structure and the intense rivalry that exists among certain unions has sometimes fostered and sometimes inhibited change, particularly because their jurisdictions overlap. A coalition of unions will offer a shipowner more favorable terms than the industry norm in order to represent the seafarers from top to bottom, usually on a newly constructed vessel. However, the same competitive conditions among unions create political insecurity and discourage their leaders from accepting change that is in the long-term interest of their members, but that may not be so perceived. Therefore, it is desirable to find other incentives for unions to support staffing changes. The earlier effort of Harvard professor John Dunlop to promote mergers and coordination among seafaring unions should be renewed.

The fact that different unions represent different workers frustrates innovative change in many other U.S. industries, including construction, railroads, shipbuilding, and airlines. For example, the well-intentioned efforts by Eastern Airlines management and the leaders of the unions that represented pilots, flight attendants, and mechanics were frustrated by this fragmented labor structure; in this particular case fragmentation made it more difficult for the parties to decide what constituted an equitable allocation of the sacrifices required to keep the airline alive and independent. Similarly, the divisions between the skilled trades within the UAW and other UAW members have either slowed or defeated innovative change in some auto plants.

Enabling Local Experimentation and Systemwide Learning. Each set of labor, business, and government institutions provides a particular mix of autonomy and interdependent decision making. Highly decentralized systems are usually better than centralized systems in allowing more experimentation and hence the development of more diverse work innovations, but centralized systems are relatively better equipped to diffuse innovations rapidly. Ideally, institutional structures permit local experimentation and yet provide industry-level learning and diffusion mechanisms. They should also provide for industry-level consensus where local consensus is not sufficient to implement change.

In the shipping industry national unions represented all seafarers within a certain craft group, except in the United States (and West Germany in a minor way). The unions bargained with employers and dealt with government agencies on an industrywide basis. Over the period studied the trend in almost every country was toward allowing more company-by-company or ship-by-ship decisions. This permitted more diversity of practice, including some innovative practices.

In the United States relatively few industries have traditionally conducted bargaining on an industrywide basis. They include Eastern coal, garments, basic steel, railroads, and trucking. In recent years these structures have been weakened as an increasing number of company agreements have deviated from the general agreement, usually to accommodate a company in financial difficulty. Similarly, in industries where bargaining was previously coordinated to produce nearly identical agreements, as among automakers, in recent years the patterns have broken down. The same general tendency has created more diversity of practice among plants within the same company.

The shipping industry and other industries in the United States provide examples of the complementary condition for local experimentation, namely, systemwide learning. In several shipping industries, including Norway, Japan, and Holland, industry-level mechanisms enabled other parts of the industry to learn about the results of project ships implemented by a leading company. These mechanisms include monitoring procedures, research centers, conferences, and the forums discussed next.

Developing Forums and Third-Party Resources. Apart from institutional structures that exist to serve more general purposes, it is often highly desirable to create forums and other institutional mechanisms to deal with change agenda, such as work reform. The utility of such mechanisms was illustrated by the contact group in Norwegian shipping and the modernization committee in Japan. In both cases not only were representatives of labor, management, and government included but also a relatively disinterested party, who could serve as a catalyst and bring additional perspectives to the change program. In Norway the additional party was a group of researchers from the Oslo Work Research Institute (WRI), and in Japan it was a university professor, who was referred to as a representative of the public.

The discussion in Chapter Nine showed that forums and third parties can contribute to the tactical management of the innovation process in several ways.

- by facilitating the development of consensus about innovations and change strategies
- by helping principals shape norms to accept local experiments and suspending judgment about their merits
- by providing substantive expertise, bringing existing knowledge to new innovative activity, deriving lessons from trials, and disseminating results throughout industry

The point of this discussion of the strategic management of the institutional context is that third-party resources need to be developed in the first place.

In the American shipping industry, where both labor and management are highly fragmented, an important need exists for forums and third-party organizations that can manage the forums. The National Research Council's Committee on Effective Manning convened a workshop attended by the presidents of five seafaring unions and officials of several others, by top executives from thirteen shipping companies, and by eight high-level representatives from the Coast Guard and Maritime Administration. The workshop, which I helped organize, occurred in October 1983 and reviewed the findings about shipboard innovations in Europe and Japan. Although its official purpose was to help the committee complete its report on effective staffing, an equally apparent and more important purpose was to begin enhancing the industry's capacity to address the need for change.

This forum dramatized both the striking absence of prior forums and the potential utility of such forums. An industry meeting of such scope was an unprecedented event in shipping. Never before had U.S. maritime labor, management, and government leaders been assembled for reflective off-the-record discussions about the problems they customarily negotiated or litigated. The meeting raised awareness in all parts of the industry about alternative staffing practices and their rationale.

Ideally, the shipping-industry workshop would also have been the first of a series of forums designed to continue the dialogue about the need for the industry to become more competitive and about the specific problems that must be addressed in order to clear the path for innovative change. The participants generally agreed that a neutral agency was required to sponsor future industrywide forums. However, the committee that convened this one-shot conference, chaired by Wayne L. Horvitz, a former head of the Federal Mediation and Conciliation Service, went out of existence when it published its report, and no follow-up forums occurred.

Despite the tensions between the Maritime Administration, labor, and shipowners, I believe that MarAd is sufficiently neutral to permit it to expand the catalytic functions it performs. As noted above, MarAd has begun to administer subsidy programs in ways that sharpen incentives for shipowners to become more cost-effective. In addition, the innovative changes that were initiated by APL and PGM, two U.S. liner companies, after 1983 had been encouraged and facilitated by a MarAd staff member. MarAd should take other initiatives: It should use its approval power and other funds for staffing research and development to encourage union and management joint planning of trials in other parts of the industry. It should enlist other agencies, such as the Work in America Institute or the Bureau of Labor-Management Cooperation and Cooperative Programs in the Department of Labor, to convene the parties and should sponsor education and network activities for shipowners and union officials. MarAd should also convene a blue-ribbon task force to define the unfunded pension liability problem and its consequences, identify possible alternative solutions, and recommend a process for deciding on a solution. It should encourage the Coast Guard to sanction trials and involve unions to a greater extent in their proceedings.

Other U.S. industries can also be well served if we in government, academia, and industry create third-party resources and structure industry-level and enterprise-level forums. Indeed, a number of examples of developments along these lines have already occurred.

In basic steel two third-party resources have played a catalytic role at the industry level. One third party was the American Productivity Center (APC), a nonprofit consulting-and-training organization set up by Jack Grayson after he had served in the administration of President Carter. American Productivity Center professionals, trusted by both labor and management, helped the parties implement the Labor-Management Participation Teams

Agreement beginning in 1981. A second neutral resource to help
steel was a bureau concerned with labor-management cooperation
in the U.S. Department of Labor. This bureau of the Department
of Labor was enlisted by the joint Steel Advisory Committee in 1983
to "make important contributions in support of the parties' joint
efforts." The potential contribution included encouraging the
"extension [of labor-management participation teams] throughout
the entire domestic steel industry" and "offering training opportunities for USWA international staff, and their corporate management counterparts represented on the committee and throughout
the steel industry." The first high-level program for union officials
and steel executives was conducted in November 1986. On the basis
of my firsthand observations as a faculty member of this program,
I judge the concept to be applicable to other U.S. industries with
urgent change agendas.

Another example of a third-party resource playing a strategic
role at the institutional level occurred in the relationship between
AT&T and the Communication Workers of America (CWA).
Michael Maccoby, director of Harvard University's Project on
Technology, Work, and Character, was retained by both parties in
1980 to help them jointly promote worker participation and
develop a new form of labor-management relationship. Over the
past six years Maccoby has performed almost the full set of
functions played by WRI in Norwegian shipping and helps confirm
how important third-party resources can be to the capacity for
innovative change. In the spring of 1982 the CWA-AT&T national
committee planned a series of meetings of the top international
union officials and chief operating and personnel vice-presidents.
I joined Maccoby in conducting these meetings, which were held at
Harvard's Kennedy School of Government. The participants
discussed case studies showing different levels and methods of
worker participation. The two principal sponsors of these meetings,
Glenn Watts, president of CWA, and Raymond Williams, vice-
president of labor relations at AT&T, wrote several years later that
this forum enabled "both management and union to openly share
their views: concern for potential problems and hopes for potential
successes." [10]

Another active third-party organization, the Work in America Institute, headed by Jerome Rosow, is making the most important contribution in the United States today in the development and dissemination of knowledge about work innovations. It is a tripartite research organization, with strong links to the academic community, and serves the widest possible spectrum of clients—enterprises, labor unions, and government agencies.

Finally, a government entity in a strategic position to bring labor and management together at the industry level is the Department of Labor's Bureau of Labor-Management Cooperation and Cooperative Programs Division, mentioned earlier in connection with the steel industry. The division is headed by a visionary deputy undersecretary, Stephen Schlossberg, who has extensive contacts in industry and labor and has been active for several years in creating forums of representatives of labor, management, government, and academia. If my judgment is right about the importance in many industries of industrywide forums for addressing the need for change, then this division should take more initiative in other industries, such as machine tools, textiles, and aircraft manufacturing, as well as shipping.

Revising Assumptions About the Roles of Labor, Management, and Government in International Competition

I have described ways the interests of multiple stakeholders can be combined and integrated to provide a more powerful set of incentives for innovative change. I have also described how institutions are structured and oriented to enable innovative change. Policy and institutional innovations such as these imply changes in our underlying assumptions about the appropriate roles of labor, management, and government.[11]

Others have also called for institutional changes and for using national economic well-being as a rationale for creating industry-level collaboration.[12] An important reason why progress in line with the recommendations in this chapter is slow is that many of the proposed changes are contrary to the prevailing assumptions about the appropriate roles of business management, labor, and government in the United States.

Our traditional conception of the interests and roles of stakeholders and therefore our ready acceptance of the adversarial relations among the institutions serving them assume that

- the enterprise is managed strictly in the interest of its shareowners
- labor's interests are distinct and predominantly in conflict with employers' interests[13]
- the government should develop defense plans, provide certain regulatory functions, and perform other limited functions, but should not have an industrial strategy

Although actual practice in the United States has progressively departed from these traditional assumptions, the concepts continue to be influential and serve as a brake on efforts to change the policy and institutional context for innovative change.

Until we recognize the enterprise as a social entity that has other stakeholders as well as shareowners whose concerns must be acknowledged and integrated, if possible, and balanced as necessary, we are not likely to reform management and labor institutions toward more cooperative relations, internal unity, and problem-solving mechanisms.

Until we recognize that under present conditions of world competition, the government can better serve the public by helping assess the competitiveness of U.S. industries and actively promoting the capacities for innovative change, we are not likely to reform economic policies, so that when combined with market pressures they provide economic incentives for innovative change that are neither too weak nor too strong.

We need to develop a system of beliefs that not only permits the parties to play these roles but that also expects them to.

Appendix

Some Notes on
Research Design and Methods

The findings reported in this book are based on a study of the development and diffusion of four innovations in eight countries over seventeen years. This appendix reviews the evolution of the study and describes the data and methods utilized in the research.

Evolution of the Theoretical Model and Empirical Findings

My attempt to present concepts, data, and findings from a study in a manner that makes them most accessible for readers tends to obscure how the study itself was carried out.

Two major aspects of the evolution of the study should be noted. One relates to the development of the theory and the other to the phasing of the analyses of the countries in the sample.

The study on which the book is based combined deductive and inductive processes and was a mixture of illustrating prior theory and generating new theory. Although I present a fully elaborated model in Chapter Two and then exemplify it in subsequent chapters, the model actually evolved over the course of

309

the study. The major structural elements of the model presented in Figure 2-1 were formulated before the field investigations were undertaken. They are reflected in the "what," "why," and "how" questions used in the interview guide presented later in this appendix. Other aspects of the model emerged early in the study, after I had immersed myself in the field data, but before I had undertaken to organize and summarize the data. The most important aspect of the model to emerge at this stage was the notion that the innovation process (the "how") was influenced by two factors, the institutional context within which it recurred and the competence of the individuals who managed it. Finally, at least one crucial aspect of the model was added late in my analysis of the findings. It was the concept of metacompetence—the ability of those within the industry to manage aspects of the motivational and institutional contexts. The addition of this element to the model made it less deterministic than it was when originally formulated and therefore increased its utility as a policy tool.

The analysis of the countries covered by my study occurred in two phases, an aspect of the methodology that is not reflected in the presentation technique I employed of simultaneously comparing and contrasting all eight countries. The first phase centered on the six northwestern European countries. The second phase extended the comparative analysis to include the United States and Japan. I did not have access to the data on the United States and Japan until after I had analyzed the European data. Interestingly, the analysis of the United States and Japanese data merely reinforced the major findings based on the comparison of the European countries—that the soundness of the guiding models and the enabling character of the institution strongly influenced innovative change.

The general analytical question pursued throughout the entire study was: How can the different innovation records be explained? This general question was broken down into a series of analytic questions, each pertaining to a factor in the theoretical model: five internal components of innovative change and two external forces. For each factor, the question was: How helpful is this factor in explaining the records of shipboard innovation in the eight countries?

The degree of support for a component proposition is assessed primarily by examining the correspondence between the eight countries' rankings on the component (for example, the soundness of the model) and their overall innovation records. The more correspondence, the more support for the general proposition. The rankings themselves varied widely in whether they were based on carefully delineated operations and assessed quantitatively or were subjective and impressionistic. Fortunately, the innovation records themselves are based on relatively objective assessments and provide a reliable ranking of the outcomes, which subsequent analysis can attempt to explain. The ranking of guiding models was also highly reliable. The ranking of the social contexts was based on judgments that were mostly subjective and impressionistic. The indexes I used to operationalize the concept of economic necessity were mostly quantitative, but the judgments about what operations to use and how to weight them (I weighted them equally) certainly are open to challenge. Some aspects of institutional arrangements were determined objectively (for example, the fragmentation of the seafaring-union structures), and others involved more impressionistic judgments (for example, the amount of consensus among groups required before work innovations could be implemented).

Given the subjective bases for the assessments of aspects of some of the components and the judgments that inevitably were required in selecting and weighting operational definitions of these components, the reader may be partly reassured to learn that at the outset of the study I generally regarded all of the competing explanatory factors as plausible. While I expected that in combination the five propositions relating to the five basic components in the model would explain most of the differences in countries' innovation records, I did not at the outset attempt to propose which proposition would be more helpful in this setting. Therefore, I pursued the analysis of the data without in any sense rooting for any particular proposition to get strong support. And, indeed, the degree of support for each proposition revealed itself slowly over a long period of analytic work.

Unit of Analysis

While the framework can be applied to social systems ranging in scope from plants to companies to industrial sectors to countries, the empirical study of shipping focuses on one of these. The unit of analysis is the national industry. The comparisons are between, say, the Norwegian and the British shipping sectors. It is not a comparison of Britain and Norway as countries. It does not center on a comparison of companies, although some selected company contrasts and comparisons are used to generate insight or clarify certain dynamics.

Treating the country shipping industry as the unit of analysis has two operational meanings. In some instances it refers to certain conditions that apply systematically to the entire shipping industry in the country, such as a subsidy, regulation, certification standard, industrywide shipowner's association, and industrywide union. In other instances it refers to the sum of the parts of the industry, for example, to the aggregation of the individual change initiatives of the dozens of shipowners in the country or to the most typical concern or reaction of the country's seafarers to a proposed shipboard organization.

Data

Some data on the eight countries were gleaned from the publications cited in the text. Some data on the U.S. industry were gathered by Christopher Allen during his tenure as a Postdoctoral Fellow at the Harvard Business School in interviews with staff members of the Maritime Administration in 1985. Most of the other country-specific data were gathered in connection with the National Research Council's investigation into staffing practices in Europe and Japan for the purpose of recommending more effective practices for the U.S. industry.

A delegation of the committee, including myself, visited Europe during June 1983. The visits in each of the six countries usually included shipowners and officials of their associations, officials of seafarers' unions, officials of government agencies, and researchers active in the industry. Individuals who had been scheduled to meet with the U.S. delegation were invariably among the most informed about conditions and developments in the industry. The European visits are listed below. The notes on each interview were drafted by the staff officer, Michael Gaffney, each night and subsequently reviewed by committee members, who checked them against their own notes. For the European trip, I have relied upon both my notes and those drafted by Michael Gaffney.

More information on shipping in Japan was gathered by Michael Gaffney on a trip to the Far East in 1985, which was similar to the one to Europe in 1983. He again made detailed notes on the content of the interviews. I have relied heavily on these notes (as well as on published material) for my understanding of the Japanese case.

I circulated an early draft of the manuscript to several persons more informed about the industry than myself to check the accuracy of my facts and reasonableness of my interpretations. One person was David Moreby, Dean of the Maritime College at Plymouth Polytechnic in Plymouth, England. He was cited by many informants as the single most informed person about the European shipping industry. A second person was Jacques Roggema, who had been active as a change agent and researcher in shipping in Norway, Holland, and the United Kingdom. The third reviewer was Michael Gaffney, now at Cornell University.

The interviews in each country were guided by the following broad questions:

1. *What* have they done? (List shipboard projects, experiments, and implemented changes, specifying both technical and organizational content, for example, what devices employed, how many in crew, how employed.)
2. *Why* did they do it? (What prompted the various parties to participate?)
3. *How* did they do it? (Describe the process by which the above has been accomplished.)
   a. What has been the role of the research company?
      (1) What basic research was undertaken?
      (2) What applied research was undertaken?
      (3) What action research (experiments) was undertaken?

    b. In each case, how was the research done?
        (1) Who sponsored it?
        (2) Who did it?
        (3) How was it communicated?
        (4) How did it lead to the next step?
    c. What has been the role of the ship operators?
        (1) The individual firms?
        (2) The shipping associations?
    d. What has been the role of the seafarers' unions?
        (1) In support of research?
        (2) In provision of regulatory variance for experiments?
        (3) In encouragement of experiments through subsidy leverage?
        (4) In subsequent regulatory amendments?

4. What has been done to mitigate undesirable side effects of manning adjustments? (Describe contractual, that is, labor-management and government, policy initiatives.)

Interviews in Northwestern European Shipping Sectors

The following are the parties interviewed by the delegation of the National Research Council that visited Europe.

Operators:
P.A.L. Shipping Services (United Kingdom)
General Council of British Shipping (United Kingdom)
Bibby Line (United Kingdom)
Swedish Shipowners' Association (Sweden)
Salen Shipping Company (Sweden)
Danish Shipowners' Association (Denmark)
DFDS Shipping (Denmark)
German Shipowners' Association (West Germany)
Leif Hoegh Line (Norway)
Norwegian Shipowners' Association (Norway)
Nedlloyd Shipping Company (Holland)
Shell Tankers (Holland)
Van Nievelt Goudriaan (Holland)
Netherlands Shipowners' Federation (Holland)

Unions:
National Union of Seamen (United Kingdom)
Merchant Navy and Airline Officers Union (United Kingdom)
Swedish Seaman's Union (Sweden)
Swedish Engineer Officers Association (Sweden)
Swedish Ship Officers Association (Sweden)
Merchant Navy Officers Association (Denmark)
Danish Radio Officers Union (Denmark)
German Employees Union (West Germany)
Transportation and Public Services Union (West Germany)
Norwegian Shipmasters Union (Norway)
Norwegian Union of Marine Engineers (Norway)
Norwegian Mates Union (Norway)

Government:
National Administration of Shipping and Navigation (Sweden)
Ship Safety Administration (West Germany)
Ministry of Transport (West Germany)
Ministry of Trade and Shipping (Norway)
Coast Guard (Holland)

Researchers:
Dr. David Moreby, Plymouth Polytechnic (United Kingdom)
Tavistock Institute (United Kingdom)
Mr. Arne Rebnes, DFDS (Denmark)
Work Research Institute (Norway)
Ship Operation of the Future (Norway)
Institute for Ergonomic and Organizational Research, Bremen
    University (West Germany)

Notes

Chapter One

1. President's Commission on Industrial Competitiveness, *Global Competition and the New Reality, Volumes I and II* (Washington, D.C.: U.S. Government Printing Office, January 1985). See Bruce R. Scott and George C. Lodge, eds., *U.S. Competitiveness in the World Economy* (Boston: Harvard Business School Press, 1985); and National Research Council, *Toward a New Era in U.S. Manufacturing: The Need for a National Vision* (Washington, D.C.: National Academy Press, 1986). Also see industry-by-industry assessments published by the International Trade Administration (ITA), U.S. Department of Commerce, for example, *A Competitive Assessment of the U.S. Manufacturing Automation Equipment Industries* (Washington, D.C.: U.S. Department of Commerce, June 1984).

2. Paul R. Lawrence and Davis Dyer, *Renewing American Industry* (New York: Free Press, 1983), 19.

3. Alan Altshuler, Martin Anderson, Daniel Jones, Daniel Roos, and James Womack, *The Future of the Automobile: The Report of MIT's International Automobile Program* (Cambridge, Mass.: MIT Press, 1984).

4. Altshuler and others, *Future of the Automobile*, 159.

317

5. Altshuler and others, *Future of the Automobile,* 161.

6. Lawrence and Dyer, *Renewing American Industry,* 72–76.

7. Many, including myself, have written elsewhere about the shape of the work innovations regarded as adaptive in the United States. According to my interpretation, the major premise underlying work-force practices in the past has been the need to *impose control* in order to achieve efficiency. Reliance on control is giving way to an effort to *elicit commitment* from workers, because it appears essential to do in order to achieve higher productivity, better use of new technology, and greater human development. Richard E. Walton, "Toward a Strategy of Eliciting Commitment Based on Policies of Mutuality," in *Human Resource Management Trends and Challenges,* R. E. Walton and Paul R. Lawrence, eds. (Boston: Harvard Business School Press, 1985) 35–65; and Richard E. Walton, "Vision-Led Management Restructuring," in *Organizational Dynamics* (Summer 1986). The first article treats innovations at the worker level and the second addresses changes in the management organization.

Similar changes have been advocated as necessary for U.S. competitiveness by Michael J. Piore and Charles F. Sabel in *The Second Industrial Divide* (New York: Basic Books, 1984); Altshuler and others, *Future of the Automobile;* Robert B. Reich, *The Next American Frontier* (New York: Times Books, 1983); and Lester C. Thurow, "Revitalizing American Industry: Managing in a Competitive World Economy," *California Management Review* 27, no. 1 (1984), 9–41. See also Goodmeasure, Inc., *The Changing American Workplace: Work Alternatives in the 80s* (New York: American Management Association, 1985); and Edward E. Lawler III, *High-Involvement Management* (San Francisco: Jossey-Bass, 1986).

8. Altshuler and others, *Future of the Automobile,* 146. Also see William J. Abernathy, Kim B. Clark, and Alan M. Kantrow, *Industrial Renaissance: Producing a Competitive Future for America* (New York: Basic Books, 1983).

9. Altshuler and others, *Future of the Automobile,* 183.

10. Harry C. Katz and Charles F. Sabel, "Industrial Relations and Industrial Adjustment: The World Car Industry," MIT working paper, April 1985.

11. Alfred S. Warren, "Quality of Work Life at General Motors," in *Teamwork: Joint Labor-Management Programs in America,* ed. Jerome M. Rosow (New York: Pergamon Press, Work in America Series, 1986), 120.

12. Sam Camens, "Labor-Management Participation Teams in Basic Steel Industry," in *Teamwork: Joint Labor-Management Programs in America,* ed. Jerome M. Rosow (New York: Pergamon Press, Work in America Series, 1986), 112.

13. Benjamin Boylston, "Employee Involvement and Cultural Change at Bethlehem Steel," in *Teamwork: Joint Labor-Management Programs in America,* ed. Jerome M. Rosow (New York: Pergamon Press, Work in America Series, 1986), 94.

14. Camens, "Labor-Management Teams," 116.

15. Camens, "Labor-Management Teams," 115.

16. Boylston, "Employee Involvement and Cultural Change at Bethlehem Steel," 89.

17. National Research Council, *Human Resource Practices for Implementing Advanced Manufacturing Technology* (Washington, D.C.: National Academy Press, 1986).

18. For a rare example of research focusing on the ability of a national industry to innovate, in this case the American shoe industry, see Jerald Hage, "Responding to Technological and Competitive Changes: Organization and Industry Factors," in *Managing Technological Innovation,* eds. Donald D. Davis and Associates (San Francisco: Jossey-Bass, 1986), 44–71.

Chapter Two

1. By using the term "innovative change," I embrace the development of an innovation, its early implementation to test its efficacy, and its diffusion throughout a social system. The distinction among these activities is useful, and I sometimes want to emphasize one or another of these phases of innovative change, especially in discussions of factors that impinge on the process itself. However, the classic distinction in the literature between developing and diffusing an innovation assumed that the innovation was essentially unchanging during its diffusion. The existence of reinvention was ignored, perhaps because many of the innova-

tions considered in formulating the models were commercial products. The social innovations treated here, like those considered by Donald A. Schön in *Beyond the Stable State* (New York: Random House, 1971), are adapted and reinvented as they spread. Therefore, the spread of new shipboard concepts throughout northwestern European countries and to Japan—from country to country, from company to company, and even from ship to ship—involved varying mixtures of adopting existing innovations and adapting them.

2. See Michael Beer, *Organization Change and Development: A Systemic View* (New York: Goodyear, 1980); and Richard E. Walton, "Planned Changes to Improve Organizational Effectiveness," *Technology in Society* 2 (1980b): 391–412.

3. See Fred E. Emery and Eric E. Trist, *Towards a Social Ecology: Contextual Appreciation of the Future in the Present* (London: Plenum, 1973); Michael Beer, Bert Spector, Paul Lawrence, Quinn Mills, and Richard Walton, *Managing Human Assets* (New York: Free Press, 1984); and J. Richard Hackman, "The Design of Work Teams," in *Handbook of Organizational Behavior*, ed. Jay Lorsch (Englewood Cliffs, N.J.: Prentice-Hall, 1986), 315–342.

4. Camens, "Labor-Management Teams," 112-113.

5. Camens, "Labor-Management Teams," 113.

6. Alfred D. Chandler, Jr., *Strategy and Structure: The History of the American Industrial Enterprise* (Cambridge, Mass.: MIT Press, 1962). Chandler provides the classic demonstration of the idea that environmental changes set the stage for new competitive strategies, which in turn lead to the realignment of the internal structure of the corporation.

7. Joseph Schumpeter, *Capitalism, Socialism, and Democracy*, 3d ed. (New York: Harper & Row, 1950); Edwin Mansfield, *Industrial Research and Technological Innovation* (New York: Norton, 1968); and John R. Hicks, *The Theory of Wages* (London: Macmillan, 1932).

8. Thorstein Veblen, *The Theory of the Leisure Class* (New York: Heller, 1899). Also, see Andrew H. Van de Ven, "Central Problems in the Management of Innovation," *Management Science* 32 (1986): 590–607.

9. These differences have continued and are found in all of the Big Three auto companies, according to a recent study. See Daniel D. Levine, "New Labor-Management Models from Detroit," *Harvard Business Review* (September–October 1986): 24.

10. Boylston, "Employee Involvement and Cultural Change at Bethlehem Steel," 90.

11. Robert E. Cole, "The Macropolitics of Organizational Change: A Comparative Analysis of the Spread of Small-Group Activities," *Administrative Science Quarterly* 30 (1985): 560-585.

12. Andrew M. Pettigrew, *The Awakening Giant: Continuity and Change in Imperial Chemical Companies* (London: Basil Blackwell, 1985).

13. For example, see Ronald Dore, *British Factory—Japanese Factory* (Berkeley: University of California Press, 1974). In addition, Geert Hofstede's *Culture's Consequences: International Differences in Work-Related Values* (London: Gage Publications, 1980) reports on his own extensive research of forty countries and the results of other studies, to support his conclusion that country differences in values have profound consequences for the ability to transfer organizational forms from one country to another. Other research on managerial attitudes in nine European countries and the United States supports the hypothesis that the national origin of managers working in European companies affects their view of what proper management should be. See, for example, Andre Laurent, "The Cultural Diversity of Western Conceptions of Management," *International Studies of Management and Organization* 13, nos. 1-2 (1983): 75-96.

14. Institutional arrangements of a country can be viewed as a manifestation of the national culture. See John Child and Monir Tyeh, "Theoretical Perspectives in Cross-National Research," *International Studies of Management and Organization* 12, no. 4 (1982): 23-70. Recognizing that social values and institutional factors may be systematically related, they are nevertheless separated in this book, because they impact innovation through different routes—social beliefs affecting motivation and institutions affecting processes.

The type of institutional influence contemplated in the present theory can be illustrated by several recent studies: Joseph L.

Badaracco, Jr., *Loading the Dice: A Five-Country Study of Vinyl Chloride Regulation* (Boston: Harvard Business School Press, 1985); Robert B. Reich, "Bailout: A Comparative Study in Law and Industrial Structure," *Yale Journal on Regulation* 2, no. 2 (1985): 163–224; and Peter Katzenstein, *Small States in World Markets* (Ithaca, N.Y.: Cornell University Press, 1985).

Robert Reich's analysis of the bailout of key businesses— AEG-Telefunken, British Leyland, Toyo Kogyo, and Chrysler—in four countries is highly relevant. Each of these four companies had previously experienced substantial losses over a period of time but had failed to shift their resources to potentially more profitable uses. After government action to bail out the company was initiated, each company shrank employment and plant capacity and shifted resources to more productive uses. Some companies, however, adapted better and more quickly than others. Toyo Kogyo adapted most effectively—it shifted the most and shrank the least. Employment declined by 27 percent, and the manufacturing processes and products were completely transformed. At the other extreme, British Leyland proved least effective—it shrank more than it shifted, cutting its work force by over 50 percent without fundamentally altering its processes or products. Telefunken and Chrysler fell in the middle of the spectrum of adaptive responses.

Reich's primary explanation for these differences centered on institutional arrangements, involving the enterprise, labor, financial institutions, and government. In particular, he argued that linkages among financial supporters (creditors) of the enterprise provided the creditors with a better basis for information and control, which in turn affected the promptness of adaptive responses. He also argued that tighter interdependencies (rather than arm's-length relations) between financial institutions and the enterprise and between labor unions and the enterprise resulted in a greater willingness by creditors and labor to make the sacrifices entailed in shrinking employment and shifting resources.

The Badaracco study drew conclusions parallel to those of Reich on the critical role of institutional arrangements at the sector level. Badaracco's research problem did not involve economic adaptation or social innovation. Instead, it involved the setting of tighter industry standards for vinyl chloride and polyvinyl chloride

(PVC) exposure levels in the workplace. He compared the handling of the same basic problem in the United States, France, the United Kingdom, West Germany, and Japan. In all countries the effort was triggered in 1973 by news of a major finding that linked cancer to PVC exposure in a Goodrich plant. Although the standards ultimately set in the five countries were similar, the methods they employed contained instructive differences. The United States established new standards by adversarial processes heavily reliant on lawyers, which produced an early once-and-for-all decision. The European and Japanese processes involved cooperation between industry management, labor, and government and produced a series of incremental decisions as parties gained confidence in the feasibility of compliance. Badaracco found that institutional arrangements in some countries had "loaded the dice" (as he put it) in favor of cooperative versus adversarial processes between government and industry. In particular, Badaracco found that cooperative processes were promoted by (1) stronger hierarchies (centralized control) within the government and within the industry association and (2) active networks of informal personal contacts between the companies and government agencies concerned.

Katzenstein analyzed the industrial adjustment strategies of seven small European states—Sweden, Norway, Denmark, Holland, Belgium, Switzerland, and Austria—comparing them with one another as well as with the large industrial countries. He attempted to explain how they adjusted their economies to rapid changes in technology and global competition. Katzenstein was interested in shifts in the size and importance of the different industries comprising their small, open, and vulnerable economies. These adjustments are broader adjustments than the ones I focus on, but the factors that promote the broad adjustments also can enable the firm-level or sector-level innovations of particular interest here. He attributed the effective adjustment of these open economies to their institutional arrangements, which he labeled "democratic corporatism." This system, he argued, is distinguished by three traits: "an ideology of social partnership expressed at the national level; a relatively centralized and concentrated system of interest groups; and voluntary and informal coordination of conflicting objectives, through continuous bargaining between interest groups, state bureaucracies, and political parties" (p. 32).

A related aspect of interorganizational systems studied for its effect on technical innovation is the strength of the formal and informal communication networks among organizations. Also see L. Nabseth and G. F. Ray, eds., *The Diffusion of New Industrial Processes: An International Study* (London: Cambridge University Press, 1974); and John A. Czepial, "Patterns of Interorganizational Communications and the Diffusion of a Major Technological Innovation in a Competitive Industrial Community," *Academy of Management Journal* 18, no. 1 (March 1975): 6–24. Also see James G. March and John P. Olsen, "The New Institutionalism: Organizational Factors in Political Life," *The American Political Service Review* 78 (1984): 734–749.

The dimensions of the institutional framework discussed here have their counterparts within organizations, as is shown by Rosabeth Moss Kanter's study of innovation in corporate organization (*The Change Masters,* New York: Simon & Schuster, 1983). Kanter found that highly segmented organizations that emphasized boundaries between functions, between management and labor, and between central staffs and field operations were less innovative than those that were characterized by strong integrative mechanisms, encouraged fluidity of boundaries, and promoted the free flow of information. Pettigrew's comprehensive study of changes in ICI, *The Awakening Giant,* provides persuasive support for the same ideas. Also, for example, see Cole, "The Macropolitics of Organizational Change," which reports on a comparative study of quality circles in Japan, Sweden, and the United States and concludes that industry-level organizations can play a key role in communicating and supporting change.

15. Thus, whereas specific beliefs about the content of innovations are relevant to the third proposition, social motivation, the broader ideologies about how society ought to function are integral to understanding the roles that institutions play in the innovation process. A comparative study of five mature industrial countries and four newly industrialized countries, *Ideology and National Competitiveness,* eds. George Lodge and Ezra Vogel (Boston: Harvard Business School Press, 1986), found that the

countries' adjustment policies were systematically related to prevailing beliefs about certain issues, such as individualism versus communitarianism, and the appropriate roles of business and government in society. Ideologies manifested themselves in certain institutional forms, which in turn biased the content of the policies they produced.

16. Many recent proposals for better industrial adaptation in the United States have emphasized the role of managerial choice and behavior. See Thomas A. Kochan, Harry C. Katz, and Robert B. McKersie, *The Transformation of American Industrial Relations* (New York: Basic Books, 1986); Robert H. Hayes and Steven C. Wheelwright, *Restoring Our Competitive Edge: Competing Through Manufacturing* (New York: Wiley, 1984); Kanter, *Change Masters;* and Lawrence and Dyer, *Renewing American Industry.*

Much of the literature on organization change and diffusion of innovation also underscores the role of choice by diffusion agents and by adopters. See Schön, *Beyond the Stable State;* Gerald Zaltman and Robert Duncan, *Strategies of Planned Change* (New York: Wiley, 1977); and Gerald Zaltman, Robert Duncan, and Jonny Holbek, *Innovations and Organizations* (New York: Wiley, 1973).

17. A study of the fates of early efforts to spread work innovations throughout a dozen companies that pioneered them found an extraordinarily high failure rate during the late 1960s and early 1970s. The pilot experiments, which typically occurred in single units and were successful in their own terms, generated tension and conflict with the wider organization. Thus, the other parts of the organizations studied resisted the spread of the innovations. Richard E. Walton, "The Diffusion of New Work Structures: Explaining Why Success Didn't Take," *Organizational Dynamics* (Winter 1975): 3-22.

18. See Robert Zager and Michael P. Rosow, eds., *The Innovation Organization: Productivity Programs in Action* (New York: Pergamon Press, 1982). See, for example, the chapter by Eric Trist and Charles Dwyer, "The Limits of Laissez-Faire as a Sociotechnical Change Strategy" (pp. 149-183), for an analysis of failed diffusion efforts in a manufacturing company. For an assessment of failed innovative change in coal mining, see Paul S.

Goodman, *Assessing Organizational Change: The Rushton Quality of Work Experiment* (New York: Wiley, 1979). Also see Richard E. Walton, "Successful Strategies for Diffusing Work Innovations," *Journal of Contemporary Business* (Spring 1977): 1–22; and Trevor A. Williams, *Learning to Manage Our Futures* (New York: Wiley, 1982).

19. The proposed theoretical framework may be readily adapted to explain the diffusion of those technical innovations that have economic and social implications and require institutional approval. A National Research Council report, *Diffusion of Biomass Energy Technologies in Developing Countries* (Washington, D.C.: National Academy Press, 1984) notes that "new technologies with indigenous systems of source allocation, work organization, goods distributions, social and authority structures, and prevailing values and religious beliefs clearly have the best chance of success" (p. 3).

20. A recent work that draws attention to theoretical and practical significance of different levels is the work by Kochan, Katz, and McKersie (*The Transformation of American Industrial Relations*). Although their distinctions are slightly different from those employed in the present theory, they too emphasize the importance of understanding the interrelationship among the several levels at which policies apply and social action occurs.

21. The framework used by Pettigrew in his study of ICI (*The Awakening Giant*) and the one proposed here are remarkably similar in their emphasis on the interrelationships among the content, context, and processes of change. One of the major conclusions of Pettigrew's study, which isolated five ICI cases of strategic change, was how the content of the change (new model) was influenced by contextual factors (including economic, structural, political, and cultural) and by the change processes ("of signalling new areas for concern and enclosing those signals in issues for attention and decision, of mobilizing energy and enthusiasm in an additive fashion to ensure that new problem areas found and defined eventually gained sufficient legitimacy and power to result in contextually appropriate action") (page 453).

22. The theory presented here attempts to integrate two types of theoretical models of organization change. Structural variance

models specify the conditions that accompany change and action; process models show how change occurs. See L. B. Mohr, *Explaining Organizational Behavior: The Limits and Possibilities of Theory and Research* (San Francisco: Jossey-Bass, 1982); Andrew H. Van de Ven and Marshall Scott Poole, "Paradoxical Requirements for a Theory of Organizational Change," Discussion Paper No. 58, Strategic Management Research Center (Minneapolis: University of Minnesota, September 1986); William Foote Whyte, "Culture, Social Learning, and Economic Progress," paper presented to meeting of the American Sociological Association in Washington, D.C., August 26-30, 1985.

Also see Kochan, Katz, and McKersie (*The Transformation of American Industrial Relations*), who contrast their theory of industrial relations systems with the earlier theory by John T. Dunlop in *Industrial Relations Systems* (New York: Holt, Rinehart & Winston, 1958) on this dimension. Their theory views the evolution of a country's industrial relations system as influenced importantly by strategic action, whereas Dunlop's theory, which has served as the classic work on this subject, emphasized contextual determinants.

Chapter Three

1. Sidney Roger, "American Seamen on the Hoegh *Mallard*," in Robert Schrank, editor, *Industrial Democracy at Sea* (Cambridge, Mass.: MIT Press, 1983), 4-5.

2. U.S. Department of Commerce, Maritime Administration, *Merchant Fleets of the World, 1966* and *1973* and *1983* (Washington, D.C.: U.S. Government Printing Office, 1967, 1974, 1984a).

3. U.S. Congress, Office of Technology Assessment, *An Assessment of Marine Trade and Technology* (Washington, D.C.: U.S. Government Printing Office, 1983): 19-34.

4. Lane C. Kendall, *The Business of Shipping* (Centreville, Md.: Cornell Maritime Press, 1983).

5. Maritime Administration, *Merchant Fleets, 1967* and *1984*.

6. Office of Technology Assessment, *Marine Trade and Technology*, 27.

7. UNCTAD, *Review of Maritime Transport* (Paris: UNCTAD, 1985).

8. Alan E. Branch, *Economics of Shipping Practice and Management* (London: Chapman & Hall, 1982), 55.

9. U.S. Congress, Congressional Budget Office, *U.S. Shipping and Shipbuilding: Trends and Policy Choices* (Washington, D.C.: U.S. Government Printing Office, August 1984): 24–25.

10. Office of Technology Assessment, *Marine Trade and Technology*, 193.

11. U.S. Department of Transportation, Maritime Administration, *Maritime Subsidies* (Washington, D.C.: U.S. Government Printing Office, 1981a).

12. U.S. Department of Transportation, *Maritime Subsidies.*

13. Maritime Administration, *Merchant Fleets*, 1967.

14. Maritime Administration, *Merchant Fleets*, 1974.

15. Maritime Administration, *Merchant Fleets*, 1984.

16. Kendall, *Business of Shipping*, 204.

17. National Research Council, *Effective Manning of the U.S. Merchant Fleet* (Washington, D.C.: National Academy Press, 1984), 31–34.

18. Branch, *Economics of Shipping*, 56–57; and Roger, "American Seamen on the Hoegh *Mallard*," 105–107.

19. National Research Council, *Effective Manning of the U.S. Merchant Fleet*, 20.

20. Branch, *Economics of Shipping*, 159–163.

21. Rosalyn Winther and Paul Bartlett, "A Balanced Life," *Seatrade* 11, no. 8 (August 1981): 3.

22. In these descriptions of work innovations and their rationale, I draw heavily on the joint work of M. H. Smith and Jacques Roggema. Their four articles published in *Maritime Policy and Management* during 1979 and 1980 are thorough and carefully reasoned treatments of these four types of innovations. (These articles are listed in the Bibliography.) In addition, see J. Roggema and M. H. Smith, "Organizational Change in the Shipping Industry: Issues in the Transformation of Basic Assumptions," *Human Relations* 36, no. 8 (1983): 765–790. I also found Michael Gaffney's papers on this subject very helpful, especially "Reduced Manning in the Liner Trades: Technological Capabilities and

Organizational Implications," *Proceedings of the Conference on the Management of Change Aboard Ship* (Maine Maritime Academy: Center for Advanced Maritime Studies, 1981a).

23. Ragnar Johansen, "Democratizing Work and Social Life on Ships: A Report from the Experiment on Board M.S. *Balao*," in *Working on the Quality of Working Life,* ed. Hans van Beinum (Boston: Martinum Nijhoff Publishing, 1979), 122.

24. Roger, "American Seamen on the Hoegh *Mallard*," 73-74.

25. Roger, "American Seamen on the Hoegh *Mallard*," 90.

26. *Seaways,* "Manning—A Major Concern and Major Cost" (April 1983): 4-5.

27. Roggema and Smith, "Organizational Change in the Shipping Industry," 772.

28. Roger, "American Seamen on the Hoegh *Mallard*," 18-19.

29. Roger, "American Seamen on the Hoegh *Mallard*," 69-70.

30. Michael Grey, *Seatrade* 13 (1983): 9.

31. Roggema and Smith, "Organizational Change in the Shipping Industry," 770-771.

32. Burger Vilkund, "Workplace Changes and Union Power," in *Industrial Democracy at Sea,* ed. Robert Schrank, 193-202.

33. Michael Gaffney, "The Potential for Organizational Development in the U.S. Merchant Marine," *Proceedings of the Conference on the Management of Change Aboard Ship* (Maine Maritime Academy: Center for Advanced Maritime Studies, 1981b).

34. Roger, "American Seamen on the Hoegh *Mallard*," 14-15.

Chapter Four

1. Peter Dundelach and Nils Mortensen, "Denmark, Norway, and Sweden," in *New Forms of Work Organization* (Geneva: International Labour Office, 1979), 38.

2. "Japan to Test Seventeen-Man Crew" (*Norwegian Shipping News,* October 15, 1982): 26.

3. A very early experiment in shipboard practices was conducted in 1962 and 1963, before the period covered by the study. It occurred on a newly commissioned Danish tanker equipped with the latest automation. A social science consultant was utilized by the shipowner to train the crew. The consultant also sought to help the crew build a new role system toward more flexible work assignments and more participative decision making. On the basis of his direct observations on a voyage from Japan to the Persian Gulf, he declared the experiment a success. However, apparently the changes were not long sustained, and they did not lead to other changes in the industry. The seafaring unions opposed the experiment.

4. Gaffney, "Potential for Organizational Development."

5. National Research Council, *Effective Manning of the U.S. Merchant Fleet*, 17.

6. For a recent excellent comprehensive review of labor practices in the U.S. shipping industry, see Clifford B. Donn, "Federal Subsidies, Technological Change, and Collective Bargaining in the Ocean-Going Maritime Industry," a paper presented to the Atlantic Economic Association Conference, August 1986.

Chapter Five

1. Einar Thorsrud, "Changing Organizational Patterns in Norwegian Shipping," *Proceedings of Safety of Life at Sea* (Oslo, Norway, October 20–21, 1980): 5.

2. In this section I draw heavily on the research of M. H. Smith and J. Roggema contained in "Emerging Organizational Values in Shipping: Part 1, Crew Stability," *Maritime Policy and Management* 6, no. 2 (1979a): 129–143.

3. Paul Woodward, "U.K. Crew Costs Put Fleet in Jeopardy," *Seatrade,* (March 1983): 109.

4. David H. Moreby, "The Future of Ship Organizations," SAPANUT 2 no. 3 (1981): 5.

5. Simplicity versus complexity is one of the five major characteristics Everett M. Rogers identified as contributing most to the diffusion of innovations. See the third edition of *Diffusion of Innovations* (New York: Free Press, 1983).

6. Johansen, "Democratizing Work and Social Life on Ships."

7. N. K. Hammerstrong, "Organizational Experiment in M/S Hoegh *Mistral* and M/T Hoegh *Multina*," unpublished, undated company memo.

Chapter Six

1. M. H. Smith, "Shipboard Change: The Reaction of Seafarers," unpublished Sealife Programme report, December 1979, p. 15.

2. "Feature: Scandinavian Ship Management," *Lloyd's Ship Manager* (May 1981): 29.

3. M. H. Smith, "The Implementation of a Shipboard Management Programme," unpublished Sealife Programme report, October 1981, p. 8.

4. "Changing Shipping Organizations," unpublished Sealife Programme report, May 1978, p. 7.

5. Smith, "Shipboard Change," 5.

6. American Center for the Quality of Work Life (ACQWL), *Industrial Democracy in Europe: A 1977 Survey* (Washington, D.C.: ACQWL, 1978): p. 62.

7. ACQWL, 72-73.

8. ACQWL, 38.

9. ACQWL, 57.

10. ACQWL, 91.

11. ACQWL, 93.

12. Moreby, "Future of Ship Organization."

13. Einar Thorsrud, "Organizational Change and Workers' Exchange," in *Industrial Democracy at Sea,* ed. Robert Schrank, 117-134.

14. Smith, "Shipboard Change," 16.

15. Roger, "American Seamen on the Hoegh *Mallard*," 30.

16. J. H. Guy, "Pitfalls on the Road to Social Integration," *Lloyd's Ship Manager* (March 1983): 9.

17. Smith, "Shipboard Change," 15.

Chapter Seven

1. Woodward, "U.K. Crew Costs," 109.

2. Shortages of seafarers were also experienced in Japan and the United States during the time from 1966 to 1970. In the U.S. case, it was directly related to the Vietnam logistics support, for which the government paid. The U.S. seafaring labor negotiations strengthened retirement plans and provided for new training facilities, controlled by unions, and major increases in total wages and benefit packages.

3. Winther and Bartlett, "A Balanced Life," 3.

4. *Lloyd's Anversios* (Colchester, Essex: Lloyd's of London Press, November 18, 1982), 4; and *Sofart,* November 10, 1976, 15.

5. Paul Bartlett, "A Sad Picture," *Seatrade* (November 1981): 4; *Lloyd's Anversios,* 4.

6. U.S. Congress, Congressional Budget Office, *U.S. Shipping and Shipbuilding;* 24–25.

7. The variety and complexity of the subsidies make comparisons difficult, especially comparisons across regions. For my comparisons within northwestern Europe, I relied on the judgments of informed observers of shipping activity in the region. See John Oakes and Paul Bartlett, "Analysis," *Seatrade* 15, no. 1 (January 1985): 21–25. For my comparisons among Japan, the United States, and European countries I referred to another publication: U.S. Department of Commerce, Maritime Administration, *U.S. Maritime Studies* (Washington, D.C.: U.S. Government Printing Office, 1981b).

8. U.S. Department of Transportation, Maritime Administration, *U.S. Maritime Administration Annual Report* (Washington, D.C.: U.S. Government Printing Office, 1984c), 55.

9. President's Commission on Industrial Competitiveness, *Global Competition,* Vol. I, 36.

Chapter Eight

1. The account of the Norwegian innovation processes, and especially that of the contact group, draws heavily upon Einar Thorsrud, "Policymaking as a Learning Process in Working Life,"

in *Working Life,* B. Gardell and G. Johansson, eds. (London: Wiley, 1981), 313–326.

2. Thorsrud, "Policymaking as Learning Process," 320.

3. Thorsrud, "Organizational Change," 121–122.

4. Lisl Klein, *A Social Scientist in Industry* (Tavistock, U.K.: Grover Press, 1976), 113–114.

5. Except where other specific sources are cited, my account of the Sealife Programme is based on an unpublished report by Peter Sharpe, "Sealife Programme: Chief Executive's Summary Report," January 1980, 33 pages.

6. Sharpe, "Sealife Programme," 7–8.

7. Sharpe, "Sealife Programme," 10.

8. Sharpe, "Sealife Programme," 13.

9. Sharpe, "Sealife Programme," 32–33.

10. Roggema and Smith, "Organizational Change in the Shipping Industry," 765–790.

11. The generally segmented, rigid, and closed nature of shipping institutions is precisely the condition that inhibits the generation of new ideas, according to Rosabeth Moss Kanter, based on her own field research in American corporations and her review of the literature on innovation. See "When a Thousand Flowers Bloom: Structural, Collective, and Social Conditions for Innovation in Organizations," in *Research in Organizational Behavior,* Vol. 9, eds. Barry Staw and Larry Cumming (Greenwich: JAI Press, forthcoming).

12. Low tolerance for diversity discourages innovation in the first instance but may increase the tendency for systemwide adoption of innovations that cross a threshold of approval or acceptance. This tendency was found for incremental but not radical technical innovations in an empirical study in the footwear industry. See Stephen F. Cohn and Romaine M. Twryn, "Organization Structure, Decision-Making Procedures, and the Adoption of Innovations," *IEEE Transactions on Engineering Management* (November 1984): 154–161. Also see Kanter, "Thousand Flowers."

13. One reason Denmark's unions are organized on a craft basis rather than an industry basis, as in neighboring Norway and Sweden, is that the guilds were highly developed before industrialization in Denmark but not in the less urbanized Norway and

Sweden. Another reason is the relative lack of larger enterprises in Denmark. Related to these differences is the difference in centralization of decision making. In Norway and Sweden the control over strike funds lies with the national confederation, but in Denmark it rests with the individual trade unions. In Norway and Sweden the general agreements need not be confirmed by the members' ballot, but in Denmark this ratification is required. See Dundelach and Mortensen, "Denmark, Norway, and Sweden," 16.

14. For an analysis of the rivalry among seafaring unions in particular and labor relations in the shipping industry in general, see Donn, "Federal Subsidies."

15. *Marine Engineering/Log* (January 1984), 21.

16. National Research Council, *Ship Operation Research and Development* (Washington, D.C.: National Academy Press, 1983).

17. National Research Council, *Effective Manning of the U.S. Merchant Fleet*, 22.

18. *New York Times*, "Political Action Gifts Shift to a New Frontier Among Committees in House" (September 19, 1983): 16.

19. Howard Kurtz, "Industry Factions Protect Their Turf," *Washington Post* (July 18, 1985): 16.

Chapter Nine

1. Smith, "Implementation of Shipboard Management," 2.

2. Smith, "Implementation of Shipboard Management," 3.

3. Smith, "Implementation of Shipboard Management," 9.

4. See, for example, Modesto A. Maidique, "Entrepreneurs, Champions, and Technological Innovations," *Sloan Management Review* 21 (Winter 1980): 59–76.

5. See Noel M. Tichey and Mary Anne Devanna, *The Transformational Leader* (New York: Wiley, 1986).

6. Also identified as a preliminary task in the management of innovation by Andrew H. Van de Ven, "Central Problems in the Management of Innovation," *Management Science* 32 (1986): 590–607.

7. Thorsrud, "Policymaking," 5. Also see Thorsrud, "Changing Organizational Patterns."

8. The pioneers should be opinion leaders. See Everett M. Rogers and F. Floyd Shoemaker, *Communication of Innovations: A Cross-Cultural Approach*, 2d ed. (New York: Free Press, 1971).

9. The sheltered experiment for social innovation is an example of what Galbraith has called "reservations," units that were physically and organizationally separated from the rest of the organization. The sheltered conditions, or conditions of isolation, permit the new ideas to be perfected and tested. See Jay Galbraith, "Designing the Innovating Organization," *Organizational Dynamics* 10 (Summer 1982): 5–25.

10. Sealife Programme, "Changing Shipping," 37.

11. The use of mechanisms that cross organizational levels and departmental boundaries has been identified as an asset for innovation generally—technical as well as organizational. See, for example, Roger Schroeder, Andrew Van de Ven, Gary Scudder, and Douglas Polley, "Observations Leading to a Process Model of Innovation," Discussion Paper No. 48, Strategic Management Center, University of Minnesota, 1986. Also see Kanter, *Change Masters*.

12. The ability to learn from others is a capacity that may be encouraged and provided for by boundary-spanning roles. See Michael Tushman, "Special Boundary Roles in the Innovation Process," *Administrative Science Quarterly* 22 (1977): 587–605.

13. Roggema and Smith, "Organizational Change in the Shipping Industry," 765–790; also Gaffney, "Reduced Manning in the Liner Trades."

Chapter Eleven

1. The most relevant bodies of literature were identified in outlining the theory in Chapter Two. Therefore, the various levels of support and nonsupport provided by shipping findings for the propositions provide corresponding degrees of support and nonsupport for the literature cited earlier in connection with the theoretical propositions. The study as a whole, if not the specific findings summarized in this chapter, is related to an additional body of literature not reviewed in depth in Chapter Two, the vast diffusion literature. Pieces of this literature were cited in Chapters

Two and Nine, but the more important relevance is a broader one. The point requires elaboration.

As Everett M. Rogers shows in his comprehensive review of diffusion studies, *Diffusion of Innovations,* 3d ed., this literature includes many different strands, each focusing on a different aspect of the field.

- Some studies focus on the original inventions, and others on their diffusion.
- Some studies focus on the strategies used by change agents to promote diffusion, and others on the decisions by adopters and nonadopters.
- Some studies focus on the attributes of innovations themselves that affect their rate of adoption, and others on the character- istics of the context that facilitate or hinder their adoption.
- Some researchers study centralized diffusion systems (in which overall control of diffusion decisions are made by central authorities or agencies), and others study decentralized diffusion systems (with wide sharing of power among parts of the system).

The present study is not within any one or two of these research traditions. Rather than attempt to make a substantial contribution to any one of these more focused bodies of literature, each of which is substantial and well developed, the present study attempts to develop a broader action-oriented theory that embraces and interrelates some of the phenomena central to each of many of the types of research on innovation and diffusion.

An analysis of the key construct in the proposed theory, the capacity of a social system for innovative change, helps clarify why the present study must incorporate many of the specific aspects of innovation usually isolated for study.

The term *innovative change* is designed to embrace both the development of the innovation and its diffusion, emphasizing that often the diffusion involves many combinations of adoption and reinvention.

The term *capacity of a social system* embraces both enabling capabilities of agents who can provide innovative change indirectly and the capabilities of those who can implement—develop, reinvent, and adopt—the change. The term also embraces both innovation attributes that affect the rate of diffusion (including attributes that can be deliberately designed into guiding models) and characteristics of the contact that influence the rate of diffusion (including economic, social, and institutional factors).

Going beyond the construct itself, the shipping study included aspects of two types of diffusion settings often differentiated for research purposes: centralized diffusion systems and decentralized systems. In shipping, it was an open question how much initiative change would be or could be controlled by central bodies in a country's shipping industry, and how much initiative could be taken by individual companies with diffusion resulting from experience along horizontal networks among companies. In fact, diffusion patterns were a combination of the centralized and decentralized types.

Finally, the research strategy employed in shipping embraced the spirit of both variance research, to establish what conditions help explain the amount of innovative change, and process research, to explain causes and sequences of a series of events over time.

Thus, in general, the present book represents an expansion of the study of diffusion more than a significant addition to any specific aspects of the existing diffusion literature. Nevertheless, some relatively important specific findings pertinent to the diffusion and change literature are discussed in this chapter. They relate to a confirmation of the strong influence of institutional (structural) factors, a new perspective on the role of process competence in larger social systems, and insights into the reciprocal and dynamic relationship among social beliefs, organizational forms, and experience.

2. See Richard E. Walton, "Establishing and Maintaining High Commitment Work Systems," in *Organizational Life Cycles: Issues in the Creation, Transformation, and Decline of Organizations,* eds. Robert Miles, John Kimberly, and Associates (San Francisco: Jossey-Bass, 1980), 208–290, which explains the successes and failures of innovative work structures in four plants. Also, see case studies of organizational change in an insurance company, an oil tanker, a factory, hospitals, and a military unit in Peter A. Clark,

Action Research and Organizational Change (London: Harper & Row, 1972). Another relevant set of case studies of change projects in Martin Marietta, Pacific Northwest Bell, Ford, General Motors, Harman Miller, General Foods, Harman International, Citibank, and Rushton Mining are contained in Zager and Rosow, *Innovative Organization*. Also see John Simmons and William Mares, *Working Together* (New York: Knopf, 1983).

3. See George Lodge and Richard Walton, "The American Corporation and Its New Relationships," unpublished paper, Harvard Business School, November 1986.

Chapter Twelve

1. Camens, "Labor-Management Teams," 110–111.

2. Camens, "Labor-Management Teams," 117.

3. Donald F. Ephlin, "United Auto Workers: Pioneers in Labor-Management Partnerships," in *Teamwork: Joint Labor-Management Programs in America,* ed. Jerome M. Rosow (New York: Pergamon Press, Work in America Series, 1986), 133–145.

4. See Jocelyn Gutchess, *Employment Security in Action: Strategies that Work* (New York: Pergamon Press, Work in America Series, 1985). Also see Work in America Institute, *Employment Security in a Free Economy* (New York: Pergamon Press, Work in America Institute Policy Study, 1984).

5. Katz, *Shifting Gears,* 168.

6. Katz, *Shifting Gears,* 169.

7. Robert R. McKersie and Laurence C. Hunter, *Pay, Productivity, and Collective Bargaining* (London: Macmillan, 1973).

8. Rudolph A. Oswald, "Joint Labor-Management Programs: A Labor Viewpoint," in *Teamwork: Joint Labor-Management Programs in America,* ed. Jerome M. Rosow (New York: Pergamon Press, Work in America Series, 1986), 28–29.

9. Oswald, "Joint Labor-Management Programs," 30.

10. Raymond Williams and Glenn Watts, "The Process of Working Together: CWA's/AT&T's Approach to QWL," in *Teamwork: Joint Labor-Management Programs in America,* ed.

Jerome M. Rosow (New York: Pergamon Press, Work in America
Series, 1986), 79.

11. George C. Lodge, *The American Disease* (New York:
Knopf, 1984).

12. There is growing recognition that these traditional
conceptions are outmoded. As an indication of the growing sense
that we need to define new, more interdependent roles for our major
institutions, the President's Commission on Industrial Competitiveness, chaired by Hewlett Packard's chief executive officer, John
Young, and composed of thirty leaders from business, labor,
government, and academia, called for a review of the largely
ineffective existing advisory committees affiliated with the
departments of commerce, labor, and the treasury and the Office of
U.S. Trade Representatives. The report called on the president to
consider expanding the role of trade associations, labor representatives, representatives of academia, and other interested parties in the
membership of these citizen advisory committees to government
agencies to enhance their ability to address competitiveness issues.

Also see Davis Dyer, Malcolm Salter, and Alan Webber,
Changing Alliances: The Politics of an American Industry (Boston:
Harvard Business School Press, 1987). Based on their study of the
automobile industries in America, Japan, and Europe, these
authors call for the negotiation of the enterprise's *competitive*
strategy—by management and labor.

13. Jack Barbash has captured the conventional union
conception of its role: "In the American union view, bargaining
effectiveness is better enforced through countervailing power rather
than through the kind of integration in the management system
which codetermination imposes" (p. 91). Thus, the union can do
more for its member as griever and adversary than as partner.
Quotation is drawn from Jack Barbash, "The Work Humanization
Movement: U.S. and European Experiences Compared," in *Labor
Relations in Advanced Industrial Societies: Issues and Problems*,
Benjamin Martin and Everett M. Kassalow, eds. (Washington,
D.C.: Carnegie Endowment for International Peace, 1980), 184–195.

For examples of research leading to proposals for new roles
for labor unions in the United States, see Michael J. Piore,
"Computer Technologies, Market Structure, and Strategic Union

Choices," in *Challenges and Choices Facing American Labor,* ed. Thomas A. Kochan (Cambridge, Mass.: MIT Press, 1985), 193–204; and Thomas A. Kochan, Harry C. Katz, and Nancy R. Mower, "Worker Participation and American Unions," in *Challenges and Choices Facing American Labor,* ed. Thomas A. Kochan (Cambridge, Mass.: MIT Press, 1985), 260–306.

Bibliography

Abernathy, William J., Kim B. Clark, and Alan M. Kantrow. *Industrial Renaissance: Producing a Competitive Future for America.* New York: Basic Books, 1983.

Altshuler, Alan, Martin Anderson, Daniel Jones, Daniel Roos, and James Womack. *The Future of the Automobile: The Report of MIT's International Automobile Program.* Cambridge, Mass.: MIT Press, 1984.

American Center for the Quality of Work Life (ACQWL). *Industrial Democracy in Europe: A 1977 Survey.* Washington, D.C.: ACQWL, 1978.

Badaracco, Joseph L., Jr. *Loading the Dice: A Five-Country Study of Vinyl Chloride Regulation.* Boston: Harvard Business School Press, 1985.

Barbash, Jack. "The Work Humanization Movement: U.S. and European Experiences Compared." In *Labor Relations in Advanced Industrial Societies: Issues and Problems,* edited by Benjamin Martin and Everett M. Kassalow. Washington, D.C.: Carnegie Endowment for International Peace, 1980.

Bartlett, Paul. "A Sad Picture." *Seatrade* 11, no. 11 (November 1981): 4.

Beer, Michael. *Organization Change and Development: A Systemic View.* New York: Goodyear, 1980.

341

Beer, Michael, Bert Spector, Paul Lawrence, Quinn Mills, and Richard Walton. *Managing Human Assets.* New York: Free Press, 1984.

Boylston, Benjamin. "Employee Involvement and Cultural Change at Bethlehem Steel." In *Teamwork: Joint Labor-Management Programs in America,* edited by Jerome M. Rosow. New York: Pergamon Press, Work in America Series, 1986.

Branch, Alan E. *Economics of Shipping Practice and Management.* London: Chapman & Hall, 1982.

Camens, Sam. "Labor-Management Participation Teams in Basic Steel Industry." In *Teamwork: Joint Labor-Management Programs in America,* edited by Jerome M. Rosow. New York: Pergamon Press, Work in America Series, 1986.

Chandler, Alfred D., Jr. *Strategy and Structure: The History of the American Industrial Enterprise.* Cambridge, Mass.: MIT Press, 1962.

Child, John, and Monir Tyeh. "Theoretical Perspectives in Cross-National Research," *International Studies of Management and Organization* 12, no. 4 (1982): 23–70.

Clark, Peter A. *Action Research and Organizational Change.* London: Harper & Row, 1972.

Cohn, Stephen F., and Romaine M. Twryn. "Organization Structure, Decision-Making Procedures, and the Adoption of Innovations." *IEEE Transactions on Engineering Management* (November 1984): 154–161.

Cole, Robert E. "The Macropolitics of Organizational Change: A Comparative Analysis of the Spread of Small-Group Activities." *Administrative Science Quarterly,* 30 (1985): 560–585.

Czepial, John A. "Patterns of Interorganizational Communications and the Diffusion of a Major Technological Innovation in a Competitive Industrial Community." *Academy of Management Journal* 18, no. 1 (March 1975): 6–24.

Donn, Clifford B. "Federal Subsidies, Technological Change, and Collective Bargaining in the Ocean-Going Maritime Industry." A paper presented to the Atlantic Economic Association Conference, August 1986.

Dore, Ronald. *British Factory—Japanese Factory.* Berkeley: University of California Press, 1974.

Dundelach, Peter, and Nils Mortensen. "Denmark, Norway, and Sweden." In *New Forms of Work Organization.* Geneva: International Labour Office, 1979.

Dyer, Davis, Malcolm Salter, and Alan Webber. *Changing Alliances: The Politics of an American Industry.* Boston: Harvard Business School Press, 1987.

Emery, Fred E., and Eric E. Trist. *Towards a Social Ecology: Contextual Appreciation of the Future in the Present.* London: Plenum, 1973.

Ephlin, Donald F. "United Auto Workers: Pioneers in Labor-Management Partnerships." In *Teamwork: Joint Labor-Management Programs in America,* edited by Jerome M. Rosow. New York: Pergamon Press, Work in America Series, 1986.

Gaffney, Michael. "The Potential for Organizational Development in the U.S. Merchant Marine." *Proceedings of the Conference on the Management of Change Aboard Ship.* Maine Maritime Academy: Center for Advanced Maritime Studies, 1981a.

Gaffney, Michael. "Reduced Manning in the Liner Trades: Technological Capabilities and Organizational Implications." *Proceedings of the Conference on the Management of Change Aboard Ship.* Maine Maritime Academy: Center for Advanced Maritime Studies, 1981b.

Galbraith, Jay. "Designing the Innovating Organization." *Organizational Dynamics* 10 (Summer 1982): 5-25.

Goodman, Paul S. *Assessing Organizational Change: The Rushton Quality of Work Life Experiment.* New York: Wiley, 1979.

Goodmeasure, Inc. *The Changing American Workplace: Work Alternatives in the '80s.* New York: American Management Association, 1985.

Grey, Michael. *Seatrade* 13 (1983): 9.

Guy, J. H. "Pitfalls on the Road to Social Integration." *Lloyd's Ship Manager* (March 1983): 9-10.

Hackman, J. Richard. "The Design of Work Teams." In *Handbook of Organizational Behavior,* edited by Jay Lorsch. Englewood Cliffs, N.J.: Prentice-Hall, 1986.

Hage, Jerald. "Responding to Technological and Competitive Changes: Organization and Industry Factors." In *Managing Technological Innovation: Organizational Strategies for*

Implementing Advanced Manufacturing Technologies, edited by Donald D. Davis and Associates. San Francisco: Jossey-Bass, 1986.

Hammerstrong, N. K. "Organizational Experiment in M/S Hoegh *Mistral* and M/T Hoegh *Multina.*" Unpublished, undated company memo.

Hayes, Robert H., and Steven C. Wheelwright. *Restoring Our Competitive Edge: Competing Through Manufacturing.* New York: Wiley, 1984.

Hicks, John R. *The Theory of Wages.* London: Macmillan, 1932.

Hofstede, Geert. *Culture's Consequences: International Differences in Work-Related Values.* London: Gage Publications, 1980.

"Japan to Test Seventeen-Man Crew." *Norwegian Shipping News* (October 15, 1982): 26.

Johansen, Ragnar. "Democratizing Work and Social Life on Ships: A Report from the Experiment on Board M.S. *Balao.*" In *Working on the Quality of Working Life,* edited by Hans van Beinum. Boston: Martinus Nijhoff Publishing, 1979.

Kanter, Rosabeth Moss. *The Change Masters.* New York: Simon & Schuster, 1983.

Kanter, Rosabeth Moss. "When a Thousand Flowers Bloom: Structural, Collective, and Social Conditions for Innovation in Organizations." In *Research in Organizational Behavior, Vol. 9,* edited by Barry Staw and Larry Cumming. Greenwich: JAI Press, forthcoming.

Katz, Harry C. *Shifting Gears: Changing Labor Relations in the U.S. Automobile Industry.* Cambridge, Mass.: MIT Press, 1985.

Katz, Harry C., and Charles F. Sabel. "Industrial Relations and Industrial Adjustment: The World Car Industry." MIT working paper, April 1985.

Katzenstein, Peter. *Small States in World Markets.* Ithaca, N.Y.: Cornell University Press, 1985.

Kendall, Lane C. *The Business of Shipping.* Centreville, Md.: Cornell Maritime Press, 1983.

Klein, Lisl. *A Social Scientist in Industry.* Tavistock, U.K.: Grover Press, 1976.

Kochan, Thomas A., Harry C. Katz, and Nancy R. Mower. "Worker Participation and American Unions." In *Challenges and Choices*

Facing American Labor, edited by Thomas A. Kochan. Cambridge, Mass.: MIT Press, 1985.

Koishi, Yasumichi. "Work Simplification Through the Transformation of Work on Board," *Maritime Policy and Management* 8, no. 4 (1981): 261.

Kurtz, Howard. "Industry Factions Protect Their Turf." *Washington Post* (July 18, 1985): 16.

Lawler, Edward E., III. *High-Involvement Management: Participative Strategies for Improving Organizational Performance.* San Francisco: Jossey-Bass, 1986.

Lawrence, Paul R., and Davis Dyer. *Renewing American Industry.* New York: Free Press, 1983.

Lloyd's Anversios. Colchester, Essex: Lloyd's of London Press, Ltd., November 18, 1982.

Lloyd's Register of Shipping Tables. Colchester, Essex: Lloyd's of London Press, Ltd., 1984.

Lloyd's Ship Manager. "Feature: Scandinavian Ship Management." May 1981, pp. 29–33.

Lodge, George C. *The American Disease.* New York: Knopf, 1984.

Lodge, George, and Richard Walton. "The American Corporation and Its New Relationships." Unpublished paper, Harvard Business School, November 1986.

Lodge, George, and Ezra Vogel, eds. *Ideology and National Competitiveness.* Boston: Harvard Business School Press, 1986.

McKersie, Robert R., and Laurence C. Hunter. *Pay, Productivity and Collective Bargaining.* London: Macmillan, 1973.

Maidique, Modesto A. "Entrepreneurs, Champions, and Technological Innovations." *Sloan Management Review* 21 (Winter 1980): 59–76.

Mansfield, Edwin. *Industrial Research and Technological Innovation.* New York: Norton, 1968.

Marine Engineering/Log (January 1984): 21.

Moreby, David H. "The Future of Ship Organization." *SAPANUT* 2, no. 3 (1981): 1–13.

National Research Council. *Ship Operation Research and Development.* Washington, D.C.: National Academy Press, 1983.

National Research Council. *Effective Manning of the U.S.*

Merchant Fleet. Washington, D.C.: National Academy Press, 1984.

National Research Council. *Human Resource Practices for Implementing Advanced Manufacturing Technology.* Washington, D.C.: National Academy Press, 1986.

New York Times. "Political Action Gifts Shift to a New Frontier Among Committees in House." September 19, 1983, p. 16.

Oakes, John, and Paul Bartlett. "Analysis." *Seatrade* 15, no. 1 (January 1985): 21–25.

O'Loughlin, Carleen. *The Economics of Seatransport.* London: Penguin Press, 1967.

Organization for Economic Cooperation and Development (OECD). *Review of Maritime Transport.* Paris: OECD Publications, 1969.

Organization for Economic Cooperation and Development (OECD). *Review of Maritime Transport.* Paris: OECD Publications, 1974.

Organization for Economic Cooperation and Development (OECD). *Review of Maritime Transport.* Paris: OECD Publications, 1983.

Organization for Economic Cooperation and Development (OECD). *Review of Maritime Transport.* Paris: OECD Publications, 1984.

Organization for Economic Cooperation and Development (OECD). *Labor Force Statistics.* Paris: OECD Publications, 1985.

Oswald, Rudolph A. "Joint Labor-Management Programs: A Labor Viewpoint." In *Teamwork: Joint Labor-Management Programs in America,* edited by Jerome M. Rosow. New York: Pergamon Press, Work in America Series, 1986.

Pettigrew, Andrew M. *The Awakening Giant: Continuity and Change in Imperial Chemical Industries.* London: Basil Blackwell, 1985.

Piore, Michael J. "Computer Technologies, Market Structure, and Strategic Union Choices." In *Challenges and Choices Facing American Labor,* edited by Thomas A. Kochan. Cambridge, Mass.: MIT Press, 1985.

Piore, Michael J., and Charles F. Sabel. *The Second Industrial Divide.* New York: Basic Books, 1984.

President's Commission on Industrial Competitiveness. *Global Competition: The New Reality, Volumes I and II.* Washington, D.C.: U.S. Government Printing Office, January 1985.

Reich, Robert B. *The Next American Frontier.* New York: Times Books, 1983.

Reich, Robert B. "Bailout: A Comparative Study in Law and Industrial Structure." *Yale Journal on Regulation* 2, no. 2 (1985): 163–224.

Roger, Sidney. "American Seamen on the Hoegh *Mallard.*" In *Industrial Democracy at Sea,* edited by Robert Schrank. Cambridge, Mass.: MIT Press, 1983.

Rogers, Everett M. *Diffusion of Innovations.* 3d ed. New York: Free Press, 1983.

Rogers, Everett M., and F. Floyd Shoemaker. *Communication of Innovations: A Cross-Cultural Approach.* 2d ed. New York: Free Press, 1971.

Roggema, Jacques, and M. H. Smith. "Organizational Change in the Shipping Industry: Issues in the Transformation of Basic Assumptions." *Human Relations* 36, no. 8 (1983): 765–790.

Schön, Donald A. *Beyond the Stable State.* New York: Random House, 1971.

Schroeder, Roger, Andrew Van de Van, Gary Scudder, and Douglas Polley. "Observations Leading to a Process Model of Innovation." Discussion Paper No. 48, Strategic Management Center, University of Minnesota, 1986.

Schumpeter, Joseph. *Capitalism, Socialism, and Democracy.* 3d ed. New York: Harper & Row, 1950.

Sealife Programme. "Changing Shipping Organizations." Unpublished Sealife Programme report, London, May 1978.

Seaways. "Manning—A Major Concern and Major Cost." (April 1983): 4–5.

Sharpe, Peter. "Sealife Programme: Chief Executive's Summary Report." Unpublished Sealife Programme report, January 1980.

Simmons, John, and William Mares. *Working Together.* New York: Knopf, 1983.

Smith, M. H. "Shipboard Change: The Reaction of Seafarers." Unpublished Sealife Programme report, December 1979.

Smith, M. H. "The Implementation of a Shipboard Management Programme." Unpublished Sealife Programme report, October 1981.

Smith, M. H., and J. Roggema. "Crew Stability and Shipboard Management." Unpublished Sealife Programme report, 1978.

Smith, M. H., and J. Roggema. "Emerging Organizational Values in Shipping: Part 1, Crew Stability." *Maritime Policy and Management* 6, no. 2 (1979a): 129-143.

Smith, M. H., and J. Roggema. "Emerging Organizational Values in Shipping: Part 2, Towards a Redistribution of Responsibility Onboard Ship." *Maritime Policy and Management* 6, no. 2 (1979b): 145-156.

Smith, M. H., and J. Roggema. "Emerging Organizational Values in Shipping: Part 3, The Matrix Organization—Towards a Multiple Skill Structure." *Maritime Policy and Management* 7, no. 4 (1980a): 241-254.

Smith, M. H., and J. Roggema. "Emerging Organizational Values in Shipping: Part 4, Decentralization—The Redefinition of Authority in Shipping Company Organization." *Maritime Policy and Management* 7, no. 4 (1980b): 255-269.

Thorsrud, Einar. "Changing Organizational Patterns in Norwegian Shipping." In *Proceedings of Safety of Life at Sea* conference at Oslo, Norway, October 20-21, 1980.

Thorsrud, Einar. "Policymaking as a Learning Process in Working Life." In *Working Life,* edited by B. Gardell and G. Johansson. London: Wiley, 1981.

Thorsrud, Einar. "Organizational Change and Workers' Exchange." In *Industrial Democracy at Sea,* edited by Robert Schrank. Cambridge, Mass.: MIT Press, 1983.

Thurow, Lester C. "Revitalizing American Industry: Managing in a Competitive World Economy." *California Management Review* 27, no. 1 (1984): 9-41.

Tichey, Noel M., and Mary Anne Devanna. *The Transformational Leader.* New York: Wiley, 1986.

Trist, Eric, and Charles Dwyer. "The Limits of Laissez-Faire as a Sociotechnical Change Strategy." In *The Innovation Organization: Productivity Programs in Action,* edited by Robert Zager and Michael P. Rosow. New York: Pergamon Press, 1982.

Tushman, Michael. "Special Boundary Roles in the Innovation Process." *Administrative Science Quarterly* 22 (1977): 587–605.

UNCTAD. *Review of Maritime Transport.* Paris: UNCTAD, 1979.

UNCTAD. *Review of Maritime Transport.* Paris: UNCTAD, 1982.

UNCTAD. *Review of Maritime Transport.* Paris: UNCTAD, 1985.

U.S. Congress, Congressional Budget Office. *U.S. Shipping and Shipbuilding: Trends and Policy Choices.* Washington, D.C.: U.S. Government Printing Office, August 1984.

U.S. Congress, Office of Technology Assessment. *An Assessment of Marine Trade and Technology.* Washington, D.C.: U.S. Government Printing Office, October 1983.

U.S. Department of Commerce, Maritime Administration. *Merchant Fleets of the World, 1966.* Washington, D.C.: U.S. Government Printing Office, 1967.

U.S. Department of Commerce, Maritime Administration. *Merchant Fleets of the World, 1973.* Washington, D.C.: U.S. Government Printing Office, 1974.

U.S. Department of Commerce, Maritime Administration. *Merchant Fleets of the World, 1978.* Washington, D.C.: U.S. Government Printing Office, 1979.

U.S. Department of Commerce, Maritime Administration. *Maritime Subsidies.* Washington, D.C.: U.S. Government Printing Office, 1981a.

U.S. Department of Commerce, Maritime Administration. *Maritime Studies.* Washington, D.C.: U.S. Government Printing Office, 1981b.

U.S. Department of Commerce, Maritime Administration. *Merchant Fleets of the World, 1980.* Washington, D.C.: U.S. Government Printing Office, 1981c.

U.S. Department of Commerce, Maritime Administration. *Merchant Fleets of the World, 1981.* Washington, D.C.: U.S. Government Printing Office, 1982.

U.S. Department of Commerce, Maritime Administration. *Merchant Fleets of the World, 1986.* Washington, D.C.: U.S. Government Printing Office, 1985a.

U.S. Department of Commerce, Maritime Administration. *Statistical Analysis of World Fleets.* Washington, D.C.: U.S. Government Printing Office, 1985b.

U.S. Department of Transportation, Maritime Administration. *Merchant Fleets of the World, 1983.* Washington, D.C.: U.S. Government Printing Office, 1984a.

U.S. Department of Transportation, Maritime Administration. *U.S. Maritime Administration Annual Report.* Washington, D.C.: U.S. Government Printing Office, 1984b.

U.S. Department of Transportation, Maritime Administration. *Statistical Analysis of World Fleets.* Washington, D.C.: U.S. Government Printing Office, 1985.

Veblen, Thorstein. *The Theory of the Leisure Class.* New York: Heller, 1899.

Vilkund, Burger. "Workplace Changes and Union Power." In *Industrial Democracy at Sea,* edited by Robert Schrank. Cambridge, Mass.: MIT Press, 1983.

Walton, Richard E. "The Diffusion of New Work Structures: Explaining Why Success Didn't Take." *Organizational Dynamics* (Winter 1975): 3–22.

Walton, Richard E. "Successful Strategies for Diffusing Work Innovations." *Journal of Contemporary Business* (Spring 1977): 1–22.

Walton, Richard E. "Establishing and Maintaining High Commitment Work Systems." In *The Organizational Life Cycles: Issues in the Creation, Transformation, and Decline of Organizations,* edited by Robert Miles, John Kimberly, and Associates. San Francisco: Jossey-Bass, 1980a.

Walton, Richard E. "Planned Changes to Improve Organizational Effectiveness." *Technology in Society* 2 (1980b): 391–412.

Walton, Richard E. "Toward a Strategy of Eliciting Commitment Based on Policies of Mutuality." In *Human Resource Management Trends and Challenges,* edited by R. E. Walton and Paul R. Lawrence. Boston: Harvard Business School Press, 1985.

Walton, Richard E. "Vision-Led Management Restructuring." *Organizational Dynamics* (Summer 1986): 5–16.

Warren, Alfred S. "Quality of Work Life at General Motors." In *Teamwork: Joint Labor-Management Programs in America,* edited by Jerome M. Rosow. New York: Pergamon Press, Work in America Series, 1986.

Williams, Raymond, and Glenn Watts. "The Process of Working Together: CWA's/AT&T's Approach to QWL." In *Teamwork: Joint Labor-Management Programs in America,* edited by Jerome M. Rosow. New York: Pergamon Press, Work in America Series, 1986.

Williams, Trevor A. *Learning to Manage Our Futures.* New York: Wiley, 1982.

Winther, Rosalyn, and Paul Bartlett. "A Balanced Life." *Seatrade* 11, no. 8 (August 1981): 3–4.

Woodward, Paul. "U.K. Crew Costs Put Fleet in Jeopardy." *Seatrade* (March 1983): 109.

Work in America Institute. *Employment Security in a Free Economy.* New York: Pergamon Press, Work in America Institute Policy Study, 1984.

Zager, Robert, and Michael P. Rosow, eds. *The Innovative Organization: Productivity Programs in Action.* New York: Pergamon Press, 1982.

Zaltman, Gerald, and Robert Duncan. *Strategies of Planned Change.* New York: Wiley, 1977.

Zaltman, Gerald, Robert Duncan, and Jonny Holbek. *Innovations and Organizations.* New York: Wiley, 1973.

Index

353